THE WHO'S BUYING SERIES
BY THE NEW STRATEGIST EDITORS

Who's Buying

Household Furnishings, Services and Supplies

5th EDITION

New Strategist Publications, Inc.
P.O. Box 242, Ithaca, New York 14851
800/848-0842; 607/273-0913
www.newstrategist.com

ISBN 978-1-933588-59-9
ISBN 1-933588-59-4

Printed in the United States of America

Contents

About the Data in Who's Buying Household Furnishings, Services, and Supplies 5

1.   Percent Reporting Expenditure and Amount Spent, Average Week or Quarter 2005 9

Household Spending Trends 2000 to 2005 10

2.   Household Spending Trends, 2000 to 2005 11

Household Spending on Household Furnishings, Services, and Supplies, 2005 13

3.   Household Furnishings, Services, and Supplies Spending, 2000 to 2005 15

Household Spending on Household Furnishings, Services, and Supplies by Demographic Characteristic, 2005

4.   Household Furnishings, Services, Supplies: Average Spending by Age, 2005 16

5.   Household Furnishings, Services, Supplies: Indexed Spending by Age, 2005 17

6.   Household Furnishings, Services, Supplies: Total Spending by Age, 2005 18

7.   Household Furnishings, Services, Supplies: Market Shares by Age, 2005 19

8.   Household Furnishings, Services, Supplies: Average Spending by Income, 2005 20

9.   Household Furnishings, Services, Supplies: Indexed Spending by Income, 2005 21

10. Household Furnishings, Services, Supplies: Total Spending by Income, 2005 22

11. Household Furnishings, Services, Supplies: Market Shares by Income, 2005 23

12. Household Furnishings, Services, Supplies: Average Spending
     by High-Income Consumer Units, 2005 24

13. Household Furnishings, Services, Supplies: Indexed Spending
     by High-Income Consumer Units, 2005 25

14. Household Furnishings, Services, Supplies: Total Spending
     by High-Income Consumer Units, 2005 26

15. Household Furnishings, Services, Supplies: Market Shares
     by High-Income Consumer Units, 2005 27

16. Household Furnishings, Services, Supplies: Average Spending
     by Household Type, 2005 28

17. Household Furnishings, Services, Supplies: Indexed Spending
     by Household Type, 2005 29

18. Household Furnishings, Services, Supplies: Total Spending by Household Type, 2005 30

19. Household Furnishings, Services, Supplies: Market Shares by Household Type, 2005 31

20. Household Furnishings, Services, Supplies: Average Spending
     by Race and Hispanic Origin, 2005 32

21. Household Furnishings, Services, Supplies: Indexed Spending
     by Race and Hispanic Origin, 2005 33

22. Household Furnishings, Services, Supplies: Total Spending
     by Race and Hispanic Origin, 2005 34

23. Household Furnishings, Services, Supplies: Market Shares
     by Race and Hispanic Origin, 2005 35

24. Household Furnishings, Services, Supplies: Average Spending by Region, 2005 36

25. Household Furnishings, Services, Supplies: Indexed Spending by Region, 2005 37

26. Household Furnishings, Services, Supplies: Total Spending by Region, 2005 38

27. Household Furnishings, Services, Supplies: Market Shares by Region, 2005 39

28. Household Furnishings, Services, Supplies: Average Spending by Education, 2005 40

29. Household Furnishings, Services, Supplies: Indexed Spending by Education, 2005 41

30. Household Furnishings, Services, Supplies: Total Spending by Education, 2005 42

31. Household Furnishings, Services, Supplies: Market Shares by Education, 2005 43

Household Spending on Household Furnishings, Services, and Supplies by Product Category, 2005

32. Appliance Repair, including Service Center 44
33. Appliances, Major 46
34. Babysitting and Child Care in Own or Other Home...48
35. Bathroom Linens 50
36. Bedrom Furniture (except Mattresses and Springs) 52
37. Bedroom Linens 54
38. Cleansing and Toilet Tissue, Paper Towels, and Napkins 56
39. Closet and Storage Items 58
40. Curtains and Draperies 60
41. Day Care Centers, Nursery Schools, Preschools 62
42. Decorative Items for the Home 64
43. Floor Coverings, Nonpermanent 66
44. Floor Coverings, Wall-to-Wall 68
45. Gardening and Lawn Care Services 70
46. Housekeeping Services 72
47. Housewares 74
48. Infants' Equipment and Furniture 76
49. Kitchen and Dining Room Furniture 78
50. Kitchen and Dining Room Linens 80
51. Kitchen Appliances, Small Electric 82
52. Lamps and Lighting Fixtures 84
53. Laundry Equipment 86
54. Laundry and Cleaning Supplies 88
55. Lawn and Garden Equipment 90
56. Lawn and Garden Supplies 92
57. Living Room Chairs 94
58. Living Room Tables 96
59. Mattresses and Springs 98
60. Moving, Storage, and Freight Express 100
61. Outdoor Equipment 102
62. Outdoor Furniture 104
63. Plants and Fresh Flowers, Indoor 106
64. Postage 108
65. Power Tools 110
66. Security System Service Fees 112
67. Sewing Materials for Household Items 114
68. Sofas 116
69. Stationery, Stationery Supplies, and Giftwrap 118
70. Termite and Pest Control Products and Services 120
71. Wall Units, Cabinets, and Other Furniture 122

Appendix: Spending by Product and Service Ranked by Amount Spent, 2005 124

Glossary 130

About the Data in Who's Buying Household Furnishings, Services, and Supplies

Introduction

The spending data in *Who's Buying Household Furnishings, Services, and Supplies* are based on the Bureau of Labor Statistics' Consumer Expenditure Survey, an ongoing, nationwide survey of household spending. The Consumer Expenditure Survey is a complete accounting of household expenditures, including everything from big-ticket items, such as homes and cars, to small purchases like laundry detergent and videos. The survey does not include expenditures by government, business, or institutions. The lag time between data collection and dissemination is about two years. The data in this report are from the 2005 Consumer Expenditure Survey, unless otherwise noted.

To produce this report, New Strategist Publications analyzed the Consumer Expenditure Survey's average household spending data in a variety of ways, calculating household spending indexes, aggregate (or total) household spending, and market shares. Spending data by age, household income, household type, race, Hispanic origin, region of residence, and education are shown in this report. These analyses are presented in two formats—for all product categories by demographic characteristic and for all demographic characteristics by product category.

Definition of consumer unit

The Consumer Expenditure Survey uses the consumer unit rather than the household as its sampling unit. The term "household" is used interchangeably with the term "consumer unit" in this report for convenience, although they are not exactly the same. Some households contain more than one consumer unit.

The Bureau of Labor Statistics defines consumer units as either: (1) members of a household who are related by blood, marriage, adoption, or other legal arrangements; (2) a person living alone or sharing a household with others or living as a roomer in a private home or lodging house or in permanent living quarters in a hotel or motel, but who is financially independent; or (3) two or more persons living together who pool their income to make joint expenditure decisions. The bureau defines financial independence in terms of "the three major expense categories: housing, food, and other living expenses. To be considered financially independent, at least two of the three major expense categories have to be provided by the respondent."

The Census Bureau uses the household as its sampling unit in the decennial census and in the monthly Current Population Survey. The Census Bureau's household "consists of all persons who occupy a housing unit. A house, an apartment or other groups of rooms, or a single room is regarded as a housing unit when it is occupied or intended for occupancy as separate living quarters; that is, when the occupants do not live and eat with any other persons in the structure and there is direct access from the outside or through a common hall."

The definition goes on to specify that "a household includes the related family members and all the unrelated persons, if any, such as lodgers, foster children, wards, or employees who share the housing unit. A person living alone in a housing unit or a group of unrelated persons sharing a housing unit as partners is also counted as a household. The count of households excludes group quarters."

Because there can be more than one consumer unit in a household, consumer units outnumber households by several million. Young adults under age 25 head most of the additional consumer units.

How to use the tables in this report

The starting point for all calculations are the unpublished, detailed average household spending data collected by the Consumer Expenditure Survey. These numbers are shown on the report's average spending tables and on each of the product-specific tables. New Strategist's editors calculated the other figures in the report based on the average figures. The indexed spending tables and the indexed spending column (Best Customers) on the product-specific tables reveal whether spending by households in a given segment is above or below the average for all households and by how much. The total (or aggregate) spending tables show the overall size of the market. The market share tables and market share column (Biggest Customers) on the product-specific tables reveal how much spending each household segment controls. These analyses are described in detail below.

• **Average Spending** The average spending figures show the average annual spending of households on furnishings, supplies, and services for the home in 2005. The Consumer Expenditure Survey produces average spending data for all households in a segment, e.g., all households with a householder aged 25 to 34, not just for those purchasing an item. When examining spending data, it is important to remember that by including both purchasers and nonpurchasers in the calculation, the average is less than the amount spent on the item by buyers. (See Table 1 for the percentage of households spending on home furnishings, services, and supplies in 2005 and how much the purchasers spent.)

Because average spending figures include both buyers and nonbuyers, they reveal spending patterns by demographic characteristic. By knowing who is most likely to spend on an item, marketers can target their advertising and promotions more efficiently, and businesses can determine the market potential of a product or service in a city or neighborhood. By multiplying the average amount households spend on lawn and garden supplies by the number of households in an area, for example, a store owner can estimate the potential size of the local market for these items.

• **Indexed Spending (Best Customers)** The indexed spending figures compare the spending of each household segment with that of the average household. To compute the indexes, New Strategist divides the average amount each household segment spends on an item by average household spending and multiplies the resulting figure by 100.

An index of 100 is the average for all households. An index of 125 means the spending of a household segment is 25 percent above average (100 plus 25). An index of 75 indicates spending that is 25 percent below the average for all households (100 minus 25). Indexed spending figures identify the best customers for a product or service. Households with an index of 178 for bedroom linens, for example, are a strong market for this product. Those with an index below 100 are either a weak or an underserved market.

Spending indexes can reveal hidden markets—household segments with a high propensity to buy a particular product or service but which are overshadowed by household segments that account for a larger share of the market. Householders aged 65 to 74, for example, account for a smaller share of spending on postage than householders aged 35 to 44 (15 versus 19 percent). But a look at the indexed spending figures reveals that, in fact, the older householders are the best customers. Householders aged 65 to 74 spend 55 percent more than the average household on postage (with an index of 155) versus 9 percent below average spending by householders aged 35 to 44 (with an index of 91). The postal service can use this type of information to craft advertising and promotions to appeal to its best customers.

Note that because of sampling errors, small differences in index values may be insignificant. But the broader patterns revealed by indexes can guide marketers to the best customers.

• **Total (Aggregate) Spending** To produce the total (aggregate) spending figures, New Strategist multiplies average spending by the number of households in a segment. The result is the dollar size of the total household market and of each market segment. All totals are shown in thousands of dollars. To convert the numbers in the total spending tables to dollars, you must append "000" to the number. For example, households headed by people aged 35 to 44 spent nearly $6 billion ($5,839,196,000) on major appliances in 2005.

When comparing the total spending figures in this report with total spending estimates from the Bureau of Economic Analysis, other government agencies, or trade associations, keep in mind that the Consumer Expenditure Survey includes only household spending, not spending by businesses or institutions. Sales data also will differ from household spending totals because sales figures for consumer products include the value of goods sold to industries, government, and foreign markets, which may be a significant proportion of sales.

• **Market Shares (Biggest Customers)** New Strategist produces market share figures by converting total (aggregate) spending data into percentages. To calculate the percentage of total spending on an item that is controlled by each demographic segment—i.e., its market share—each segment's total spending on an item is divided by aggregate household spending on the item.

Market shares reveal the biggest customers—the demographic segments that account for the largest share of spending on a particular product or service. In 2005, for example, households headed by college graduates accounted for 52 percent of spending on gardening and lawn care services. By targeting only the most educated consumers, lawn care companies could reach the majority of their customers. There is a danger here, however. By single-mindedly targeting the biggest customers, businesses cannot nurture potential growth markets. With competition for customers more heated than ever, targeting potential markets is increasingly important to business survival.

• **Product-Specific Tables** The product-specific tables reveal at a glance the demographic characteristics of spending by individual product category. These tables show average spending, indexed spending (Best Customers), and market shares (Biggest Customers) by age, income, household type, race and Hispanic origin, region of residence, and education. If you want to see the spending pattern for an individual product at a glance, these are the tables for you.

History and methodology of the Consumer Expenditure Survey

The Consumer Expenditure Survey is an ongoing study of the day-to-day spending of American households. In taking the survey, government interviewers collect spending data on products and services as well as the amount and sources of household income, changes in saving and debt, and demographic and economic characteristics of household members. The Bureau of the Census collects data for the Consumer Expenditure Survey under contract with the Bureau of Labor Statistics, which is responsible for analysis and release of the survey data.

Since the late nineteenth century, the federal government has conducted expenditure surveys about every ten years. Although the results have been used for a variety of purposes, their primary application is to track consumer prices. In 1980, the Consumer Expenditure Survey became continuous with annual release of data (with a lag time of about two years between data collection and release). The survey is used to update prices for the market basket of products and services used in calculating the Consumer Price Index.

The Consumer Expenditure Survey consists of two separate surveys: an interview survey and a diary survey. In the interview portion of the survey, respondents are asked each quarter for five consecutive quarters to report their expenditures for the previous three months. The purchase of big-ticket items such as houses, cars, and major appliances, or recurring expenses such as insurance premiums, utility payments, and rent are recorded by the interview survey. The interview component covers about 95 percent of all expenditures.

Expenditures on small, frequently purchased items are recorded during a two-week period by the diary survey. These detailed records include expenses for food and beverages purchased in grocery stores and at restaurants, as well as other items such as tobacco, housekeeping supplies, nonprescription drugs, and personal care products and services. The diary survey is intended to capture expenditures respondents are likely to forget or recall incorrectly over longer periods of time.

Two separate, nationally representative samples are used for the interview and diary surveys. For the interview survey, about 7,500 consumer units are interviewed on a rotating panel basis each quarter for five consecutive quarters. Another 7,500 consumer units keep weekly diaries of spending for two consecutive weeks. Data collection is carried out in 105 areas of the country.

The Bureau of Labor Statistics reviews, audits, and cleanses the data, then weights them to reflect the number and characteristics of all U.S. consumer units. Like any sample survey, the Consumer Expenditure Survey is subject to two major types of error. Nonsampling error occurs when respondents misinterpret questions or interviewers are inconsistent in the way they ask questions or record answers. Respondents may forget items, recall expenses incorrectly, or deliberately give wrong answers. A respondent may remember how much he or she spent at the grocery store but forget the items picked up at a local convenience store. Nonsampling error can also be caused by mistakes during the various stages of data processing and refinement.

Sampling error occurs when a sample does not accurately represent the population it is supposed to represent. This kind of error is present in every sample-based survey and is minimized by using a proper sampling procedure. Standard error tables documenting the extent of sampling error in the Consumer Expenditure Survey are available from the Bureau of Labor Statistics at http://www.bls.gov/cex/csxstnderror.htm.

Although the Consumer Expenditure Survey is the best source of information about the spending behavior of American households, it should be treated with caution because of the above problems.

For more information

To find out more about the Consumer Expenditure Survey, contact the specialists at the Bureau of Labor Statistics at (202) 691-6900, or visit the Consumer Expenditure Survey home page at http://www.bls.gov/cex/. The web site includes news releases, technical documentation, and current and historical summary-level data. The detailed average spending data shown in this report are available from the Bureau of Labor Statistics only by special request.

For a comprehensive look at detailed household spending data for all products and services, see the 12th edition of *Household Spending: Who Spends How Much on What*. New Strategist's books are available in hardcopy or as downloads by visiting http://www.newstrategist.com or by calling 1-800-848-0842.

Table 1. Percent Reporting Expenditure and Amount Spent, Average Week or Quarter 2005

(percent of consumer units reporting expenditure and amount spent by purchasers during an average week or quarter, 2005)

	average quarter	
	percent reporting expenditure	**amount spent by purchasers**
HOUSEHOLD FURNISHINGS	**53.5%**	**$639.54**
Appliances, kitchen, small electric	7.4	63.47
Appliances, major	8.5	617.10
Bathroom linens	6.9	47.86
Bedroom furniture excl. mattresses and springs	2.5	957.76
Bedroom linens	11.0	106.27
Closet and storage items	1.8	66.90
Curtains and draperies	2.6	178.94
Decorative items for the home	7.7	185.17
Floor coverings, nonpermanent	3.1	244.04
Floor coverings, wall-to-wall	0.3	1,843.38
Housewares	10.0	75.90
Kitchen and dining room furniture	1.5	830.96
Kitchen and dining room linens	2.0	26.65
Lamps and lighting fixtures	3.7	131.84
Lawn and garden equipment	2.7	478.95
Living room chairs	2.2	608.45
Living room tables	1.7	265.03
Mattresses and springs	1.9	773.53
Outdoor equipment	0.8	312.80
Outdoor furniture	1.9	67.75
Plants and fresh flowers, indoor	12.9	88.51
Sewing materials for household items	3.9	65.52
Sofas	2.4	1,109.02
Wall units, cabinets, and other furniture	3.2	477.70

	average week	
	percent reporting expenditure	**amount spent by purchasers**
HOUSEHOLD SUPPLIES	**55.8%**	**$21.05**
Cleansing and toilet tissue, paper towels, and napkins	27.4	6.69
Laundry and cleaning supplies	30.0	8.60
Lawn and garden supplies	7.5	24.30
Postage	10.2	12.89
Stationery, stationery supplies, giftwrap	18.7	8.75

	average quarter	
	percent reporting expenditure	**amount spent by purchasers**
HOUSEHOLD SERVICES	**61.0%**	**$326.47**
Appliance repair, including service center	2.6	141.31
Babysitting and childcare in other home	1.3	562.30
Babysitting and childcare in own home	2.0	523.48
Day care centers, nursery schools, preschools	5.0	1,116.12
Gardening, lawn care service	13.9	172.67
Housekeeping services	5.8	395.79
Moving, storage, and freight express	2.0	460.10
Security system service fee	3.9	105.91
Termite/pest control services	3.3	119.25

Note: Expenditures shown are total net outlays at the time of purchase, whether or not the item was financed.
Source: Calculations by New Strategist based on the 2005 Consumer Expenditure Survey

Household Spending Trends 2000 to 2005

Between 2000 and 2005, spending by the average household rose by a substantial 8 percent, after adjusting for inflation. In 2005, the average household spent $46,409, according to the Bureau of Labor Statistics' Consumer Expenditure Survey.

Spending surged on a number of items between 2000 and 2005. Not surprisingly, one of the biggest gainers was gasoline. The average household spent 38 percent more on gasoline in 2005 than in 2000, after adjusting for inflation. The average household spent $1,361 on out-of-pocket health insurance costs, 22 percent more than in 2000. Spending on property taxes was up 19 percent, and spending on natural gas increased by 36 percent. As college costs soared, average household spending on education rose by a substantial 31 percent. Households boosted their spending on a handful of discretionary categories. Spending on entertainment was up 13 percent, primarily due to a 26 percent increase in spending on the category audio and visual equipment and services. Behind this gain is the growing popularity of high-priced HDTVs. Spending on food away from home (primarily restaurant meals) climbed 9 percent.

The average household cut its spending on a number of products and services between 2000 and 2005. Apparel spending fell 10 percent, after adjusting for inflation. Spending on household personal services (a category dominated by day care) fell 13 percent because fewer households have day care expenses now that the small generation X dominates families with preschoolers. The category "other lodging," which includes hotels and motels on trips, fell 7 percent as households cut back on travel spending. Average household spending on public transportation (a category dominated by airfares) was also down 7 percent. Spending on gifts for people in other households fell by a substantial 11 percent between 2000 and 2005.

■ Household spending has recovered from the recession of 2001 and the sluggish economy that followed, but nondiscretionary items—such as gasoline, health insurance, and property taxes—are experiencing some of the biggest spending gains.

Households are spending less on some items, more on others.

(percent change in spending by the average household on selected products and services, 2000 to 2005; in 2005 dollars)

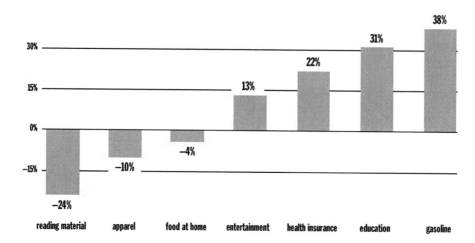

Table 2. Household Spending Trends, 2000 to 2005

(average annual spending of consumer units, 2000 and 2005; percent change, 2000–05; in 2005 dollars)

	2005	2000	percent change 2000–05
Number of consumer units (in 000s)	117,356	109,367	7.3%
Average annual spending of CUs	$46,409	$43,127	7.6
FOOD	**5,931**	**5,847**	**1.4**
Food at home	**3,297**	**3,425**	**−3.7**
Cereals and bakery products	445	514	−13.4
Cereals and cereal products	143	177	−19.2
Bakery products	302	337	−10.4
Meats, poultry, fish, and eggs	764	901	−15.2
Beef	228	270	−15.6
Pork	153	189	−19.0
Other meats	103	114	−9.6
Poultry	134	164	−18.3
Fish and seafood	113	125	−9.6
Eggs	33	39	−15.4
Dairy products	378	368	2.7
Fresh milk and cream	146	148	−1.4
Other dairy products	232	219	5.9
Fruits and vegetables	552	591	−6.6
Fresh fruits	182	185	−1.6
Fresh vegetables	175	180	−2.8
Processed fruits	106	130	−18.5
Processed vegetables	89	95	−6.3
Other food at home	1,158	1,051	10.2
Sugar and other sweets	119	133	−10.5
Fats and oils	85	94	−9.6
Miscellaneous foods	609	495	23.0
Nonalcoholic beverages	303	283	7.1
Food prepared by consumer unit on trips	41	45	−8.9
Food away from home	**2,634**	**2,422**	**8.8**
ALCOHOLIC BEVERAGES	**426**	**422**	**0.9**
HOUSING	**15,167**	**13,964**	**8.6**
Shelter	**8,805**	**8,064**	**9.2**
Owned dwellings	5,958	5,217	14.2
Mortgage interest and charges	3,317	2,991	10.9
Property taxes	1,541	1,291	19.4
Maintenance, repair, insurance, other expenses	1,101	935	17.8
Rented dwellings	2,345	2,306	1.7
Other lodging	502	542	−7.4
Utilities, fuels, and public services	**3,183**	**2,821**	**12.8**
Natural gas	473	348	35.9
Electricity	1,155	1,033	11.8
Fuel oil and other fuels	142	110	29.1
Telephone	1,048	994	5.4
Water and other public services	366	336	8.9
Household services	**801**	**775**	**3.4**
Personal services	322	370	−13.0
Other household services	479	406	18.0
Housekeeping supplies	**611**	**546**	**11.9**
Laundry and cleaning supplies	134	148	−9.5
Other household products	320	256	25.0
Postage and stationery	157	143	9.8
Household furnishings and equipment	**1,767**	**1,756**	**0.6**
Household textiles	132	120	10.0
Furniture	467	443	5.4
Floor coverings	56	50	12.0

	2005	2000	percent change 2000–05
Major appliances	$223	$214	4.2%
Small appliances and miscellaneous housewares	105	99	6.1
Miscellaneous household equipment	782	829	−5.7
APPAREL AND RELATED SERVICES	**1,886**	**2,104**	**−10.4**
Men and boys	**440**	**499**	**−11.8**
Men, aged 16 or older	349	390	−10.5
Boys, aged 2 to 15	91	109	−16.5
Women and girls	**754**	**822**	**−8.3**
Women, aged 16 or older	633	688	−8.0
Girls, aged 2 to 15	121	134	−9.7
Children under age 2	**82**	**93**	**−11.8**
Footwear	**320**	**389**	**−17.7**
Other apparel products and services	**290**	**302**	**−4.0**
TRANSPORTATION	**8,344**	**8,408**	**−0.8**
Vehicle purchases	**3,544**	**3,875**	**−8.5**
Cars and trucks, new	1,931	1,819	6.2
Cars and trucks, used	1,531	2,006	−23.7
Other vehicles	82	49	67.3
Gasoline and motor oil	**2,013**	**1,463**	**37.6**
Other vehicle expenses	**2,339**	**2,586**	**−9.6**
Vehicle finance charges	297	372	−20.2
Maintenance and repairs	671	707	−5.1
Vehicle insurance	913	882	3.5
Vehicle rentals, leases, licenses, other charges	458	625	−26.7
Public transportation	**448**	**484**	**−7.4**
HEALTH CARE	**2,664**	**2,342**	**13.7**
Health insurance	1,361	1,114	22.2
Medical services	677	644	5.1
Drugs	521	472	10.4
Medical supplies	105	112	−6.3
ENTERTAINMENT	**2,388**	**2,112**	**13.1**
Fees and admissions	588	584	0.7
Audio and visual equipment and services	888	705	26.0
Pets, toys, hobbies, and playground equipment	420	379	10.8
Other entertainment products and services	492	445	10.6
PERSONAL CARE PRODUCTS, SERVICES	**541**	**639**	**−15.3**
READING	**126**	**166**	**−24.1**
EDUCATION	**940**	**716**	**31.3**
TOBACCO PRODUCTS, SMOKING SUPPLIES	**319**	**362**	**−11.9**
MISCELLANEOUS	**808**	**880**	**−8.2**
CASH CONTRIBUTIONS	**1,663**	**1,351**	**23.1**
PERSONAL INSURANCE AND PENSIONS	**5,204**	**3,814**	**36.4**
Life and other personal insurance	381	452	−15.7
Pensions and Social Security*	4,823	3,362	43.5
PERSONAL TAXES	**2,408**	**3,533**	**−31.8**
Federal income taxes	1,696	2,731	−37.9
State and local income taxes	534	637	−16.2
Other taxes	177	166	6.6
GIFTS FOR PEOPLE IN OTHER HOUSEHOLDS	**1,091**	**1,228**	**−11.2**

Spending on pensions and Social Security in 2005 is not comparable with 2000 because of changes in methodology.

Note: Spending by category will not add to total spending because gift spending is also included in the preceding product and service categories and personal taxes are not included in the total.

Source: Bureau of Labor Statistics, 2000 and 2005 Consumer Expenditure Surveys, Internet site http://www.bls.gov/cex/; calculations by New Strategist

Household Spending on Household Furnishings, Services, and Supplies, 2005

Between 2000 and 2005, average household spending on home furnishings and supplies climbed 6 percent to $1,880, after adjusting for inflation. Spending on household services fell 7 percent during those years, to $593. The increase in spending on household furnishings and supplies was surprisingly modest, considering the housing boom. Spending may have been restrained by oversized mortgage payments, limiting the amount of discretionary dollars available to new homeowners. The decline in spending on household services was due to the entry of the small generation x into the childrearing lifestage. With a smaller proportion of households spending on day care, household service spending fell.

The average household boosted its spending on many household items between 2000 and 2005. Spending on bedroom linens was up a substantial 29 percent, after adjusting for inflation. Spending on closet and storage items rose 57 percent during those years. But spending fell on such items as curtains and draperies, decorative items for the home, mattresses and springs, wall-to-wall carpeting, and plants and fresh flowers. The average household cut spending on most household services, including day care. Spending on termite and pest control rose 25 percent, however.

Within the home furnishings category, the average household spends the most on major appliances—an average of $223 in 2005. Within the household services category, the average household spends the most on day care, an annual average of $225 in 2005. These average spending figures appear low because the Bureau of Labor Statistics calculates the average for all households, whether or not they purchased items in the category. The Percent Reporting table shows how much purchasers spend on these items. During an average quarter of 2005, for example, 8.5 percent of households purchased major appliances, spending $617 on them during the quarter. Five percent of households paid for day care during an average quarter of 2005, spending $1,116 for the quarter (or $4,464 annually).

Spending by age

Households headed by people ranging in age from 35 to 64 spend the most on household furnishings and supplies. Behind the higher spending is the fact that homeownership becomes the norm for householders in their thirties and rises with age. Householders aged 55 to 64 spend the most on major appliances, lawn and garden equipment, and wall-to-wall carpeting. Householders aged 25 to 44 devote the most to household services, spending 36 to 52 percent more than the average household. Day care expenses are behind this spending. Householders aged 25 to 44 account for 83 percent of spending on day care centers.

Spending by household income

The most affluent households spend much more than average on household furnishings, services, and supplies. In 2005, households with incomes of $100,000 or more spent more than twice the average on household furnishings and supplies and household services. This income group accounts for only 15 percent of households but controls at least 50 percent of the market for floor coverings, housekeeping services, and outdoor furniture. They control 56 percent of the market for lamps and lighting fixtures.

Spending by household type

Married couples spend 36 percent more than average on household furnishings, supplies, and services. But spending varies by category depending on family composition. Married couples without children at home (many of them empty-nesters) spend well above average on a number of household items. They are the biggest spenders on gardening and lawn care services and indoor plants and fresh flowers. Married couples with preschoolers spend more than eight times the average on day care centers and more than six times the average on infants' equipment and furniture.

Spending by race and Hispanic origin

Blacks and Hispanics spend less than average on household furnishings and household services. Asians spend an average amount on furnishings and 20 percent more than average on household services. Behind this higher spending is day care, on which Asians spend 58 percent more than the average household. Blacks spend 15 percent more than average on home security system service fees. Hispanics spend twice the average on infants' furniture, 17 percent more on laundry and cleaning supplies, and 62 percent more on babysitting services.

Spending by region

Households in the West spend the most on household furnishings and supplies (with an index of 120), while those in the Northeast spend the least (with an index of 92). Western households are the biggest spenders on infants' equipment because so many Hispanics, with relatively large families, live in the region. Households in the South spend 50 percent more than average on termite and pest control.

Spending by education

Spending on household furnishings, services, and supplies rises with education because educated householders have higher incomes. College graduates spend more than twice the average on housekeeping services. They also spend more than twice the average on floor coverings, controlling 55 percent of the market. College graduates spend less than the average household on lawn and garden equipment.

Table 3. Household Furnishings, Services, and Supplies Spending, 2000 to 2005

(average annual spending of households on household furnishings, services, and supplies, and percent distribution of spending by type, 2000 to 2005; percent change, 2000–05; in 2005 dollars)

	2005		2000		
	average household spending	percent distribution	average household spending (in 2005$)	percent distribution	percent change 2000–05
Household furnishings and supplies	**$1,879.74**	**100.0%**	**$1,765.04**	**100.0%**	**6.5%**
Appliances, major	223.33	11.9	214.31	12.1	4.2
Decorative items for the home	189.76	10.1	201.09	11.4	−5.6
Laundry and cleaning supplies	134.13	7.1	148.30	8.4	−9.6
Sofas	106.91	5.7	101.11	5.7	5.7
Cleansing and toilet tissue, paper towels, and napkins	94.91	5.0	77.63	4.4	22.3
Lawn and garden supplies	94.26	5.0	75.95	4.3	24.1
Bedroom furniture, excl. mattresses and springs	93.86	5.0	78.38	4.4	19.7
Stationery, stationery supplies, giftwrap	85.27	4.5	72.19	4.1	18.1
Housewares	80.36	4.3	73.57	4.2	9.2
Postage	67.89	3.6	68.73	3.9	−1.2
Bedroom linens	65.03	3.5	50.49	2.9	28.8
Wall units, cabinets, and other furniture	61.91	3.3	57.40	3.3	7.9
Mattresses and springs	57.86	3.1	59.99	3.4	−3.5
Power tools	53.67	2.9	24.18	1.4	122.0
Living room chairs	52.57	2.8	49.72	2.8	5.7
Lawn and garden equipment	50.96	2.7	53.10	3.0	−4.0
Kitchen and dining room furniture	50.19	2.7	52.69	3.0	−4.8
Plants and fresh flowers, indoor	45.53	2.4	64.66	3.7	−29.6
Floor coverings, nonpermanent	29.87	1.6	17.26	1.0	73.0
Outdoor equipment	28.69	1.5	20.86	1.2	37.6
Floor coverings, wall-to-wall	26.34	1.4	33.07	1.9	−20.4
Infants' equipment and furniture	22.29	1.2	16.14	0.9	38.1
Bathroom linens	21.86	1.2	19.90	1.1	9.8
Lamps and lighting fixtures	19.67	1.0	12.25	0.7	60.6
Kitchen appliances, small electric	18.66	1.0	19.33	1.1	−3.4
Curtains and draperies	18.61	1.0	23.89	1.4	−22.1
Outdoor furniture	18.02	1.0	17.19	1.0	4.8
Living room tables	17.81	0.9	19.50	1.1	−8.6
Laundry and cleaning equipment	16.47	0.9	11.43	0.6	44.1
Closet and storage items	14.34	0.8	9.11	0.5	57.5
Sewing materials for household items	10.09	0.5	11.06	0.6	−8.8
Kitchen and dining room linens	8.63	0.5	10.56	0.6	−18.3
Household services	**593.11**	**100.0**	**639.38**	**36.2**	**−7.2**
Day care centers, nursery schools, preschools	225.01	37.9	236.38	13.4	−4.8
Gardening and lawn care services	95.73	16.1	99.98	5.7	−4.2
Housekeeping services	92.14	15.5	88.76	5.0	3.8
Babysitting and childcare in own or other home	70.25	11.8	73.49	4.2	−4.4
Moving, storage, and freight express	36.44	6.1	36.78	2.1	−0.9
Care for the elderly, invalids, handicapped	24.79	4.2	57.14	3.2	−56.6
Termite and pest control	17.80	3.0	14.27	0.8	24.8
Security system service fee	16.48	2.8	21.17	1.2	−22.2
Appliance repair, including service center	14.47	2.4	11.41	0.6	26.8

Source: Bureau of Labor Statistics, 2000 and 2005 Consumer Expenditure Surveys; calculations by New Strategist

Table 4. Household Furnishings, Services, and Supplies: Average spending by age, 2005

(average annual spending of consumer units (CU) on household furnishings, services, and supplies, by age of consumer unit reference person, 2005)

	total consumer units	under 25	25 to 34	35 to 44	45 to 54	55 to 64	65 to 74	75+
Number of consumer units (in 000s)	117,356	8,543	19,635	23,835	24,393	18,104	11,505	11,342
Number of persons per CU	2.5	2.1	2.8	3.2	2.7	2.1	1.9	1.5
Average before-tax income of CU	$58,712.00	$27,494.00	$55,066.00	$72,699.00	$75,266.00	$64,156.00	$45,202.00	$28,552.00
Average spending of CU, total	46,408.80	27,776.50	45,068.47	55,189.79	55,854.14	49,592.08	38,573.50	27,018.17
Household furnishings and supplies	**1,879.74**	**918.07**	**1,641.96**	**2,276.99**	**2,056.74**	**2,418.96**	**1,831.18**	**1,035.57**
Appliances, kitchen, small electric	18.66	12.26	19.40	20.83	19.93	20.29	18.13	12.86
Appliances, major	223.33	95.29	183.93	247.01	239.38	298.03	216.54	191.75
Bathroom linens	21.86	10.76	23.37	26.40	31.41	18.75	15.76	8.99
Bedroom furniture, excl. mattresses and springs	93.86	78.17	143.45	129.25	70.16	85.99	80.48	22.57
Bedroom linens	65.03	30.72	73.87	79.05	84.09	64.00	44.88	28.21
Cleansing and toilet tissue, paper towels, and napkins	94.91	48.95	76.35	110.96	104.82	109.44	102.98	78.33
Closet and storage items	14.34	5.02	11.55	28.46	16.71	10.71	8.39	3.46
Curtains and draperies	18.61	7.41	19.71	25.97	14.30	23.89	22.74	6.31
Decorative items for the home	189.76	92.63	120.16	209.17	206.54	343.73	219.97	44.86
Floor coverings	56.20	17.31	41.18	54.55	90.79	82.56	33.71	21.29
Floor coverings, nonpermanent	29.87	6.02	20.47	20.46	63.70	38.51	21.68	5.61
Wall-to-wall carpeting	26.34	11.29	20.71	34.08	27.09	44.06	12.03	15.69
Housewares	80.36	53.21	66.27	74.46	96.94	107.01	89.83	53.11
Infants' equipment	13.99	17.15	23.14	16.16	10.69	19.80	1.94	1.06
Infants' furniture	8.30	10.68	20.74	8.94	5.36	5.62	1.87	0.75
Kitchen and dining room furniture	50.19	22.75	59.75	75.88	48.22	57.74	33.17	9.82
Kitchen and dining room linens	8.63	2.71	5.37	8.45	8.86	10.62	14.90	9.38
Lamps and lighting fixtures	19.67	5.05	26.96	26.20	18.52	19.37	18.73	8.21
Laundry and cleaning equipment	16.47	8.80	13.43	18.78	21.05	21.06	12.60	10.25
Laundry and cleaning supplies	134.13	63.31	127.33	161.23	154.45	149.58	122.37	89.42
Lawn and garden equipment	50.96	15.02	17.94	61.02	44.67	100.94	67.13	31.39
Lawn and garden supplies	94.26	15.33	58.82	108.30	137.24	122.57	90.15	59.32
Living room chairs	52.57	18.52	31.01	65.01	44.32	79.79	75.07	40.83
Living room tables	17.81	8.05	22.59	27.32	12.89	16.80	22.39	4.47
Mattresses and springs	57.86	38.07	69.32	68.20	54.28	67.18	54.75	27.18
Outdoor equipment	28.69	3.59	19.83	23.49	52.81	39.99	15.49	20.48
Outdoor furniture	18.02	1.98	10.23	33.58	19.12	22.67	13.07	6.10
Plants and fresh flowers, indoor	45.53	18.71	31.02	52.77	52.77	59.79	54.12	28.54
Postage	67.89	30.93	39.13	62.03	73.53	91.94	105.16	73.12
Power tools	53.67	27.88	23.93	121.54	41.13	55.14	22.74	40.29
Sewing materials for household items	10.09	2.84	4.91	7.34	14.23	17.08	12.68	7.60
Sofas	106.91	93.46	122.56	136.68	100.29	114.64	95.35	40.96
Stationery, stationery supplies, giftwrap	85.27	36.34	77.23	106.38	98.67	106.09	78.32	39.74
Wall units, cabinets, and other furniture	61.91	25.17	57.48	81.58	68.57	76.15	65.77	14.92
Household services	**593.11**	**275.70**	**805.83**	**903.36**	**422.09**	**458.08**	**473.70**	**516.41**
Appliance repair, including service center	14.47	1.88	10.02	14.47	16.94	17.83	19.60	15.74
Babysitting and childcare in own or other home	70.25	84.34	136.98	165.50	32.17	3.97	1.62	1.21
Care for the elderly, invalids, handicapped, etc.	24.79	0.41	0.30	1.86	8.34	21.99	82.40	115.17
Day care centers, nursery schools, preschools	225.01	151.75	513.40	496.51	91.28	40.01	10.60	10.81
Gardening, lawn care service	95.73	12.90	36.87	72.54	93.62	148.93	138.24	185.25
Housekeeping services	92.14	2.80	56.77	88.78	99.58	130.36	104.97	137.68
Moving, storage, and freight express	36.44	13.55	25.87	27.89	41.67	49.22	75.53	18.69
Security system service fee	16.48	5.40	14.19	18.61	17.55	20.45	19.48	12.65
Termite and pest control services	17.80	2.67	11.43	17.20	20.94	25.32	21.26	19.21

Source: Bureau of Labor Statistics, unpublished tables from the 2005 Consumer Expenditure Survey

Table 5. Household Furnishings, Services, and Supplies: Indexed spending by age, 2005

(indexed average annual spending of consumer units (CU) on household furnishings, services, and supplies by age of consumer unit reference person, 2005; index definition: an index of 100 is the average for all consumer units; an index of 132 means that spending by consumer units in that group is 32 percent above the average for all consumer units; an index of 68 indicates spending that is 32 percent below the average for all consumer units)

	total consumer units	under 25	25 to 34	35 to 44	45 to 54	55 to 64	65 to 74	75+
Average spending of CU, total	$46,409	$27,777	$45,068	$55,190	$55,854	$49,592	$38,574	$27,018
Average spending of CU, index	100	60	97	119	120	107	83	58
Household furnishings and supplies	100	49	87	121	109	129	97	55
Appliances, kitchen, small electric	100	66	104	112	107	109	97	69
Appliances, major	100	43	82	111	107	133	97	86
Bathroom linens	100	49	107	121	144	86	72	41
Bedroom furniture, excl. mattresses and springs	100	83	153	138	75	92	86	24
Bedroom linens	100	47	114	122	129	98	69	43
Cleansing and toilet tissue, paper towels, and napkins	100	52	80	117	110	115	109	83
Closet and storage items	100	35	81	198	117	75	59	24
Curtains and draperies	100	40	106	140	77	128	122	34
Decorative items for the home	100	49	63	110	109	181	116	24
Floor coverings	100	31	73	97	162	147	60	38
Floor coverings, nonpermanent	100	20	69	68	213	129	73	19
Wall-to-wall carpeting	100	43	79	129	103	167	46	60
Housewares	100	66	82	93	121	133	112	66
Infants' equipment	100	123	165	116	76	142	14	8
Infants' furniture	100	129	250	108	65	68	23	9
Kitchen and dining room furniture	100	45	119	151	96	115	66	20
Kitchen and dining room linens	100	31	62	98	103	123	173	109
Lamps and lighting fixtures	100	26	137	133	94	98	95	42
Laundry and cleaning equipment	100	53	82	114	128	128	77	62
Laundry and cleaning supplies	100	47	95	120	115	112	91	67
Lawn and garden equipment	100	29	35	120	88	198	132	62
Lawn and garden supplies	100	16	62	115	146	130	96	63
Living room chairs	100	35	59	124	84	152	143	78
Living room tables	100	45	127	153	72	94	126	25
Mattresses and springs	100	66	120	118	94	116	95	47
Outdoor equipment	100	13	69	82	184	139	54	71
Outdoor furniture	100	11	57	186	106	126	73	34
Plants and fresh flowers, indoor	100	41	68	116	116	131	119	63
Postage	100	46	58	91	108	135	155	108
Power tools	100	52	45	226	77	103	42	75
Sewing materials for household items	100	28	49	73	141	169	126	75
Sofas	100	87	115	128	94	107	89	38
Stationery, stationery supplies, giftwrap	100	43	91	125	116	124	92	47
Wall units, cabinets, and other furniture	100	41	93	132	111	123	106	24
Household services	100	46	136	152	71	77	80	87
Appliance repair, including service center	100	13	69	100	117	123	135	109
Babysitting and childcare in own or other home	100	120	195	236	46	6	2	2
Care for the elderly, invalids, handicapped, etc.	100	2	1	8	34	89	332	465
Day care centers, nursery schools, preschools	100	67	228	221	41	18	5	5
Gardening, lawn care service	100	13	39	76	98	156	144	194
Housekeeping services	100	3	62	96	108	141	114	149
Moving, storage, and freight express	100	37	71	77	114	135	207	51
Security system service fee	100	33	86	113	106	124	118	77
Termite and pest control services	100	15	64	97	118	142	119	108

Source: Calculations by New Strategist based on the Bureau of Labor Statistics' 2005 Consumer Expenditure Survey

Table 6. Household Furnishings, Services, and Supplies: Total spending by age, 2005

(total annual spending on household furnishings, services, and supplies, by consumer unit (CU) age groups, 2005; consumer units and dollars in thousands)

	total consumer units	under 25	25 to 34	35 to 44	45 to 54	55 to 64	65 to 74	75+
Number of consumer units	117,356	8,543	19,635	23,835	24,393	18,104	11,505	11,342
Total spending of all CUs	$5,446,351,133	$237,294,640	$884,919,408	$1,315,448,645	$1,362,450,037	$897,815,016	$443,788,118	$306,440,084
Household furnishings and supplies	220,598,767	7,843,072	32,239,885	54,272,057	50,170,059	43,792,852	21,067,726	11,745,435
Appliances, kitchen, small electric	2,189,863	104,737	380,919	496,483	486,152	367,330	208,586	145,858
Appliances, major	26,209,115	814,062	3,611,466	5,887,483	5,839,196	5,395,535	2,491,293	2,174,829
Bathroom linens	2,565,402	91,923	458,870	629,244	766,184	339,450	181,319	101,965
Bedroom furniture, except mattresses and springs	11,015,034	667,806	2,816,641	3,080,674	1,711,413	1,556,763	925,922	255,989
Bedroom linens	7,631,661	262,441	1,450,437	1,884,157	2,051,207	1,158,656	516,344	319,958
Cleansing and toilet tissue, paper towels, and napkins	11,138,258	418,180	1,499,132	2,644,732	2,556,874	1,981,302	1,184,785	888,419
Closet and storage items	1,682,885	42,886	226,784	678,344	407,607	193,894	96,527	39,243
Curtains and draperies	2,183,995	63,304	387,006	618,995	348,820	432,505	261,624	71,568
Decorative items for the home	22,269,475	791,338	2,359,342	4,985,567	5,038,130	6,222,888	2,530,755	508,802
Floor coverings	6,595,407	147,879	808,569	1,300,199	2,214,640	1,494,666	387,834	241,471
Floor coverings, nonpermanent	3,505,424	51,429	401,928	487,664	1,553,834	697,185	249,428	63,629
Wall-to-wall carpeting	3,091,157	96,450	406,641	812,297	660,806	797,662	138,405	177,956
Housewares	9,430,728	454,573	1,301,211	1,774,754	2,364,657	1,937,309	1,033,494	602,374
Infants' equipment	1,641,810	146,512	454,354	385,174	260,761	358,459	22,320	12,023
Infants' furniture	974,055	91,239	407,230	213,085	130,746	101,744	21,514	8,507
Kitchen and dining room furniture	5,890,098	194,353	1,173,191	1,808,600	1,176,230	1,045,325	381,621	111,378
Kitchen and dining room linens	1,012,782	23,152	105,440	201,406	216,122	192,264	171,425	106,388
Lamps and lighting fixtures	2,308,393	43,142	529,360	624,477	451,758	350,674	215,489	93,118
Laundry and cleaning equipment	1,932,853	75,178	263,698	447,621	513,473	381,270	144,963	116,256
Laundry and cleaning supplies	15,740,960	540,857	2,500,125	3,842,917	3,767,499	2,707,996	1,407,867	1,014,202
Lawn and garden equipment	5,980,462	128,316	352,252	1,454,412	1,089,635	1,827,418	772,331	356,025
Lawn and garden supplies	11,061,977	130,964	1,154,931	2,581,331	3,347,695	2,219,007	1,037,176	672,807
Living room chairs	6,169,405	158,216	608,881	1,549,513	1,081,098	1,444,518	863,680	463,094
Living room tables	2,090,110	68,771	443,555	651,172	314,426	304,147	257,597	50,699
Mattresses and springs	6,790,218	325,232	1,361,098	1,625,547	1,324,052	1,216,227	629,899	308,276
Outdoor equipment	3,366,944	30,669	389,362	559,884	1,288,194	723,979	178,212	232,284
Outdoor furniture	2,114,755	16,915	200,866	800,379	466,394	410,418	150,370	69,186
Plants and fresh flowers, indoor	5,343,219	159,840	609,078	1,257,773	1,287,219	1,082,438	622,651	323,701
Postage	7,967,299	264,235	768,318	1,478,485	1,793,617	1,664,482	1,209,866	829,327
Power tools	6,298,497	238,179	469,866	2,896,906	1,003,284	998,255	261,624	456,969
Sewing materials for household items	1,184,122	24,262	96,408	174,949	347,112	309,216	145,883	86,199
Sofas	12,546,530	798,429	2,406,466	3,257,768	2,446,374	2,075,443	1,097,002	464,568
Stationery, stationery supplies, giftwrap	10,006,946	310,453	1,516,411	2,535,567	2,406,857	1,920,653	901,072	450,731
Wall units, cabinets, and other furniture	7,265,510	215,027	1,128,620	1,944,459	1,672,628	1,378,620	756,684	169,223
Household services	69,605,017	2,355,305	15,822,472	21,531,586	10,296,041	8,293,080	5,449,919	5,857,122
Appliance repair, incl. service center	1,698,141	16,061	196,743	344,892	413,217	322,794	225,498	178,523
Babysitting and childcare in own or other home	8,244,259	720,517	2,689,602	3,944,693	784,723	71,873	18,638	13,724
Care for the elderly, invalids, handicapped, etc.	2,909,255	3,503	5,891	44,333	203,438	398,107	948,012	1,306,258
Day care centers, nursery schools, and preschools	26,406,274	1,296,400	10,080,609	11,834,316	2,226,593	724,341	121,953	122,607
Gardening, lawn care service	11,234,490	110,205	723,942	1,728,991	2,283,673	2,696,229	1,590,451	2,101,106
Housekeeping services	10,813,182	23,920	1,114,679	2,116,071	2,429,055	2,360,037	1,207,680	1,561,567
Moving, storage, and freight express	4,276,453	115,758	507,957	664,758	1,016,456	891,079	868,973	211,982
Security system service fee	1,934,027	46,132	278,621	443,569	428,097	370,227	224,117	143,476
Termite and pest control services	2,088,937	22,810	224,428	409,962	510,789	458,393	244,596	217,880

Note: Numbers will not add to total because not all categories are shown and because of rounding.
Source: Calculations by New Strategist based on the Bureau of Labor Statistics' 2005 Consumer Expenditure Survey

Table 7. Household Furnishings, Services, and Supplies: Market shares by age, 2005

(percentage of total annual spending on household furnishings, services, and supplies accounted for by consumer unit age groups, 2005)

	total consumer units	under 25	25 to 34	35 to 44	45 to 54	55 to 64	65 to 74	75+
Share of total consumer units	100.0%	7.3%	16.7%	20.3%	20.8%	15.4%	9.8%	9.7%
Share of total before-tax income	100.0	3.4	15.7	25.1	26.6	16.9	7.5	4.7
Share of total spending	100.0	4.4	16.2	24.2	25.0	16.5	8.1	5.6
Household furnishings and supplies	100.0	3.6	14.6	24.6	22.7	19.9	9.6	5.3
Appliances, kitchen, small electric	100.0	4.8	17.4	22.7	22.2	16.8	9.5	6.7
Appliances, major	100.0	3.1	13.8	22.5	22.3	20.6	9.5	8.3
Bathroom linens	100.0	3.6	17.9	24.5	29.9	13.2	7.1	4.0
Bedroom furniture, excl. mattresses and springs	100.0	6.1	25.6	28.0	15.5	14.1	8.4	2.3
Bedroom linens	100.0	3.4	19.0	24.7	26.9	15.2	6.8	4.2
Cleansing and toilet tissue, paper towels, and napkins	100.0	3.8	13.5	23.7	23.0	17.8	10.6	8.0
Closet and storage items	100.0	2.5	13.5	40.3	24.2	11.5	5.7	2.3
Curtains and draperies	100.0	2.9	17.7	28.3	16.0	19.8	12.0	3.3
Decorative items for the home	100.0	3.6	10.6	22.4	22.6	27.9	11.4	2.3
Floor coverings	100.0	2.2	12.3	19.7	33.6	22.7	5.9	3.7
Floor coverings, nonpermanent	100.0	1.5	11.5	13.9	44.3	19.9	7.1	1.8
Wall-to-wall carpeting	100.0	3.1	13.2	26.3	21.4	25.8	4.5	5.8
Housewares	100.0	4.8	13.8	18.8	25.1	20.5	11.0	6.4
Infants' equipment	100.0	8.9	27.7	23.5	15.9	21.8	1.4	0.7
Infants' furniture	100.0	9.4	41.8	21.9	13.4	10.4	2.2	0.9
Kitchen and dining room furniture	100.0	3.3	19.9	30.7	20.0	17.7	6.5	1.9
Kitchen and dining room linens	100.0	2.3	10.4	19.9	21.3	19.0	16.9	10.5
Lamps and lighting fixtures	100.0	1.9	22.9	27.1	19.6	15.2	9.3	4.0
Laundry and cleaning equipment	100.0	3.9	13.6	23.2	26.6	19.7	7.5	6.0
Laundry and cleaning supplies	100.0	3.4	15.9	24.4	23.9	17.2	8.9	6.4
Lawn and garden equipment	100.0	2.1	5.9	24.3	18.2	30.6	12.9	6.0
Lawn and garden supplies	100.0	1.2	10.4	23.3	30.3	20.1	9.4	6.1
Living room chairs	100.0	2.6	9.9	25.1	17.5	23.4	14.0	7.5
Living room tables	100.0	3.3	21.2	31.2	15.0	14.6	12.3	2.4
Mattresses and springs	100.0	4.8	20.0	23.9	19.5	17.9	9.3	4.5
Outdoor equipment	100.0	0.9	11.6	16.6	38.3	21.5	5.3	6.9
Outdoor furniture	100.0	0.8	9.5	37.8	22.1	19.4	7.1	3.3
Plants and fresh flowers, indoor	100.0	3.0	11.4	23.5	24.1	20.3	11.7	6.1
Postage	100.0	3.3	9.6	18.6	22.5	20.9	15.2	10.4
Power tools	100.0	3.8	7.5	46.0	15.9	15.8	4.2	7.3
Sewing materials for household items	100.0	2.0	8.1	14.8	29.3	26.1	12.3	7.3
Sofas	100.0	6.4	19.2	26.0	19.5	16.5	8.7	3.7
Stationery, stationery supplies, giftwrap	100.0	3.1	15.2	25.3	24.1	19.2	9.0	4.5
Wall units, cabinets, and other furniture	100.0	3.0	15.5	26.8	23.0	19.0	10.4	2.3
Household services	100.0	3.4	22.7	30.9	14.8	11.9	7.8	8.4
Appliance repair, including service center	100.0	0.9	11.6	20.3	24.3	19.0	13.3	10.5
Babysitting and childcare in own or other home	100.0	8.7	32.6	47.8	9.5	0.9	0.2	0.2
Care for the elderly, invalids, handicapped, etc.	100.0	0.1	0.2	1.5	7.0	13.7	32.6	44.9
Day care centers, nursery schools, preschools	100.0	4.9	38.2	44.8	8.4	2.7	0.5	0.5
Gardening, lawn care service	100.0	1.0	6.4	15.4	20.3	24.0	14.2	18.7
Housekeeping services	100.0	0.2	10.3	19.6	22.5	21.8	11.2	14.4
Moving, storage, and freight express	100.0	2.7	11.9	15.5	23.8	20.8	20.3	5.0
Security system service fee	100.0	2.4	14.4	22.9	22.1	19.1	11.6	7.4
Termite and pest control services								

Note: Numbers may not add to total because of rounding.
Source: Calculations by New Strategist based on the Bureau of Labor Statistics' 2005 Consumer Expenditure Survey

Table 8. Household Furnishings, Services, and Supplies: Average spending by income, 2005

(average annual spending on household furnishings, services, and supplies, by before-tax income of consumer units (CU), 2005)

	total consumer units	under $20,000	$20,000–$39,999	$40,000–$49,999	$50,000–$69,999	$70,000–$79,999	$80,000–$99,999	$100,000 or more
Number of consumer units (in 000s)	117,356	26,890	28,637	11,451	16,956	6,725	9,448	17,248
Number of persons per CU	2.5	1.7	2.2	2.6	2.8	3.0	3.1	3.2
Average before-tax income of CU	$58,712.00	$10,830.16	$29,639.14	$44,659.00	$59,110.00	$74,523.00	$88,931.00	$167,851.00
Average spending of CU, total	46,408.80	19,643.94	31,211.19	40,264.61	49,028.61	57,696.84	65,280.30	99,127.82
Household furnishings and supplies	**1,879.74**	**726.87**	**1,158.83**	**1,566.86**	**1,781.19**	**2,169.34**	**2,676.96**	**4,521.69**
Appliances, kitchen, small electric	18.66	8.94	14.14	21.81	20.74	20.83	23.04	33.93
Appliances, major	223.33	74.47	125.70	175.37	232.38	242.60	317.13	579.81
Bathroom linens	21.86	12.52	13.06	20.74	23.70	33.67	38.97	32.22
Bedroom furniture, excl. mattresses and springs	93.86	43.00	63.63	96.28	88.98	150.84	149.65	173.77
Bedroom linens	65.03	14.37	60.27	69.66	78.56	67.97	101.57	106.24
Cleansing and toilet tissue, paper towels, and napkins	94.91	65.11	71.20	83.05	104.95	112.90	120.50	149.51
Closet and storage items	14.34	2.97	7.34	6.43	23.66	12.15	15.34	37.57
Curtains and draperies	18.61	8.19	8.75	16.17	18.31	43.07	22.15	41.65
Decorative items for the home	189.76	50.99	86.17	170.64	152.91	185.51	321.51	530.50
Floor coverings	56.20	16.30	21.84	40.42	48.30	49.22	66.28	190.88
Floor coverings, nonpermanent	29.87	4.82	8.31	13.72	28.84	24.70	24.77	121.24
Wall-to-wall carpeting	26.34	11.48	13.54	26.70	19.45	24.52	41.51	69.64
Housewares	80.36	35.11	42.95	44.09	74.73	125.76	141.42	179.95
Infants' equipment	13.99	3.40	11.93	19.42	5.89	21.30	20.96	29.92
Infants' furniture	8.30	1.99	4.51	5.90	9.41	8.28	14.81	21.36
Kitchen and dining room furniture	50.19	11.74	22.72	37.50	43.22	81.94	72.16	146.63
Kitchen and dining room linens	8.63	3.16	5.26	5.07	11.44	10.76	12.35	18.07
Lamps and lighting fixtures	19.67	4.28	8.21	12.18	13.07	19.33	18.44	74.91
Laundry and cleaning equipment	16.47	7.85	12.09	13.49	18.41	23.70	13.74	34.61
Laundry and cleaning supplies	134.13	81.11	107.27	140.84	156.31	154.57	163.57	198.07
Lawn and garden equipment	50.96	17.73	37.35	42.90	55.40	45.05	53.41	127.31
Lawn and garden supplies	94.26	42.94	46.47	69.13	84.05	98.96	111.65	258.57
Living room chairs	52.57	24.04	24.96	42.85	37.70	43.36	54.88	166.27
Living room tables	17.81	4.44	10.47	12.79	13.85	28.29	18.78	53.46
Mattresses and springs	57.86	25.46	32.06	47.57	52.77	86.44	104.18	126.52
Outdoor equipment	28.69	2.68	13.40	26.54	34.36	54.99	27.86	75.74
Outdoor furniture	18.02	1.20	5.76	5.24	11.70	13.48	27.02	76.09
Plants and fresh flowers, indoor	45.53	15.34	28.65	28.82	42.76	47.04	68.26	121.37
Postage	67.89	36.37	57.51	66.30	67.71	83.16	98.54	105.96
Power tools	53.67	21.53	70.96	38.24	26.62	31.19	81.14	111.76
Sewing materials for household items	10.09	4.96	6.76	7.57	10.30	11.80	15.74	21.31
Sofas	106.91	38.25	51.31	94.63	85.85	110.28	140.76	315.25
Stationery, stationery supplies, giftwrap	85.27	29.61	52.12	68.79	93.91	86.25	147.92	182.86
Wall units, cabinets, and other furniture	61.91	16.79	33.97	36.43	39.24	64.65	93.23	199.62
Household services	**593.11**	**188.99**	**313.33**	**426.28**	**504.18**	**687.85**	**995.33**	**1,628.60**
Appliance repair, including service center	14.47	5.71	9.82	7.95	16.11	16.51	23.29	32.92
Babysitting and childcare in own or other home	70.25	14.69	34.47	56.68	58.10	101.33	118.75	198.53
Care for the elderly, invalids, handicapped, etc.	24.79	20.99	29.25	39.48	3.50	38.29	15.33	34.41
Day care centers, nursery schools, preschools	225.01	43.33	96.31	157.29	233.48	295.24	512.71	573.63
Gardening, lawn care service	95.73	45.56	60.48	62.62	71.68	82.51	117.78	271.16
Housekeeping services	92.14	34.17	29.58	37.31	54.28	64.94	117.82	356.53
Moving, storage, and freight express	36.44	14.05	32.10	38.38	34.33	54.32	30.79	75.49
Security system service fee	16.48	4.89	10.38	14.47	15.97	14.58	27.42	41.27
Termite and pest control services	17.80	5.59	10.93	12.10	16.73	20.13	31.44	44.66

Note: Numbers will not add to total because not all categories are shown.
Source: Bureau of Labor Statistics, unpublished tables from the 2005 Consumer Expenditure Survey; calculations by New Strategist

Table 9. Household Furnishings, Services, and Supplies: Indexed spending by income, 2005

(indexed average annual spending of consumer units (CU) on household furnishings, services, and supplies by before-tax income of consumer unit, 2005; index definition: an index of 100 is the average for all consumer units; an index of 132 means that spending by consumer units in that group is 32 percent above the average for all consumer units; an index of 68 indicates spending that is 32 percent below the average for all consumer units)

	total consumer units	under $20,000	$20,000–$39,999	$40,000–$49,999	$50,000–$69,999	$70,000–$79,999	$80,000–$99,999	$100,000 or more
Average spending of CU, total	$46,409	$19,644	$31,211	$40,265	$49,029	$57,697	$65,280	$99,128
Average spending of CU, index	100	42	67	87	106	124	141	214
Household furnishings and supplies	**100**	**39**	**62**	**83**	**95**	**115**	**142**	**241**
Appliances, kitchen, small electric	100	48	76	117	111	112	123	182
Appliances, major	100	33	56	79	104	109	142	260
Bathroom linens	100	57	60	95	108	154	178	147
Bedroom furniture, excl. mattresses and springs	100	46	68	103	95	161	159	185
Bedroom linens	100	22	93	107	121	105	156	163
Cleansing and toilet tissue, paper towels, and napkins	100	69	75	88	111	119	127	158
Closet and storage items	100	21	51	45	165	85	107	262
Curtains and draperies	100	44	47	87	98	231	119	224
Decorative items for the home	100	27	45	90	81	98	169	280
Floor coverings	100	29	39	72	86	88	118	340
Floor coverings, nonpermanent	100	16	28	46	97	83	83	406
Wall-to-wall carpeting	100	44	51	101	74	93	158	264
Housewares	100	44	53	55	93	156	176	224
Infants' equipment	100	24	85	139	42	152	150	214
Infants' furniture	100	24	54	71	113	100	178	257
Kitchen and dining room furniture	100	23	45	75	86	163	144	292
Kitchen and dining room linens	100	37	61	59	133	125	143	209
Lamps and lighting fixtures	100	22	42	62	66	98	94	381
Laundry and cleaning equipment	100	48	73	82	112	144	83	210
Laundry and cleaning supplies	100	60	80	105	117	115	122	148
Lawn and garden equipment	100	35	73	84	109	88	105	250
Lawn and garden supplies	100	46	49	73	89	105	118	274
Living room chairs	100	46	47	82	72	82	104	316
Living room tables	100	25	59	72	78	159	105	300
Mattresses and springs	100	44	55	82	91	149	180	219
Outdoor equipment	100	9	47	93	120	192	97	264
Outdoor furniture	100	7	32	29	65	75	150	422
Plants and fresh flowers, indoor	100	34	63	63	94	103	150	267
Postage	100	54	85	98	100	122	145	156
Power tools	100	40	132	71	50	58	151	208
Sewing materials for household items	100	49	67	75	102	117	156	211
Sofas	100	36	48	89	80	103	132	295
Stationery, stationery supplies, giftwrap	100	35	61	81	110	101	173	214
Wall units, cabinets, and other furniture	100	27	55	59	63	104	151	322
Household services	**100**	**32**	**53**	**72**	**85**	**116**	**168**	**275**
Appliance repair, including service center	100	39	68	55	111	114	161	228
Babysitting and childcare in own or other home	100	21	49	81	83	144	169	283
Care for the elderly, invalids, handicapped, etc.	100	85	118	159	14	154	62	139
Day care centers, nursery schools, preschools	100	19	43	70	104	131	228	255
Gardening, lawn care service	100	48	63	65	75	86	123	283
Housekeeping services	100	37	32	40	59	70	128	387
Moving, storage, and freight express	100	39	88	105	94	149	84	207
Security system service fee	100	30	63	88	97	88	166	250
Termite and pest control services	100	31	61	68	94	113	177	251

Source: Calculations by New Strategist based on the Bureau of Labor Statistics' 2005 Consumer Expenditure Survey

Table 10. Household Furnishings, Services, and Supplies: Total spending by income, 2005

(total annual spending on household furnishings, services, and supplies, by before-tax income group of consumer units (CU), 2005; consumer units and dollars in thousands)

	total consumer units	under $20,000	$20,000– $39,999	$40,000– $49,999	$50,000– $69,999	$70,000– $79,999	$80,000– $99,999	$100,000 or more
Number of consumer units	117,356	26,890	28,637	11,451	16,956	6,725	9,448	17,248
Total spending of all CUs	$5,446,351,133	$528,225,562	$893,794,801	$461,070,049	$831,329,111	$388,011,249	$616,768,274	$1,709,756,639
Household furnishings and supplies	220,598,767	19,545,465	33,185,477	17,942,114	30,201,858	14,588,812	25,291,918	77,990,109
Appliances, kitchen, small electric	2,189,863	240,505	404,943	249,746	351,667	140,082	217,682	585,225
Appliances, major	26,209,115	2,002,443	3,599,799	2,008,162	3,940,235	1,631,485	2,996,244	10,000,563
Bathroom linens	2,565,402	336,727	374,107	237,494	401,857	226,431	368,189	555,731
Bedroom furniture, excl. mattresses and springs	11,015,034	1,156,394	1,822,216	1,102,502	1,508,745	1,014,399	1,413,893	2,997,185
Bedroom linens	7,631,661	386,543	1,725,920	797,677	1,332,063	457,098	959,633	1,832,428
Cleansing and toilet tissue, paper towels, and napkins	11,138,258	1,750,914	2,038,883	951,006	1,779,532	759,253	1,138,484	2,578,748
Closet and storage items	1,682,885	79,754	210,177	73,630	401,179	81,709	144,932	648,007
Curtains and draperies	2,183,995	220,207	250,634	185,163	310,464	289,646	209,273	718,379
Decorative items for the home	22,269,475	1,371,077	2,467,673	1,953,999	2,592,742	1,247,555	3,037,626	9,150,064
Floor coverings	6,595,407	438,221	625,555	462,849	818,975	331,005	626,213	3,292,298
Floor coverings, nonpermanent	3,505,424	129,481	237,929	157,108	489,011	166,108	234,027	2,091,148
Wall-to-wall carpeting	3,091,157	308,710	387,626	305,742	329,794	164,897	392,186	1,201,151
Housewares	9,430,728	944,147	1,230,039	504,875	1,267,122	845,736	1,336,136	3,103,778
Infants' equipment	1,641,810	91,324	341,620	222,378	99,871	143,243	198,030	516,060
Infants' furniture	974,055	53,643	129,163	67,561	159,556	55,683	139,925	368,417
Kitchen and dining room furniture	5,890,098	315,725	650,760	429,413	732,838	551,047	681,768	2,529,074
Kitchen and dining room linens	1,012,782	84,846	150,705	58,057	193,977	72,361	116,683	311,671
Lamps and lighting fixtures	2,308,393	115,179	235,247	139,473	221,615	129,994	174,221	1,292,048
Laundry and cleaning equipment	1,932,853	211,003	346,353	154,474	312,160	159,383	129,816	596,953
Laundry and cleaning supplies	15,740,960	2,181,105	3,072,029	1,612,759	2,650,392	1,039,483	1,545,409	3,416,311
Lawn and garden equipment	5,980,462	476,716	1,069,598	491,248	939,362	302,961	504,618	2,195,843
Lawn and garden supplies	11,061,977	1,154,743	1,330,892	791,608	1,425,152	665,506	1,054,869	4,459,815
Living room chairs	6,169,405	646,536	714,648	490,675	639,241	291,596	518,506	2,867,825
Living room tables	2,090,110	119,474	299,884	146,458	234,841	190,250	177,433	922,078
Mattresses and springs	6,790,218	684,600	918,166	544,724	894,768	581,309	984,293	2,182,217
Outdoor equipment	3,366,944	72,180	383,748	303,910	582,608	369,808	263,221	1,306,364
Outdoor furniture	2,114,755	32,390	164,969	60,003	198,385	90,653	255,285	1,312,400
Plants and fresh flowers, indoor	5,343,219	412,488	820,371	330,018	725,039	316,344	644,920	2,093,390
Postage	7,967,299	978,091	1,646,907	759,201	1,148,091	559,251	931,006	1,827,598
Power tools	6,298,497	579,043	2,032,193	437,886	451,369	209,753	766,611	1,927,636
Sewing materials for household items	1,184,122	133,437	193,605	86,684	174,647	79,355	148,712	367,555
Sofas	12,546,530	1,028,434	1,469,327	1,083,608	1,455,673	741,633	1,329,900	5,437,432
Stationery, stationery supplies, giftwrap	10,006,946	796,224	1,492,607	787,714	1,592,338	580,031	1,397,548	3,153,969
Wall units, cabinets, and other furniture	7,265,510	451,351	972,740	417,160	665,353	434,771	880,837	3,443,046
Household services	69,605,017	5,081,929	8,972,971	4,881,332	8,548,876	4,625,791	9,403,878	28,090,093
Appliance repair, incl. service center	1,698,141	153,633	281,237	91,035	273,161	111,030	220,054	567,804
Babysitting and childcare in own or other home	8,244,259	395,074	987,241	649,043	985,144	681,444	1,121,950	3,424,245
Care for the elderly, invalids, handicapped, etc.	2,909,255	564,312	837,763	452,085	59,346	257,500	144,838	593,504
Day care centers, nursery schools, preschools	26,406,274	1,165,039	2,757,985	1,801,128	3,958,887	1,985,489	4,844,084	9,893,970
Gardening, lawn care service	11,234,490	1,225,211	1,732,020	717,062	1,215,406	554,880	1,112,785	4,676,968
Housekeeping services	10,813,182	918,911	846,989	427,237	920,372	436,722	1,113,163	6,149,429
Moving, storage, and freight express	4,276,453	377,925	919,356	439,489	582,099	365,302	290,904	1,302,052
Security system service fee	1,934,027	131,455	297,236	165,696	270,787	98,051	259,064	711,825
Termite and pest control services	2,088,937	150,369	313,143	138,557	283,674	135,374	297,045	770,296

Note: Numbers will not add to total because not all categories are shown and because of rounding.
Source: Calculations by New Strategist based on the Bureau of Labor Statistics' 2005 Consumer Expenditure Survey

Table 11. Household Furnishings, Services, and Supplies: Market shares by income, 2005

(percentage of total annual spending on household furnishings, services, and supplies accounted for by before-tax income group of consumer units, 2005)

	total consumer units	under $20,000	$20,000–$39,999	$40,000–$49,999	$50,000–$69,999	$70,000–$79,999	$80,000–$99,999	$100,000 or more
Share of total consumer units	100.0%	22.9%	24.4%	9.8%	14.4%	5.7%	8.1%	14.7%
Share of total before-tax income	100.0	4.2	12.3	7.4	14.5	7.3	12.2	42.0
Share of total spending	100.0	9.7	16.4	8.5	15.3	7.1	11.3	31.4
Household furnishings and supplies	100.0	8.9	15.0	8.1	13.7	6.6	11.5	35.4
Appliances, kitchen, small electric	100.0	11.0	18.5	11.4	16.1	6.4	9.9	26.7
Appliances, major	100.0	7.6	13.7	7.7	15.0	6.2	11.4	38.2
Bathroom linens	100.0	13.1	14.6	9.3	15.7	8.8	14.4	21.7
Bedroom furniture, excl. mattresses and springs	100.0	10.5	16.5	10.0	13.7	9.2	12.8	27.2
Bedroom linens	100.0	5.1	22.6	10.5	17.5	6.0	12.6	24.0
Cleansing and toilet tissue, paper towels, and napkins	100.0	15.7	18.3	8.5	16.0	6.8	10.2	23.2
Closet and storage items	100.0	4.7	12.5	4.4	23.8	4.9	8.6	38.5
Curtains and draperies	100.0	10.1	11.5	8.5	14.2	13.3	9.6	32.9
Decorative items for the home	100.0	6.2	11.1	8.8	11.6	5.6	13.6	41.1
Floor coverings	100.0	6.6	9.5	7.0	12.4	5.0	9.5	49.9
Floor coverings, nonpermanent	100.0	3.7	6.8	4.5	14.0	4.7	6.7	59.7
Wall-to-wall carpeting	100.0	10.0	12.5	9.9	10.7	5.3	12.7	38.9
Housewares	100.0	10.0	13.0	5.4	13.4	9.0	14.2	32.9
Infants' equipment	100.0	5.6	20.8	13.5	6.1	8.7	12.1	31.4
Infants' furniture	100.0	5.5	13.3	6.9	16.4	5.7	14.4	37.8
Kitchen and dining room furniture	100.0	5.4	11.0	7.3	12.4	9.4	11.6	42.9
Kitchen and dining room linens	100.0	8.4	14.9	5.7	19.2	7.1	11.5	30.8
Lamps and lighting fixtures	100.0	5.0	10.2	6.0	9.6	5.6	7.5	56.0
Laundry and cleaning equipment	100.0	10.9	17.9	8.0	16.2	8.2	6.7	30.9
Laundry and cleaning supplies	100.0	13.9	19.5	10.2	16.8	6.6	9.8	21.7
Lawn and garden equipment	100.0	8.0	17.9	8.2	15.7	5.1	8.4	36.7
Lawn and garden supplies	100.0	10.4	12.0	7.2	12.9	6.0	9.5	40.3
Living room chairs	100.0	10.5	11.6	8.0	10.4	4.7	8.4	46.5
Living room tables	100.0	5.7	14.3	7.0	11.2	9.1	8.5	44.1
Mattresses and springs	100.0	10.1	13.5	8.0	13.2	8.6	14.5	32.1
Outdoor equipment	100.0	2.1	11.4	9.0	17.3	11.0	7.8	38.8
Outdoor furniture	100.0	1.5	7.8	2.8	9.4	4.3	12.1	62.1
Plants and fresh flowers, indoor	100.0	7.7	15.4	6.2	13.6	5.9	12.1	39.2
Postage	100.0	12.3	20.7	9.5	14.4	7.0	11.7	22.9
Power tools	100.0	9.2	32.3	7.0	7.2	3.3	12.2	30.6
Sewing materials for household items	100.0	11.3	16.4	7.3	14.7	6.7	12.6	31.0
Sofas	100.0	8.2	11.7	8.6	11.6	5.9	10.6	43.3
Stationery, stationery supplies, giftwrap	100.0	8.0	14.9	7.9	15.9	5.8	14.0	31.5
Wall units, cabinets, and other furniture	100.0	6.2	13.4	5.7	9.2	6.0	12.1	47.4
Household services	100.0	7.3	12.9	7.0	12.3	6.6	13.5	40.4
Appliance repair, including service center	100.0	9.0	16.6	5.4	16.1	6.5	13.0	33.4
Babysitting and childcare in own or other home	100.0	4.8	12.0	7.9	11.9	8.3	13.6	41.5
Care for the elderly, invalids, handicapped, etc.	100.0	19.4	28.8	15.5	2.0	8.9	5.0	20.4
Day care centers, nursery schools, preschools	100.0	4.4	10.4	6.8	15.0	7.5	18.3	37.5
Gardening, lawn care service	100.0	10.9	15.4	6.4	10.8	4.9	9.9	41.6
Housekeeping services	100.0	8.5	7.8	4.0	8.5	4.0	10.3	56.9
Moving, storage, and freight express	100.0	8.8	21.5	10.3	13.6	8.5	6.8	30.4
Security system service fee	100.0	6.8	15.4	8.6	14.0	5.1	13.4	36.8
Termite and pest control services	100.0	7.2	15.0	6.6	13.6	6.5	14.2	36.9

Note: Numbers may not add to total because of rounding.
Source: Calculations by New Strategist based on the Bureau of Labor Statistics' 2005 Consumer Expenditure Survey

Table 12. Household Furnishings, Services, and Supplies: Average spending by high-income consumer units, 2005

(average annual spending on household furnishings, services, and supplies, by before-tax income of consumer units with high incomes, 2005)

	total consumer units	$100,000 or more	$100,000– $119,999	$120,000– $149,999	$150,000 or more
Number of consumer units (in 000s)	117,356	17,248	6,065	4,719	6,464
Number of persons per consumer unit	2.5	3.2	3.2	3.2	3.2
Average before-tax income of consumer units	$58,712.00	$167,851.00	$108,670.00	$132,190.00	$249,411.00
Average spending of consumer units, total	46,408.80	99,127.82	78,350.98	88,974.37	125,933.98
Household furnishings and supplies	**1,879.74**	**4,521.69**	**3,239.92**	**4,073.40**	**6,032.26**
Appliances, kitchen, small electric	18.66	33.93	26.96	29.71	43.56
Appliances, major	223.33	579.81	471.86	448.88	774.16
Bathroom linens	21.86	32.22	30.09	17.11	45.20
Bedroom furniture, excl. mattresses and springs	93.86	173.77	100.92	169.73	245.07
Bedroom linens	65.03	106.24	63.56	80.79	163.24
Cleansing and toilet tissue, paper towels, and napkins	94.91	149.51	128.54	135.38	178.70
Closet and storage items	14.34	37.57	46.17	22.87	40.62
Curtains and draperies	18.61	41.65	26.97	40.81	56.03
Decorative items for the home	189.76	530.50	194.24	280.39	1,015.88
Floor coverings	56.20	190.88	85.46	124.41	338.32
Floor coverings, nonpermanent	29.87	121.24	32.95	91.06	226.11
Wall-to-wall carpeting	26.34	69.64	52.50	33.36	112.21
Housewares	80.36	179.95	135.39	151.75	240.60
Infants' equipment	13.99	29.92	27.56	22.14	37.73
Infants' furniture	8.30	21.36	16.24	19.40	27.61
Kitchen and dining room furniture	50.19	146.63	69.12	133.38	229.02
Kitchen and dining room linens	8.63	18.07	30.11	5.11	16.75
Lamps and lighting fixtures	19.67	74.91	30.61	47.35	136.60
Laundry and cleaning equipment	16.47	34.61	36.27	32.71	34.52
Laundry and cleaning supplies	134.13	198.07	190.43	199.86	203.63
Lawn and garden equipment	50.96	127.31	80.15	255.80	77.78
Lawn and garden supplies	94.26	258.57	249.81	288.22	244.70
Living room chairs	52.57	166.27	96.21	197.71	209.06
Living room tables	17.81	53.46	30.75	64.21	66.93
Mattresses and springs	57.86	126.52	106.88	88.16	172.96
Outdoor equipment	28.69	75.74	92.40	134.28	17.88
Outdoor furniture	18.02	76.09	47.04	41.62	128.52
Plants and fresh flowers, indoor	45.53	121.37	86.32	95.18	173.39
Postage	67.89	105.96	104.33	106.96	106.69
Power tools	53.67	111.76	130.81	46.91	142.17
Sewing materials for household items	10.09	21.31	17.75	17.66	27.32
Sofas	106.91	315.25	216.43	400.98	345.39
Stationery, stationery supplies, giftwrap	85.27	182.86	145.68	194.17	207.97
Wall units, cabinets, and other furniture	61.91	199.62	124.86	179.76	284.26
Household services	**593.11**	**1,628.60**	**1,068.37**	**1,204.18**	**2,464.06**
Appliance repair, including service center	14.47	32.92	26.18	29.36	41.84
Babysitting and childcare in own or other home	70.25	198.53	121.53	136.35	316.19
Care for the elderly, invalids, handicapped, etc.	24.79	34.41	33.55	4.50	57.05
Day care centers, nursery schools, preschools	225.01	573.63	478.90	465.44	741.48
Gardening, lawn care service	95.73	271.16	140.62	171.40	466.47
Housekeeping services	92.14	356.53	145.66	268.37	618.75
Moving, storage, and freight express	36.44	75.49	63.70	45.88	108.16
Security system service fee	16.48	41.27	20.19	44.76	58.49
Termite and pest control services	17.80	44.66	38.04	38.12	55.63

Note: Numbers will not add to total because not all categories are shown.
Source: Bureau of Labor Statistics, unpublished tables from the 2005 Consumer Expenditure Survey

Table 13. Household Furnishings, Services, and Supplies: Indexed spending by high-income consumer units, 2005

(indexed average annual spending of consumer units with high incomes on household furnishings, services, and supplies, by before-tax income of consumer unit, 2005; index definition: an index of 100 is the average for all consumer units; an index of 132 means that spending by consumer units in that group is 32 percent above the average for all consumer units; an index of 68 indicates spending that is 32 percent below the average for all consumer units)

	total consumer units	$100,000 or more	$100,000– $119,999	$120,000– $149,999	$150,000 or more
Average spending of consumer units, total	$46,409	$99,128	$78,351	$88,974	$125,934
Average spending of consumer units, index	100	214	169	192	271
Household furnishings and supplies	100	241	172	217	321
Appliances, kitchen, small electric	100	182	144	159	233
Appliances, major	100	260	211	201	347
Bathroom linens	100	147	138	78	207
Bedroom furniture, excl. mattresses and springs	100	185	108	181	261
Bedroom linens	100	163	98	124	251
Cleansing and toilet tissue, paper towels, and napkins	100	158	135	143	188
Closet and storage items	100	262	322	159	283
Curtains and draperies	100	224	145	219	301
Decorative items for the home	100	280	102	148	535
Floor coverings	100	340	152	221	602
Floor coverings, nonpermanent	100	406	110	305	757
Wall-to-wall carpeting	100	264	199	127	426
Housewares	100	224	168	189	299
Infants' equipment	100	214	197	158	270
Infants' furniture	100	257	196	234	333
Kitchen and dining room furniture	100	292	138	266	456
Kitchen and dining room linens	100	209	349	59	194
Lamps and lighting fixtures	100	381	156	241	694
Laundry and cleaning equipment	100	210	220	199	210
Laundry and cleaning supplies	100	148	142	149	152
Lawn and garden equipment	100	250	157	502	153
Lawn and garden supplies	100	274	265	306	260
Living room chairs	100	316	183	376	398
Living room tables	100	300	173	361	376
Mattresses and springs	100	219	185	152	299
Outdoor equipment	100	264	322	468	62
Outdoor furniture	100	422	261	231	713
Plants and fresh flowers, indoor	100	267	190	209	381
Postage	100	156	154	158	157
Power tools	100	208	244	87	265
Sewing materials for household items	100	211	176	175	271
Sofas	100	295	202	375	323
Stationery, stationery supplies, giftwrap	100	214	171	228	244
Wall units, cabinets, and other furniture	100	322	202	290	459
Household services	100	275	180	203	415
Appliance repair, including service center	100	228	181	203	289
Babysitting and childcare in own or other home	100	283	173	194	450
Care for the elderly, invalids, handicapped, etc.	100	139	135	18	230
Day care centers, nursery schools, preschools	100	255	213	207	330
Gardening, lawn care service	100	283	147	179	487
Housekeeping services	100	387	158	291	672
Moving, storage, and freight express	100	207	175	126	297
Security system service fee	100	250	123	272	355
Termite and pest control services	100	251	214	214	313

Source: Calculations by New Strategist based on the Bureau of Labor Statistics' 2005 Consumer Expenditure Survey

Table 14. Household Furnishings, Services, and Supplies: Total spending by high-income consumer units, 2005

(total annual spending on household furnishings, services, and supplies, by before-tax income group of consumer units with high incomes, 2005; consumer units and dollars in thousands)

	total consumer units	$100,000 or more	$100,000–$119,999	$120,000–$149,999	$150,000 or more
Number of consumer units	117,356	17,248	6,065	4,719	6,464
Total spending of all consumer units	$5,446,351,133	$1,709,756,639	$475,198,694	$419,870,052	$814,037,247
Household furnishings and supplies	**220,598,767**	**77,990,109**	**19,650,115**	**19,222,375**	**38,992,529**
Appliances, kitchen, small electric	2,189,863	585,225	163,512	140,201	281,572
Appliances, major	26,209,115	10,000,563	2,861,831	2,118,265	5,004,170
Bathroom linens	2,565,402	555,731	182,496	80,742	292,173
Bedroom furniture, excl. mattresses and springs	11,015,034	2,997,185	612,080	800,956	1,584,132
Bedroom linens	7,631,661	1,832,428	385,491	381,248	1,055,183
Cleansing and toilet tissue, paper towels, and napkins	11,138,258	2,578,748	779,595	638,858	1,155,117
Closet and storage items	1,682,885	648,007	280,021	107,924	262,568
Curtains and draperies	2,183,995	718,379	163,573	192,582	362,178
Decorative items for the home	22,269,475	9,150,064	1,178,066	1,323,160	6,566,648
Floor coverings	6,595,407	3,292,298	518,315	587,091	2,186,900
Floor coverings, nonpermanent	3,505,424	2,091,148	199,842	429,712	1,461,575
Wall-to-wall carpeting	3,091,157	1,201,151	318,413	157,426	725,325
Housewares	9,430,728	3,103,778	821,140	716,108	1,555,238
Infants' equipment	1,641,810	516,060	167,151	104,479	243,887
Infants' furniture	974,055	368,417	98,496	91,549	178,471
Kitchen and dining room furniture	5,890,098	2,529,074	419,213	629,420	1,480,385
Kitchen and dining room linens	1,012,782	311,671	182,617	24,114	108,272
Lamps and lighting fixtures	2,308,393	1,292,048	185,650	223,445	882,982
Laundry and cleaning equipment	1,932,853	596,953	219,978	154,358	223,137
Laundry and cleaning supplies	15,740,960	3,416,311	1,154,958	943,139	1,316,264
Lawn and garden equipment	5,980,462	2,195,843	486,110	1,207,120	502,770
Lawn and garden supplies	11,061,977	4,459,815	1,515,098	1,360,110	1,581,741
Living room chairs	6,169,405	2,867,825	583,514	932,993	1,351,364
Living room tables	2,090,110	922,078	186,499	303,007	432,636
Mattresses and springs	6,790,218	2,182,217	648,227	416,027	1,118,013
Outdoor equipment	3,366,944	1,306,364	560,406	633,667	115,576
Outdoor furniture	2,114,755	1,312,400	285,298	196,405	830,753
Plants and fresh flowers, indoor	5,343,219	2,093,390	523,531	449,154	1,120,793
Postage	7,967,299	1,827,598	632,761	504,744	689,644
Power tools	6,298,497	1,927,636	793,363	221,368	918,987
Sewing materials for household items	1,184,122	367,555	107,654	83,338	176,596
Sofas	12,546,530	5,437,432	1,312,648	1,892,225	2,232,601
Stationery, stationery supplies, giftwrap	10,006,946	3,153,969	883,549	916,288	1,344,318
Wall units, cabinets, and other furniture	7,265,510	3,443,046	757,276	848,287	1,837,457
Household services	**69,605,017**	**28,090,093**	**6,479,664**	**5,682,525**	**15,927,684**
Appliance repair, including service center	1,698,141	567,804	158,782	138,550	270,454
Babysitting and childcare in own or other home	8,244,259	3,424,245	737,079	643,436	2,043,852
Care for the elderly, invalids, handicapped, etc.	2,909,255	593,504	203,481	21,236	368,771
Day care centers, nursery schools, preschools	26,406,274	9,893,970	2,904,529	2,196,411	4,792,927
Gardening, lawn care service	11,234,490	4,676,968	852,860	808,837	3,015,262
Housekeeping services	10,813,182	6,149,429	883,428	1,266,438	3,999,600
Moving, storage, and freight express	4,276,453	1,302,052	386,341	216,508	699,146
Security system service fee	1,934,027	711,825	122,452	211,222	378,079
Termite and pest control services	2,088,937	770,296	230,713	179,888	359,592

Note: Numbers will not add to total because not all categories are shown and because of rounding.
Source: Calculations by New Strategist based on the Bureau of Labor Statistics' 2005 Consumer Expenditure Survey

Table 15. Household Furnishings, Services, and Supplies: Market shares by high-income consumer units, 2005

(percentage of total annual spending on household furnishings, services, and supplies accounted for by before-tax income group of consumer units with high incomes, 2005)

	total consumer units	$100,000 or more	$100,000– $119,999	$120,000– $149,999	$150,000 or more
Share of total consumer units	100.0%	14.7%	5.2%	4.0%	5.5%
Share of total before-tax income	100.0	42.0	9.6	9.1	23.4
Share of total spending	100.0	31.4	8.7	7.7	14.9
Household furnishings and supplies	100.0	35.4	8.9	8.7	17.7
Appliances, kitchen, small electric	100.0	26.7	7.5	6.4	12.9
Appliances, major	100.0	38.2	10.9	8.1	19.1
Bathroom linens	100.0	21.7	7.1	3.1	11.4
Bedroom furniture, excl. mattresses and springs	100.0	27.2	5.6	7.3	14.4
Bedroom linens	100.0	24.0	5.1	5.0	13.8
Cleansing and toilet tissue, paper towels, and napkins	100.0	23.2	7.0	5.7	10.4
Closet and storage items	100.0	38.5	16.6	6.4	15.6
Curtains and draperies	100.0	32.9	7.5	8.8	16.6
Decorative items for the home	100.0	41.1	5.3	5.9	29.5
Floor coverings	100.0	49.9	7.9	8.9	33.2
Floor coverings, nonpermanent	100.0	59.7	5.7	12.3	41.7
Wall-to-wall carpeting	100.0	38.9	10.3	5.1	23.5
Housewares	100.0	32.9	8.7	7.6	16.5
Infants' equipment	100.0	31.4	10.2	6.4	14.9
Infants' furniture	100.0	37.8	10.1	9.4	18.3
Kitchen and dining room furniture	100.0	42.9	7.1	10.7	25.1
Kitchen and dining room linens	100.0	30.8	18.0	2.4	10.7
Lamps and lighting fixtures	100.0	56.0	8.0	9.7	38.3
Laundry and cleaning equipment	100.0	30.9	11.4	8.0	11.5
Laundry and cleaning supplies	100.0	21.7	7.3	6.0	8.4
Lawn and garden equipment	100.0	36.7	8.1	20.2	8.4
Lawn and garden supplies	100.0	40.3	13.7	12.3	14.3
Living room chairs	100.0	46.5	9.5	15.1	21.9
Living room tables	100.0	44.1	8.9	14.5	20.7
Mattresses and springs	100.0	32.1	9.5	6.1	16.5
Outdoor equipment	100.0	38.8	16.6	18.8	3.4
Outdoor furniture	100.0	62.1	13.5	9.3	39.3
Plants and fresh flowers, indoor	100.0	39.2	9.8	8.4	21.0
Postage	100.0	22.9	7.9	6.3	8.7
Power tools	100.0	30.6	12.6	3.5	14.6
Sewing materials for household items	100.0	31.0	9.1	7.0	14.9
Sofas	100.0	43.3	10.5	15.1	17.8
Stationery, stationery supplies, giftwrap	100.0	31.5	8.8	9.2	13.4
Wall units, cabinets, and other furniture	100.0	47.4	10.4	11.7	25.3
Household services	100.0	40.4	9.3	8.2	22.9
Appliance repair, including service center	100.0	33.4	9.4	8.2	15.9
Babysitting and childcare in own or other home	100.0	41.5	8.9	7.8	24.8
Care for the elderly, invalids, handicapped, etc.	100.0	20.4	7.0	0.7	12.7
Day care centers, nursery schools, preschools	100.0	37.5	11.0	8.3	18.2
Gardening, lawn care service	100.0	41.6	7.6	7.2	26.8
Housekeeping services	100.0	56.9	8.2	11.7	37.0
Moving, storage, and freight express	100.0	30.4	9.0	5.1	16.3
Security system service fee	100.0	36.8	6.3	10.9	19.5
Termite and pest control services	100.0	36.9	11.0	8.6	17.2

Note: Numbers may not add to total because of rounding.
Source: Calculations by New Strategist based on the Bureau of Labor Statistics' 2005 Consumer Expenditure Survey

Table 16. Household Furnishings, Services, and Supplies: Average spending by household type, 2005

(average annual spending of consumer units (CU) on household furnishings, services, and supplies, by type of consumer unit, 2005)

	total consumer units	total married couples	married couples, no children	married couples with children				single parent, at least one child <18	single person
				total	oldest child under 6	oldest child 6 to 17	oldest child 18 or older		
Number of consumer units (in 000s)	117,356	59,337	25,293	29,528	5,659	15,477	8,393	6,902	34,339
Number of persons per CU	2.5	3.2	2.0	3.9	3.5	4.1	3.9	2.8	1.0
Average before-tax income of CU	$58,712.00	$79,679.00	$69,453.00	$87,527.00	$76,205.00	$89,981.00	$90,635.00	$33,286.00	$30,290.00
Average spending of CU, total	46,408.80	60,401.07	53,485.78	66,441.33	58,538.11	68,421.31	68,210.57	35,364.79	26,772.96
Household furnishings and supplies	**1,879.74**	**2,548.76**	**2,350.16**	**2,766.29**	**2,553.53**	**2,866.97**	**2,737.70**	**1,190.59**	**976.43**
Appliances, kitchen, small electric	18.66	23.22	23.25	23.20	22.93	23.73	22.41	10.48	12.81
Appliances, major	223.33	316.59	305.79	333.20	186.53	399.43	306.58	71.68	103.67
Bathroom linens	21.86	25.17	16.44	30.56	25.78	29.25	36.64	29.29	12.04
Bedroom furniture, excl. mattresses and springs	93.86	126.86	104.39	147.97	230.20	141.33	104.79	117.47	44.98
Bedroom linens	65.03	85.44	73.73	99.56	82.72	110.66	89.78	64.23	29.28
Cleansing and toilet tissue, paper towels, and napkins	94.91	124.48	109.24	133.57	107.50	131.00	157.65	76.87	48.16
Closet and storage items	14.34	22.07	14.96	29.50	30.93	27.46	32.53	12.00	3.53
Curtains and draperies	18.61	26.23	20.47	31.12	26.84	41.77	14.38	10.12	10.21
Decorative items for the home	189.76	260.69	186.95	329.74	241.79	247.90	556.40	71.03	105.92
Floor coverings	56.20	83.43	75.89	97.88	85.94	119.09	66.82	25.20	25.19
Floor coverings, nonpermanent	29.87	47.51	37.56	61.11	49.70	80.60	32.87	10.29	8.43
Wall-to-wall carpeting	26.34	35.91	38.33	36.77	36.24	38.49	33.96	14.92	16.77
Housewares	80.36	107.20	109.62	106.99	120.97	92.42	125.77	56.89	45.79
Infants' equipment	13.99	20.51	8.64	31.10	90.61	9.44	30.82	5.77	6.51
Infants' furniture	8.30	13.84	12.35	14.52	57.42	4.14	4.75	2.63	0.79
Kitchen and dining room furniture	50.19	75.08	47.53	95.17	110.89	119.95	38.89	39.92	19.52
Kitchen and dining room linens	8.63	11.79	18.64	6.79	5.14	6.97	7.61	4.43	4.28
Lamps and lighting fixtures	19.67	29.33	24.01	35.31	14.66	48.21	25.47	6.32	8.56
Laundry and cleaning equipment	16.47	21.08	22.44	20.55	25.33	15.91	26.29	8.09	10.37
Laundry and cleaning supplies	134.13	172.53	140.10	195.18	182.22	194.21	206.56	136.86	65.67
Lawn and garden equipment	50.96	62.95	77.76	54.12	27.67	65.92	50.22	27.07	22.12
Lawn and garden supplies	94.26	134.89	128.11	145.67	182.24	138.18	133.91	30.97	51.74
Living room chairs	52.57	78.17	92.30	70.98	67.86	73.33	68.77	19.95	24.35
Living room tables	17.81	23.29	21.53	23.32	21.64	27.12	17.44	13.85	10.41
Mattresses and springs	57.86	75.28	74.52	75.12	59.00	82.67	72.07	31.92	35.76
Outdoor equipment	28.69	33.37	35.09	32.95	17.95	41.99	25.92	–	5.35
Outdoor furniture	18.02	29.23	26.38	33.08	29.37	40.68	21.56	4.23	5.50
Plants and fresh flowers, indoor	45.53	61.92	72.01	56.70	38.54	60.25	62.41	19.89	29.47
Postage	67.89	84.50	98.27	75.55	73.25	78.61	71.12	32.93	52.17
Power tools	53.67	53.32	59.03	51.85	30.82	61.04	48.90	16.30	57.68
Sewing materials for household items	10.09	15.05	18.57	12.90	7.81	14.49	13.39	2.85	5.46
Sofas	106.91	146.45	149.01	146.59	138.80	161.21	124.88	87.18	48.44
Stationery, stationery supplies, giftwrap	85.27	114.98	108.48	125.08	123.72	139.39	97.62	53.51	41.97
Wall units, cabinets, and other furniture	61.91	89.82	74.66	100.47	86.46	119.22	75.35	36.62	28.73
Household services	**593.11**	**831.17**	**462.69**	**1,147.93**	**2,621.83**	**1,055.40**	**324.88**	**708.22**	**247.16**
Appliance repair, including service center	14.47	20.72	20.19	21.17	16.92	20.11	26.00	6.39	6.61
Babysitting and childcare in own or other home	70.25	104.83	1.58	190.66	489.56	179.32	10.08	156.19	1.29
Care for the elderly, invalids, handicapped, etc.	24.79	16.49	27.07	0.92	–	0.03	3.18	–	32.36
Day care centers, nursery schools, preschools	225.01	350.85	10.98	638.08	1,823.55	530.54	37.11	441.14	7.31
Gardening, lawn care service	95.73	116.03	140.53	99.49	84.16	110.10	90.27	33.44	85.80
Housekeeping services	92.14	126.97	144.96	118.73	128.38	134.30	83.49	37.86	67.58
Moving, storage, and freight express	36.44	47.07	66.83	30.08	31.62	30.70	27.91	17.19	25.43
Security system service fee	16.48	21.85	22.29	21.55	31.10	19.39	19.11	9.80	11.52
Termite and pest control services	17.80	26.36	28.26	27.25	16.54	30.91	27.73	6.21	9.26

Note: Numbers will not add to total because not all categories are shown. "–" means sample is too small to make a reliable estimate.
Source: Bureau of Labor Statistics, unpublished data from the 2005 Consumer Expenditure Survey

Table 17. Household Furnishings, Services, and Supplies: Indexed spending by household type, 2005

(indexed average annual spending of consumer units (CU) on household furnishings, services, and supplies by type of consumer unit, 2005; index definition: an index of 100 is the average for all consumer units; an index of 132 means that spending by consumer units in that group is 32 percent above the average for all consumer units; an index of 68 indicates spending that is 32 percent below the average for all consumer units)

| | total consumer units | total married couples | married couples, no children | married couples with children | | | | single parent, at least one child <18 | single person |
				total	oldest child under 6	oldest child 6 to 17	oldest child 18 or older		
Average spending of CU, total	$46,409	$60,401	$3,486	$66,441	$58,538	$68,421	$68,211	$35,365	$26,773
Average spending of CU, index	100	130	115	143	126	147	147	76	58
Household furnishings and supplies	**100**	**136**	**125**	**147**	**136**	**153**	**146**	**63**	**52**
Appliances, kitchen, small electric	100	124	125	124	123	127	120	56	69
Appliances, major	100	142	137	149	84	179	137	32	46
Bathroom linens	100	115	75	140	118	134	168	134	55
Bedroom furniture, excl. mattresses and springs	100	135	111	158	245	151	112	125	48
Bedroom linens	100	131	113	153	127	170	138	99	45
Cleansing and toilet tissue, paper towels, and napkins	100	131	115	141	113	138	166	81	51
Closet and storage items	100	154	104	206	216	191	227	84	25
Curtains and draperies	100	141	110	167	144	224	77	54	55
Decorative items for the home	100	137	99	174	127	131	293	37	56
Floor coverings	100	148	135	174	153	212	119	45	45
Floor coverings, nonpermanent	100	159	126	205	166	270	110	34	28
Wall-to-wall carpeting	100	136	146	140	138	146	129	57	64
Housewares	100	133	136	133	151	115	157	71	57
Infants' equipment	100	147	62	222	648	67	220	41	47
Infants' furniture	100	167	149	175	692	50	57	32	10
Kitchen and dining room furniture	100	150	95	190	221	239	77	80	39
Kitchen and dining room linens	100	137	216	79	60	81	88	51	50
Lamps and lighting fixtures	100	149	122	180	75	245	129	32	44
Laundry and cleaning equipment	100	128	136	125	154	97	160	49	63
Laundry and cleaning supplies	100	129	104	146	136	145	154	102	49
Lawn and garden equipment	100	124	153	106	54	129	99	53	43
Lawn and garden supplies	100	143	136	155	193	147	142	33	55
Living room chairs	100	149	176	135	129	139	131	38	46
Living room tables	100	131	121	131	122	152	98	78	58
Mattresses and springs	100	130	129	130	102	143	125	55	62
Outdoor equipment	100	116	122	115	63	146	90	–	19
Outdoor furniture	100	162	146	184	163	226	120	23	31
Plants and fresh flowers, indoor	100	136	158	125	85	132	137	44	65
Postage	100	124	145	111	108	116	105	49	77
Power tools	100	99	110	97	57	114	91	30	107
Sewing materials for household items	100	149	184	128	77	144	133	28	54
Sofas	100	137	139	137	130	151	117	82	45
Stationery, stationery supplies, giftwrap	100	135	127	147	145	163	114	63	49
Wall units, cabinets, and other furniture	100	145	121	162	140	193	122	59	46
Household services	**100**	**140**	**78**	**194**	**442**	**178**	**55**	**119**	**42**
Appliance repair, including service center	100	143	140	146	117	139	180	44	46
Babysitting and childcare in own or other home	100	149	2	271	697	255	14	222	2
Care for the elderly, invalids, handicapped, etc.	100	67	109	4	–	0	13	–	131
Day care centers, nursery schools, preschools	100	156	5	284	810	236	16	196	3
Gardening, lawn care service	100	121	147	104	88	115	94	35	90
Housekeeping services	100	138	157	129	139	146	91	41	73
Moving, storage, and freight express	100	129	183	83	87	84	77	47	70
Security system service fee	100	133	135	131	189	118	116	59	70
Termite and pest control services	100	148	159	153	93	174	156	35	52

Note: "–" means sample is too small to make a reliable estimate.
Source: Calculations by New Strategist based on the Bureau of Labor Statistics' 2005 Consumer Expenditure Survey

Table 18. Household Furnishings, Services, and Supplies: Total spending by household type, 2005

(total annual spending on household furnishings, services, and supplies, by consumer unit (CU) type, 2005; consumer units and dollars in thousands)

	total consumer units	total married couples	married couples, no children	married couples with children				single parent, at least one child <18	single person
				total	oldest child under 6	oldest child 6 to 17	oldest child 18 or older		
Number of consumer units	117,356	59,337	25,293	29,528	5,659	15,477	8,393	6,902	34,339
Total spending of all CUs	$5,446,351,133	$3,584,018,291	$1,352,815,834	$1,961,879,592	$331,267,164	$1,058,956,615	$572,491,314	$244,087,781	$919,356,673
Household furnishings and supplies	**220,598,767**	**151,235,772**	**59,442,597**	**81,683,011**	**14,450,426**	**44,372,095**	**22,977,516**	**8,217,452**	**33,529,630**
Appliances, kitchen, small electric	2,189,863	1,377,805	588,062	685,050	129,761	367,269	188,087	72,333	439,883
Appliances, major	26,209,115	18,785,501	7,734,346	9,838,730	1,055,573	6,181,978	2,573,126	494,735	3,559,924
Bathroom linens	2,565,402	1,493,512	415,817	902,376	145,889	452,702	307,520	202,160	413,442
Bedroom furniture, excl. mattresses and springs	11,015,034	7,527,492	2,640,336	4,369,258	1,302,702	2,187,364	879,502	810,778	1,544,568
Bedroom linens	7,631,661	5,069,753	1,864,853	2,939,808	468,112	1,712,685	753,524	443,315	1,005,446
Cleansing and toilet tissue, paper towels, and napkins	11,138,258	7,386,270	2,763,007	3,944,055	608,343	2,027,487	1,323,156	530,557	1,653,766
Closet and storage items	1,682,885	1,309,568	378,383	871,076	175,033	424,998	273,024	82,824	121,217
Curtains and draperies	2,183,995	1,556,410	517,748	918,911	151,888	646,474	120,691	69,848	350,601
Decorative items for the home	22,269,475	15,468,563	4,728,526	9,736,563	1,368,290	3,836,748	4,669,865	490,249	3,637,187
Floor coverings	6,595,407	4,950,486	1,919,486	2,890,201	486,334	1,843,156	560,820	173,930	864,999
Floor coverings, nonpermanent	3,505,424	2,819,101	950,005	1,804,456	281,252	1,247,446	275,878	71,022	289,478
Wall-to-wall carpeting	3,091,157	2,130,792	969,481	1,085,745	205,082	595,710	285,026	102,978	575,865
Housewares	9,430,728	6,360,926	2,772,619	3,159,201	684,569	1,430,384	1,055,588	392,655	1,572,383
Infants' equipment	1,641,810	1,217,002	218,532	918,321	512,762	146,103	258,672	39,825	223,547
Infants' furniture	974,055	821,224	312,369	428,747	324,940	64,075	39,867	18,152	27,128
Kitchen and dining room furniture	5,890,098	4,455,022	1,202,176	2,810,180	627,527	1,856,466	326,404	275,528	670,297
Kitchen and dining room linens	1,012,782	699,583	471,462	200,595	29,087	107,875	63,871	30,576	146,971
Lamps and lighting fixtures	2,308,393	1,740,354	607,285	1,042,634	82,961	746,146	213,770	43,621	293,942
Laundry and cleaning equipment	1,932,853	1,250,824	567,575	606,800	143,342	246,239	220,652	55,837	356,095
Laundry and cleaning supplies	15,740,960	10,237,413	3,543,549	5,763,275	1,031,183	3,005,788	1,733,658	944,608	2,255,042
Lawn and garden equipment	5,980,462	3,735,264	1,966,784	1,598,055	156,585	1,020,244	421,496	186,837	759,579
Lawn and garden supplies	11,061,977	8,003,968	3,240,286	4,301,344	1,031,296	2,138,612	1,123,907	213,755	1,776,700
Living room chairs	6,169,405	4,638,373	2,334,544	2,095,897	384,020	1,134,928	577,187	137,695	836,155
Living room tables	2,090,110	1,381,959	544,558	688,593	122,461	419,736	146,374	95,593	357,469
Mattresses and springs	6,790,218	4,466,889	1,884,834	2,218,143	333,881	1,279,484	604,884	220,312	1,227,963
Outdoor equipment	3,366,944	1,980,076	887,531	972,948	101,579	649,879	217,547	–	183,714
Outdoor furniture	2,114,755	1,734,421	667,229	976,786	166,205	629,604	180,953	29,195	188,865
Plants and fresh flowers, indoor	5,343,219	3,674,147	1,821,349	1,674,238	218,098	932,489	523,807	137,281	1,011,970
Postage	7,967,299	5,013,977	2,485,543	2,230,840	414,522	1,216,647	596,910	227,283	1,791,466
Power tools	6,298,497	3,163,849	1,493,046	1,531,027	174,410	944,716	410,418	112,503	1,980,674
Sewing materials for household items	1,184,122	893,022	469,691	380,911	44,197	224,262	112,382	19,671	187,491
Sofas	12,546,530	8,689,904	3,768,910	4,328,510	785,469	2,495,047	1,048,118	601,716	1,663,381
Stationery, stationery supplies, giftwrap	10,006,946	6,822,568	2,743,785	3,693,362	700,131	2,157,339	819,325	369,326	1,441,208
Wall units, cabinets, and other furniture	7,265,510	5,329,649	1,888,375	2,966,678	489,277	1,845,168	632,413	252,751	986,559
Household services	**69,605,017**	**49,319,134**	**11,702,818**	**33,896,077**	**14,836,936**	**16,334,426**	**2,726,718**	**4,888,134**	**8,487,227**
Appliance repair, incl. service center	1,698,141	1,229,463	510,666	625,108	95,750	311,242	218,218	44,104	226,981
Babysitting and childcare in own or other home	8,244,259	6,220,298	39,963	5,629,808	2,770,420	2,775,336	84,601	1,078,023	44,297
Care for the elderly, invalids, handicapped, etc.	2,909,255	978,467	684,682	27,166	–	464	26,690	–	1,111,210
Day care centers, nursery schools, preschools	26,406,274	20,818,386	277,717	18,841,226	10,319,469	8,211,168	311,464	3,044,748	251,018
Gardening, lawn care service	11,234,490	6,884,872	3,554,425	2,937,741	476,261	1,704,018	757,636	230,803	2,946,286
Housekeeping services	10,813,182	7,534,019	3,666,473	3,505,859	726,502	2,078,561	700,732	261,310	2,320,630
Moving, storage, and freight express	4,276,453	2,792,993	1,690,331	888,202	178,938	475,144	234,249	118,645	873,241
Security system service fee	1,934,027	1,296,513	563,781	636,328	175,995	300,099	160,390	67,640	395,585
Termite and pest control services	2,088,937	1,564,123	714,780	804,638	93,600	478,394	232,738	42,861	317,979

Note: Numbers will not add to total because not all types of consumer units are shown, because not all categories are shown, and because of rounding. "–" means sample is too small to make a reliable estimate.
Source: Calculations by New Strategist based on the Bureau of Labor Statistics' 2005 Consumer Expenditure Survey

Table 19. Household Furnishings, Services, and Supplies: Market shares by household type, 2005

(percentage of total annual spending on household furnishings, services, and supplies accounted for by types of consumer units, 2005)

	total consumer units	total married couples	married couples, no children	married couples with children				single parent, at least one child <18	single person
				total	oldest child under 6	oldest child 6 to 17	oldest child 18 or older		
Share of total consumer units	100.0%	50.6%	21.6%	25.2%	4.8%	13.2%	7.2%	5.9%	29.3%
Share of total before-tax income	100.0	68.6	25.5	37.5	6.3	20.2	11.0	3.3	15.1
Share of total spending	100.0	65.8	24.8	36.0	6.1	19.4	10.5	4.5	16.9
Household furnishings and supplies	**100.0**	**68.6**	**26.9**	**37.0**	**6.6**	**20.1**	**10.4**	**3.7**	**15.2**
Appliances, kitchen, small electric	100.0	62.9	26.9	31.3	5.9	16.8	8.6	3.3	20.1
Appliances, major	100.0	71.7	29.5	37.5	4.0	23.6	9.8	1.9	13.6
Bathroom linens	100.0	58.2	16.2	35.2	5.7	17.6	12.0	7.9	16.1
Bedroom furniture, excl. mattresses, springs	100.0	68.3	24.0	39.7	11.8	19.9	8.0	7.4	14.0
Bedroom linens	100.0	66.4	24.4	38.5	6.1	22.4	9.9	5.8	13.2
Cleansing and toilet tissue, paper towels, and napkins	100.0	66.3	24.8	35.4	5.5	18.2	11.9	4.8	14.8
Closet and storage items	100.0	77.8	22.5	51.8	10.4	25.3	16.2	4.9	7.2
Curtains and draperies	100.0	71.3	23.7	42.1	7.0	29.6	5.5	3.2	16.1
Decorative items for the home	100.0	69.5	21.2	43.7	6.1	17.2	21.0	2.2	16.3
Floor coverings	100.0	75.1	29.1	43.8	7.4	27.9	8.5	2.6	13.1
Floor coverings, nonpermanent	100.0	80.4	27.1	51.5	8.0	35.6	7.9	2.0	8.3
Wall-to-wall carpeting	100.0	68.9	31.4	35.1	6.6	19.3	9.2	3.3	18.6
Housewares	100.0	67.4	29.4	33.5	7.3	15.2	11.2	4.2	16.7
Infants' equipment	100.0	74.1	13.3	55.9	31.2	8.9	15.8	2.4	13.6
Infants' furniture	100.0	84.3	32.1	44.0	33.4	6.6	4.1	1.9	2.8
Kitchen and dining room furniture	100.0	75.6	20.4	47.7	10.7	31.5	5.5	4.7	11.4
Kitchen and dining room linens	100.0	69.1	46.6	19.8	2.9	10.7	6.3	3.0	14.5
Lamps and lighting fixtures	100.0	75.4	26.3	45.2	3.6	32.3	9.3	1.9	12.7
Laundry and cleaning equipment	100.0	64.7	29.4	31.4	7.4	12.7	11.4	2.9	18.4
Laundry and cleaning supplies	100.0	65.0	22.5	36.6	6.6	19.1	11.0	6.0	14.3
Lawn and garden equipment	100.0	62.5	32.9	26.7	2.6	17.1	7.0	3.1	12.7
Lawn and garden supplies	100.0	72.4	29.3	38.9	9.3	19.3	10.2	1.9	16.1
Living room chairs	100.0	75.2	37.8	34.0	6.2	18.4	9.4	2.2	13.6
Living room tables	100.0	66.1	26.1	32.9	5.9	20.1	7.0	4.6	17.1
Mattresses and springs	100.0	65.8	27.8	32.7	4.9	18.8	8.9	3.2	18.1
Outdoor equipment	100.0	58.8	26.4	28.9	3.0	19.3	6.5	–	5.5
Outdoor furniture	100.0	82.0	31.6	46.2	7.9	29.8	8.6	1.4	8.9
Plants and fresh flowers, indoor	100.0	68.8	34.1	31.3	4.1	17.5	9.8	2.6	18.9
Postage	100.0	62.9	31.2	28.0	5.2	15.3	7.5	2.9	22.5
Power tools	100.0	50.2	23.7	24.3	2.8	15.0	6.5	1.8	31.4
Sewing materials for household items	100.0	75.4	39.7	32.2	3.7	18.9	9.5	1.7	15.8
Sofas	100.0	69.3	30.0	34.5	6.3	19.9	8.4	4.8	13.3
Stationery, stationery supplies, giftwrap	100.0	68.2	27.4	36.9	7.0	21.6	8.2	3.7	14.4
Wall units, cabinets, and other furniture	100.0	73.4	26.0	40.8	6.7	25.4	8.7	3.5	13.6
Household services	**100.0**	**70.9**	**16.8**	**48.7**	**21.3**	**23.5**	**3.9**	**7.0**	**12.2**
Appliance repair, including service center	100.0	72.4	30.1	36.8	5.6	18.3	12.9	2.6	13.4
Babysitting and childcare in own or other home	100.0	75.5	0.5	68.3	33.6	33.7	1.0	13.1	0.5
Care for the elderly, invalids, handicapped, etc.	100.0	33.6	23.5	0.9	–	0.0	0.9	–	38.2
Day care centers, nursery schools, preschools	100.0	78.8	1.1	71.4	39.1	31.1	1.2	11.5	1.0
Gardening, lawn care service	100.0	61.3	31.6	26.1	4.2	15.2	6.7	2.1	26.2
Housekeeping services	100.0	69.7	33.9	32.4	6.7	19.2	6.5	2.4	21.5
Moving, storage, and freight express	100.0	65.3	39.5	20.8	4.2	11.1	5.5	2.8	20.4
Security system service fee	100.0	67.0	29.2	32.9	9.1	15.5	8.3	3.5	20.5
Termite and pest control services	100.0	74.9	34.2	38.5	4.5	22.9	11.1	2.1	15.2

Note: Market shares by type of consumer unit will not add to total because not all types of consumer units are shown. "–" means sample is too small to make a reliable estimate.
Source: Calculations by New Strategist based on the Bureau of Labor Statistics' 2005 Consumer Expenditure Survey

Table 20. Household Furnishings, Services, and Supplies: Average spending by race and Hispanic origin, 2005

(average annual spending of consumer units on household furnishings, services, and supplies, by race and Hispanic origin of consumer unit reference person, 2005)

	total consumer units	Asian	black	Hispanic	non-Hispanic white and other
Number of consumer units (in 000s)	117,356	4,283	14,042	12,462	90,995
Number of persons per consumer unit	2.5	2.9	2.6	3.4	2.3
Average before-tax income of consumer units	$58,712.00	$73,995.00	$39,385.00	$47,509.00	$63,203.00
Average spending of consumer units, total	46,408.80	52,054.42	32,848.92	40,123.05	49,330.91
Household furnishings and supplies	**1,879.74**	**1,855.00**	**1,074.00**	**1,470.36**	**2,055.47**
Appliances, kitchen, small electric	18.66	20.07	9.91	16.75	20.29
Appliances, major	223.33	376.74	143.42	170.82	242.34
Bathroom linens	21.86	16.64	24.13	25.95	20.95
Bedroom furniture, excl. mattresses and springs	93.86	119.18	90.58	108.59	92.38
Bedroom linens	65.03	95.84	48.14	40.44	70.73
Cleansing and toilet tissue, paper towels, and napkins	94.91	85.59	67.83	108.92	96.95
Closet and storage items	14.34	23.19	4.07	9.58	16.49
Curtains and draperies	18.61	34.64	8.59	14.92	20.63
Decorative items for the home	189.76	84.07	114.88	105.48	212.25
Floor coverings	56.20	96.69	16.23	20.08	67.22
Floor coverings, nonpermanent	29.87	63.78	9.13	9.44	35.82
Wall-to-wall carpeting	26.34	32.92	7.10	10.64	31.41
Housewares	80.36	70.28	32.75	63.20	89.72
Infants' equipment	13.99	14.20	14.16	14.85	13.83
Infants' furniture	8.30	5.92	3.39	18.19	7.69
Kitchen and dining room furniture	50.19	85.35	21.65	68.55	52.08
Kitchen and dining room linens	8.63	7.18	1.21	5.59	10.12
Lamps and lighting fixtures	19.67	19.04	5.76	10.98	22.98
Laundry and cleaning equipment	16.47	14.94	5.95	13.17	18.45
Laundry and cleaning supplies	134.13	90.76	119.18	156.28	133.28
Lawn and garden equipment	50.96	3.52	24.00	17.45	59.65
Lawn and garden supplies	94.26	62.41	23.38	18.79	114.79
Living room chairs	52.57	29.07	26.86	33.84	59.02
Living room tables	17.81	12.88	11.75	16.75	18.89
Mattresses and springs	57.86	62.87	23.17	67.34	61.87
Outdoor equipment	28.69	41.97	9.95	23.46	32.13
Outdoor furniture	18.02	3.83	5.45	10.76	20.92
Plants and fresh flowers, indoor	45.53	37.96	14.53	19.40	53.83
Postage	67.89	51.86	35.48	42.80	76.05
Power tools	53.67	59.01	12.52	26.26	63.61
Sewing materials for household items	10.09	8.36	2.38	3.06	12.23
Sofas	106.91	125.52	81.14	106.16	110.82
Stationery, stationery supplies, giftwrap	85.27	62.34	37.25	54.76	96.52
Wall units, cabinets, and other furniture	61.91	33.08	34.31	57.19	66.76
Household services	**593.11**	**709.47**	**401.22**	**469.50**	**639.02**
Appliance repair, including service center	14.47	11.56	5.90	7.77	16.68
Babysitting and childcare in own or other home	70.25	89.64	50.83	113.75	67.17
Care for the elderly, invalids, handicapped, etc.	24.79	2.88	9.18	4.31	29.97
Day care centers, nursery schools, preschools	225.01	356.16	224.32	216.66	226.16
Gardening, lawn care service	95.73	126.04	46.71	50.42	109.41
Housekeeping services	92.14	62.80	11.53	39.35	111.66
Moving, storage, and freight express	36.44	24.17	26.48	16.85	40.61
Security system service fee	16.48	22.36	18.96	10.89	16.84
Termite and pest control services	17.80	13.86	7.31	9.50	20.52

Note: "Asian" and "black" include Hispanics and non-Hispanics who identify themselves as being of the respective race alone. "Hispanic" includes people of any race who identify themselves as Hispanic. "Other" includes people who identify themselves as non-Hispanic and as Alaska Native, American Indian, Asian (who are also included in the "Asian" column), Native Hawaiian or other Pacific Islander, as well as non-Hispanics reporting more than one race.
Source: Bureau of Labor Statistics, unpublished tables from the 2005 Consumer Expenditure Survey

Table 21. Household Furnishings, Services, and Supplies: Indexed spending by race and Hispanic origin, 2005

(indexed average annual spending of consumer units on household furnishings, services, and supplies by race and Hispanic origin of consumer unit reference person, 2005; index definition: an index of 100 is the average for all consumer units; an index of 132 means that spending by consumer units in that group is 32 percent above the average for all consumer units; an index of 68 indicates spending that is 32 percent below the average for all consumer units)

	total consumer units	Asian	black	Hispanic	non-Hispanic white and other
Average spending of consumer units, total	$46,409	$52,054	$32,849	$40,123	$49,331
Average spending of consumer units, index	100	112	71	86	106
Household furnishings and supplies	**100**	**99**	**57**	**78**	**109**
Appliances, kitchen, small electric	100	108	53	90	109
Appliances, major	100	169	64	76	109
Bathroom linens	100	76	110	119	96
Bedroom furniture, excl. mattresses and springs	100	127	97	116	98
Bedroom linens	100	147	74	62	109
Cleansing and toilet tissue, paper towels, and napkins	100	90	71	115	102
Closet and storage items	100	162	28	67	115
Curtains and draperies	100	186	46	80	111
Decorative items for the home	100	44	61	56	112
Floor coverings	100	172	29	36	120
Floor coverings, nonpermanent	100	214	31	32	120
Wall-to-wall carpeting	100	125	27	40	119
Housewares	100	87	41	79	112
Infants' equipment	100	102	101	106	99
Infants' furniture	100	71	41	219	93
Kitchen and dining room furniture	100	170	43	137	104
Kitchen and dining room linens	100	83	14	65	117
Lamps and lighting fixtures	100	97	29	56	117
Laundry and cleaning equipment	100	91	36	80	112
Laundry and cleaning supplies	100	68	89	117	99
Lawn and garden equipment	100	7	47	34	117
Lawn and garden supplies	100	66	25	20	122
Living room chairs	100	55	51	64	112
Living room tables	100	72	66	94	106
Mattresses and springs	100	109	40	116	107
Outdoor equipment	100	146	35	82	112
Outdoor furniture	100	21	30	60	116
Plants and fresh flowers, indoor	100	83	32	43	118
Postage	100	76	52	63	112
Power tools	100	110	23	49	119
Sewing materials for household items	100	83	24	30	121
Sofas	100	117	76	99	104
Stationery, stationery supplies, giftwrap	100	73	44	64	113
Wall units, cabinets, and other furniture	100	53	55	92	108
Household services	**100**	**120**	**68**	**79**	**108**
Appliance repair, including service center	100	80	41	54	115
Babysitting and childcare in own or other home	100	128	72	162	96
Care for the elderly, invalids, handicapped, etc.	100	12	37	17	121
Day care centers, nursery schools, preschools	100	158	100	96	101
Gardening, lawn care service	100	132	49	53	114
Housekeeping services	100	68	13	43	121
Moving, storage, and freight express	100	66	73	46	111
Security system service fee	100	136	115	66	102
Termite and pest control services	100	78	41	53	115

Note: "Asian" and "black" include Hispanics and non-Hispanics who identify themselves as being of the respective race alone. "Hispanic" includes people of any race who identify themselves as Hispanic. "Other" includes people who identify themselves as non-Hispanic and as Alaska Native, American Indian, Asian (who are also included in the "Asian" column), Native Hawaiian or other Pacific Islander, as well as non-Hispanics reporting more than one race.
Source: Calculations by New Strategist based on the Bureau of Labor Statistics' 2005 Consumer Expenditure Survey

Table 22. Household Furnishings, Services, and Supplies: Total spending by race and Hispanic origin, 2005

(total annual spending on household furnishings, services, and supplies, by consumer unit race and Hispanic origin groups, 2005; consumer units and dollars in thousands)

	total consumer units	Asian	black	Hispanic	non-Hispanic white and other
Number of consumer units	117,356	4,283	14,042	12,462	90,995
Total spending of all consumer units	$5,446,351,133	$222,949,081	$461,264,535	$500,013,449	$4,488,866,155
Household furnishings and supplies	**220,598,767**	**7,944,965**	**15,081,108**	**18,323,626**	**187,037,493**
Appliances, kitchen, small electric	2,189,863	85,960	139,156	208,739	1,846,289
Appliances, major	26,209,115	1,613,577	2,013,904	2,128,759	22,051,728
Bathroom linens	2,565,402	71,269	338,833	323,389	1,906,345
Bedroom furniture, excl. mattresses and springs	11,015,034	510,448	1,271,924	1,353,249	8,406,118
Bedroom linens	7,631,661	410,483	675,982	503,963	6,436,076
Cleansing and toilet tissue, paper towels, and napkins	11,138,258	366,582	952,469	1,357,361	8,821,965
Closet and storage items	1,682,885	99,323	57,151	119,386	1,500,508
Curtains and draperies	2,183,995	148,363	120,621	185,933	1,877,227
Decorative items for the home	22,269,475	360,072	1,613,145	1,314,492	19,313,689
Floor coverings	6,595,407	414,123	227,902	250,237	6,116,684
Floor coverings, nonpermanent	3,505,424	273,170	128,203	117,641	3,259,441
Wall-to-wall carpeting	3,091,157	140,996	99,698	132,596	2,858,153
Housewares	9,430,728	301,009	459,876	787,598	8,164,071
Infants' equipment	1,641,810	60,819	198,835	185,061	1,258,461
Infants' furniture	974,055	25,355	47,602	226,684	699,752
Kitchen and dining room furniture	5,890,098	365,554	304,009	854,270	4,739,020
Kitchen and dining room linens	1,012,782	30,752	16,991	69,663	920,869
Lamps and lighting fixtures	2,308,393	81,548	80,882	136,833	2,091,065
Laundry and cleaning equipment	1,932,853	63,988	83,550	164,125	1,678,858
Laundry and cleaning supplies	15,740,960	388,725	1,673,526	1,947,561	12,127,814
Lawn and garden equipment	5,980,462	15,076	337,008	217,462	5,427,852
Lawn and garden supplies	11,061,977	267,302	328,302	234,161	10,445,316
Living room chairs	6,169,405	124,507	377,168	421,714	5,370,525
Living room tables	2,090,110	55,165	164,994	208,739	1,718,896
Mattresses and springs	6,790,218	269,272	325,353	839,191	5,629,861
Outdoor equipment	3,366,944	179,758	139,718	292,359	2,923,669
Outdoor furniture	2,114,755	16,404	76,529	134,091	1,903,615
Plants and fresh flowers, indoor	5,343,219	162,583	204,030	241,763	4,898,261
Postage	7,967,299	222,116	498,210	533,374	6,920,170
Power tools	6,298,497	252,740	175,806	327,252	5,788,192
Sewing materials for household items	1,184,122	35,806	33,420	38,134	1,112,869
Sofas	12,546,530	537,602	1,139,368	1,322,966	10,084,066
Stationery, stationery supplies, giftwrap	10,006,946	267,002	523,065	682,419	8,782,837
Wall units, cabinets, and other furniture	7,265,510	141,682	481,781	712,702	6,074,826
Household services	**69,605,017**	**3,038,660**	**5,633,931**	**5,850,909**	**58,147,625**
Appliance repair, including service center	1,698,141	49,511	82,848	96,830	1,517,797
Babysitting and childcare in own or other home	8,244,259	383,928	713,755	1,417,553	6,112,134
Care for the elderly, invalids, handicapped, etc.	2,909,255	12,335	128,906	53,711	2,727,120
Day care centers, nursery schools, preschools	26,406,274	1,525,433	3,149,901	2,700,017	20,579,429
Gardening, lawn care service	11,234,490	539,829	655,902	628,334	9,955,763
Housekeeping services	10,813,182	268,972	161,904	490,380	10,160,502
Moving, storage, and freight express	4,276,453	103,520	371,832	209,985	3,695,307
Security system service fee	1,934,027	95,768	266,236	135,711	1,532,356
Termite and pest control services	2,088,937	59,362	102,647	118,389	1,867,217

Note: "Asian" and "black" include Hispanics and non-Hispanics who identify themselves as being of the respective race alone. "Hispanic" includes people of any race who identify themselves as Hispanic. "Other" includes people who identify themselves as non-Hispanic and as Alaska Native, American Indian, Asian (who are also included in the "Asian" column), Native Hawaiian or other Pacific Islander, as well as non-Hispanics reporting more than one race. Numbers may not add to total because of rounding.
Source: Calculations by New Strategist based on the Bureau of Labor Statistics' 2005 Consumer Expenditure Survey

Table 23. Household Furnishings, Services, and Supplies: Market shares by race and Hispanic origin, 2005

(percentage of total annual spending on household furnishings, services, and supplies accounted for by consumer unit race and Hispanic origin groups, 2005)

	total consumer units	Asian	black	Hispanic	non-Hispanic white and other
Share of total consumer units	100.0%	3.6%	12.0%	10.6%	77.5%
Share of total before-tax income	100.0	4.6	8.0	8.6	83.5
Share of total spending	100.0	4.1	8.5	9.2	82.4
Household furnishings and supplies	100.0	3.6	6.8	8.3	84.8
Appliances, kitchen, small electric	100.0	3.9	6.4	9.5	84.3
Appliances, major	100.0	6.2	7.7	8.1	84.1
Bathroom linens	100.0	2.8	13.2	12.6	74.3
Bedroom furniture, excl. mattresses and springs	100.0	4.6	11.5	12.3	76.3
Bedroom linens	100.0	5.4	8.9	6.6	84.3
Cleansing and toilet tissue, paper towels, and napkins	100.0	3.3	8.6	12.2	79.2
Closet and storage items	100.0	5.9	3.4	7.1	89.2
Curtains and draperies	100.0	6.8	5.5	8.5	86.0
Decorative items for the home	100.0	1.6	7.2	5.9	86.7
Floor coverings	100.0	6.3	3.5	3.8	92.7
Floor coverings, nonpermanent	100.0	7.8	3.7	3.4	93.0
Wall-to-wall carpeting	100.0	4.6	3.2	4.3	92.5
Housewares	100.0	3.2	4.9	8.4	86.6
Infants' equipment	100.0	3.7	12.1	11.3	76.7
Infants' furniture	100.0	2.6	4.9	23.3	71.8
Kitchen and dining room furniture	100.0	6.2	5.2	14.5	80.5
Kitchen and dining room linens	100.0	3.0	1.7	6.9	90.9
Lamps and lighting fixtures	100.0	3.5	3.5	5.9	90.6
Laundry and cleaning equipment	100.0	3.3	4.3	8.5	86.9
Laundry and cleaning supplies	100.0	2.5	10.6	12.4	77.0
Lawn and garden equipment	100.0	0.3	5.6	3.6	90.8
Lawn and garden supplies	100.0	2.4	3.0	2.1	94.4
Living room chairs	100.0	2.0	6.1	6.8	87.1
Living room tables	100.0	2.6	7.9	10.0	82.2
Mattresses and springs	100.0	4.0	4.8	12.4	82.9
Outdoor equipment	100.0	5.3	4.1	8.7	86.8
Outdoor furniture	100.0	0.8	3.6	6.3	90.0
Plants and fresh flowers, indoor	100.0	3.0	3.8	4.5	91.7
Postage	100.0	2.8	6.3	6.7	86.9
Power tools	100.0	4.0	2.8	5.2	91.9
Sewing materials for household items	100.0	3.0	2.8	3.2	94.0
Sofas	100.0	4.3	9.1	10.5	80.4
Stationery, stationery supplies, giftwrap	100.0	2.7	5.2	6.8	87.8
Wall units, cabinets, and other furniture	100.0	2.0	6.6	9.8	83.6
Household services	100.0	4.4	8.1	8.4	83.5
Appliance repair, including service center	100.0	2.9	4.9	5.7	89.4
Babysitting and childcare in own or other home	100.0	4.7	8.7	17.2	74.1
Care for the elderly, invalids, handicapped, etc.	100.0	0.4	4.4	1.8	93.7
Day care centers, nursery schools, preschools	100.0	5.8	11.9	10.2	77.9
Gardening, lawn care service	100.0	4.8	5.8	5.6	88.6
Housekeeping services	100.0	2.5	1.5	4.5	94.0
Moving, storage, and freight express	100.0	2.4	8.7	4.9	86.4
Security system service fee	100.0	5.0	13.8	7.0	79.2
Termite and pest control services	100.0	2.8	4.9	5.7	89.4

Note: "Asian" and "black" include Hispanics and non-Hispanics who identify themselves as being of the respective race alone. "Hispanic" includes people of any race who identify themselves as Hispanic. "Other" includes people who identify themselves as non-Hispanic and as Alaska Native, American Indian, Asian (who are also included in the "Asian" column), Native Hawaiian or other Pacific Islander, as well as non-Hispanics reporting more than one race.
Source: Calculations by New Strategist based on the Bureau of Labor Statistics' 2005 Consumer Expenditure Survey

Table 24. Household Furnishings, Services, and Supplies: Average spending by region, 2005

(average annual spending of consumer units on household furnishings, services, and supplies, by region in which consumer unit lives, 2005)

	total consumer units	Northeast	Midwest	South	West
Number of consumer units (in 000s)	117,356	22,356	27,005	42,120	25,875
Number of persons per consumer unit	2.5	2.4	2.4	2.5	2.6
Average before-tax income of consumer units	$58,712.00	$63,068.00	$56,606.00	$53,311.00	$65,938.00
Average spending of consumer units, total	46,408.80	47,920.60	45,027.11	42,504.37	52,890.92
Household furnishings and supplies	**1,879.74**	**1,725.53**	**1,840.45**	**1,757.42**	**2,251.70**
Appliances, kitchen, small electric	18.66	16.70	20.08	16.24	22.82
Appliances, major	223.33	209.73	209.78	214.33	264.10
Bathroom linens	21.86	24.65	23.26	20.69	19.97
Bedroom furniture, excl. mattresses and springs	93.86	70.18	73.21	111.86	106.57
Bedroom linens	65.03	60.49	73.38	67.56	56.47
Cleansing and toilet tissue, paper towels, and napkins	94.91	95.54	89.94	95.01	99.20
Closet and storage items	14.34	14.91	14.73	13.44	14.94
Curtains and draperies	18.61	18.38	21.06	16.48	19.71
Decorative items for the home	189.76	146.52	173.06	150.17	307.59
Floor coverings	56.20	57.89	55.90	56.03	55.31
Floor coverings, nonpermanent	29.87	27.06	23.06	36.19	29.10
Wall-to-wall carpeting	26.34	30.84	32.85	19.83	26.22
Housewares	80.36	74.53	81.85	66.97	105.53
Infants' equipment	13.99	9.37	16.10	10.83	20.94
Infants' furniture	8.30	9.78	7.76	7.39	9.06
Kitchen and dining room furniture	50.19	39.42	43.93	50.16	66.10
Kitchen and dining room linens	8.63	13.24	7.44	7.41	7.83
Lamps and lighting fixtures	19.67	18.48	18.51	19.68	21.88
Laundry and cleaning equipment	16.47	13.42	16.36	14.92	21.70
Laundry and cleaning supplies	134.13	118.08	140.04	141.27	130.39
Lawn and garden equipment	50.96	30.01	96.49	48.85	24.98
Lawn and garden supplies	94.26	101.99	98.34	77.40	110.82
Living room chairs	52.57	44.50	45.49	51.29	69.01
Living room tables	17.81	13.31	19.73	14.33	25.37
Mattresses and springs	57.86	43.22	55.15	54.67	78.54
Outdoor equipment	28.69	20.47	28.23	36.55	23.47
Outdoor furniture	18.02	15.70	16.62	14.54	27.14
Plants and fresh flowers, indoor	45.53	64.14	50.23	32.61	45.57
Postage	67.89	74.92	64.55	65.75	68.70
Power tools	53.67	30.64	43.87	51.75	86.33
Sewing materials for household items	10.09	8.48	13.22	6.57	13.94
Sofas	106.91	88.38	81.99	101.37	157.93
Stationery, stationery supplies, giftwrap	85.27	117.83	89.23	63.57	88.51
Wall units, cabinets, and other furniture	61.91	60.63	50.92	57.73	81.28
Household services	**593.11**	**558.38**	**549.95**	**588.47**	**675.75**
Appliance repair, including service center	14.47	14.55	14.96	12.75	16.68
Babysitting and childcare in own or other home	70.25	78.99	70.94	58.88	80.50
Care for the elderly, invalids, handicapped, etc.	24.79	16.36	35.27	22.01	25.68
Day care centers, nursery schools, preschools	225.01	211.10	238.51	230.21	214.50
Gardening, lawn care service	95.73	99.84	75.53	95.93	112.94
Housekeeping services	92.14	97.23	72.05	84.86	120.56
Moving, storage, and freight express	36.44	18.83	23.74	35.07	67.16
Security system service fee	16.48	13.92	11.09	22.07	15.21
Termite and pest control services	17.80	7.56	7.86	26.69	22.52

Note: Numbers will not add to total because not all categories are shown.
Source: Bureau of Labor Statistics, unpublished data from the 2005 Consumer Expenditure Survey

Table 25. Household Furnishings, Services, and Supplies: Indexed spending by region, 2005

(indexed average annual spending of consumer units on household furnishings, services, and supplies by region in which consumer unit lives, 2005; index definition: an index of 100 is the average for all consumer units; an index of 132 means that spending by consumer units in that group is 32 percent above the average for all consumer units; an index of 68 indicates spending that is 32 percent below the average for all consumer units)

	total consumer units	Northeast	Midwest	South	West
Average spending of consumer units, total	$46,409	$47,921	$45,027	$42,504	$52,891
Average spending of consumer units, index	100	103	97	92	114
Household furnishings and supplies	**100**	**92**	**98**	**93**	**120**
Appliances, kitchen, small electric	100	89	108	87	122
Appliances, major	100	94	94	96	118
Bathroom linens	100	113	106	95	91
Bedroom furniture, excl. mattresses and springs	100	75	78	119	114
Bedroom linens	100	93	113	104	87
Cleansing and toilet tissue, paper towels, and napkins	100	101	95	100	105
Closet and storage items	100	104	103	94	104
Curtains and draperies	100	99	113	89	106
Decorative items for the home	100	77	91	79	162
Floor coverings	100	103	99	100	98
Floor coverings, nonpermanent	100	91	77	121	97
Wall-to-wall carpeting	100	117	125	75	100
Housewares	100	93	102	83	131
Infants' equipment	100	67	115	77	150
Infants' furniture	100	118	93	89	109
Kitchen and dining room furniture	100	79	88	100	132
Kitchen and dining room linens	100	153	86	86	91
Lamps and lighting fixtures	100	94	94	100	111
Laundry and cleaning equipment	100	81	99	91	132
Laundry and cleaning supplies	100	88	104	105	97
Lawn and garden equipment	100	59	189	96	49
Lawn and garden supplies	100	108	104	82	118
Living room chairs	100	85	87	98	131
Living room tables	100	75	111	80	142
Mattresses and springs	100	75	95	94	136
Outdoor equipment	100	71	98	127	82
Outdoor furniture	100	87	92	81	151
Plants and fresh flowers, indoor	100	141	110	72	100
Postage	100	110	95	97	101
Power tools	100	57	82	96	161
Sewing materials for household items	100	84	131	65	138
Sofas	100	83	77	95	148
Stationery, stationery supplies, giftwrap	100	138	105	75	104
Wall units, cabinets, and other furniture	100	98	82	93	131
Household services	**100**	**94**	**93**	**99**	**114**
Appliance repair, including service center	100	101	103	88	115
Babysitting and childcare in own or other home	100	112	101	84	115
Care for the elderly, invalids, handicapped, etc.	100	66	142	89	104
Day care centers, nursery schools, preschools	100	94	106	102	95
Gardening, lawn care service	100	104	79	100	118
Housekeeping services	100	106	78	92	131
Moving, storage, and freight express	100	52	65	96	184
Security system service fee	100	84	67	134	92
Termite and pest control services	100	42	44	150	127

Source: Calculations by New Strategist based on the Bureau of Labor Statistics' 2005 Consumer Expenditure Survey

Table 26. Household Furnishings, Services, and Supplies: Total spending by region, 2005

(total annual spending on household furnishings, services, and supplies, by region in which consumer unit lives, 2005; consumer units and dollars in thousands)

	total consumer units	Northeast	Midwest	South	West
Number of consumer units	117,356	22,356	27,005	42,120	25,875
Total spending of all consumer units	$5,446,351,133	$1,071,312,934	$1,215,957,106	$1,790,284,064	$1,368,552,555
Household furnishings and supplies	**220,598,767**	**38,575,949**	**49,701,352**	**74,022,530**	**58,262,738**
Appliances, kitchen, small electric	2,189,863	373,345	542,260	684,029	590,468
Appliances, major	26,209,115	4,688,724	5,665,109	9,027,580	6,833,588
Bathroom linens	2,565,402	551,075	628,136	871,463	516,724
Bedroom furniture, excl. mattresses and springs	11,015,034	1,568,944	1,977,036	4,711,543	2,757,499
Bedroom linens	7,631,661	1,352,314	1,981,627	2,845,627	1,461,161
Cleansing and toilet tissue, paper towels, and napkins	11,138,258	2,135,892	2,428,830	4,001,821	2,566,800
Closet and storage items	1,682,885	333,328	397,784	566,093	386,573
Curtains and draperies	2,183,995	410,903	568,725	694,138	509,996
Decorative items for the home	22,269,475	3,275,601	4,673,485	6,325,160	7,958,891
Floor coverings	6,595,407	1,294,189	1,509,580	2,359,984	1,431,146
Floor coverings, nonpermanent	3,505,424	604,953	622,735	1,524,323	752,963
Wall-to-wall carpeting	3,091,157	689,459	887,114	835,240	678,443
Housewares	9,430,728	1,666,193	2,210,359	2,820,776	2,730,589
Infants' equipment	1,641,810	209,476	434,781	456,160	541,823
Infants' furniture	974,055	218,642	209,559	311,267	234,428
Kitchen and dining room furniture	5,890,098	881,274	1,186,330	2,112,739	1,710,338
Kitchen and dining room linens	1,012,782	295,993	200,917	312,109	202,601
Lamps and lighting fixtures	2,308,393	413,139	499,863	828,922	566,145
Laundry and cleaning equipment	1,932,853	300,018	441,802	628,430	561,488
Laundry and cleaning supplies	15,740,960	2,639,796	3,781,780	5,950,292	3,373,841
Lawn and garden equipment	5,980,462	670,904	2,605,712	2,057,562	646,358
Lawn and garden supplies	11,061,977	2,280,088	2,655,672	3,260,088	2,867,468
Living room chairs	6,169,405	994,842	1,228,457	2,160,335	1,785,634
Living room tables	2,090,110	297,558	532,809	603,580	656,449
Mattresses and springs	6,790,218	966,226	1,489,326	2,302,700	2,032,223
Outdoor equipment	3,366,944	457,627	762,351	1,539,486	607,286
Outdoor furniture	2,114,755	350,989	448,823	612,425	702,248
Plants and fresh flowers, indoor	5,343,219	1,433,914	1,356,461	1,373,533	1,179,124
Postage	7,967,299	1,674,912	1,743,173	2,769,390	1,777,613
Power tools	6,298,497	684,988	1,184,709	2,179,710	2,233,789
Sewing materials for household items	1,184,122	189,579	357,006	276,728	360,698
Sofas	12,546,530	1,975,823	2,214,140	4,269,704	4,086,439
Stationery, stationery supplies, giftwrap	10,006,946	2,634,207	2,409,656	2,677,568	2,290,196
Wall units, cabinets, and other furniture	7,265,510	1,355,444	1,375,095	2,431,588	2,103,120
Household services	**69,605,017**	**12,483,143**	**14,851,400**	**24,786,356**	**17,485,031**
Appliance repair, including service center	1,698,141	325,280	403,995	537,030	431,595
Babysitting and childcare in own or other home	8,244,259	1,765,900	1,915,735	2,480,026	2,082,938
Care for the elderly, invalids, handicapped, etc.	2,909,255	365,744	952,466	927,061	664,470
Day care centers, nursery schools, preschools	26,406,274	4,719,352	6,440,963	9,696,445	5,550,188
Gardening, lawn care service	11,234,490	2,232,023	2,039,688	4,040,572	2,922,323
Housekeeping services	10,813,182	2,173,674	1,945,710	3,574,303	3,119,490
Moving, storage, and freight express	4,276,453	420,963	641,099	1,477,148	1,737,765
Security system service fee	1,934,027	311,196	299,485	929,588	393,559
Termite and pest control services	2,088,937	169,011	212,259	1,124,183	582,705

Note: Numbers will not add to total because not all categories are shown and because of rounding.
Source: Calculations by New Strategist based on the Bureau of Labor Statistics' 2005 Consumer Expenditure Survey

Table 27. Household Furnishings, Services, and Supplies: Market shares by region, 2005

(percentage of total annual spending on household furnishings, services, and supplies accounted for by consumer units by region of residence, 2005)

	total consumer units	Northeast	Midwest	South	West
Share of total consumer units	100.0%	19.0%	23.0%	35.9%	22.0%
Share of total before-tax income	100.0	20.5	22.2	32.6	24.8
Share of total spending	100.0	19.7	22.3	32.9	25.1
Household furnishings and supplies	100.0	17.5	22.5	33.6	26.4
Appliances, kitchen, small electric	100.0	17.0	24.8	31.2	27.0
Appliances, major	100.0	17.9	21.6	34.4	26.1
Bathroom linens	100.0	21.5	24.5	34.0	20.1
Bedroom furniture, excl. mattresses and springs	100.0	14.2	17.9	42.8	25.0
Bedroom linens	100.0	17.7	26.0	37.3	19.1
Cleansing and toilet tissue, paper towels, and napkins	100.0	19.2	21.8	35.9	23.0
Closet and storage items	100.0	19.8	23.6	33.6	23.0
Curtains and draperies	100.0	18.8	26.0	31.8	23.4
Decorative items for the home	100.0	14.7	21.0	28.4	35.7
Floor coverings	100.0	19.6	22.9	35.8	21.7
Floor coverings, nonpermanent	100.0	17.3	17.8	43.5	21.5
Wall-to-wall carpeting	100.0	22.3	28.7	27.0	21.9
Housewares	100.0	17.7	23.4	29.9	29.0
Infants' equipment	100.0	12.8	26.5	27.8	33.0
Infants' furniture	100.0	22.4	21.5	32.0	24.1
Kitchen and dining room furniture	100.0	15.0	20.1	35.9	29.0
Kitchen and dining room linens	100.0	29.2	19.8	30.8	20.0
Lamps and lighting fixtures	100.0	17.9	21.7	35.9	24.5
Laundry and cleaning equipment	100.0	15.5	22.9	32.5	29.0
Laundry and cleaning supplies	100.0	16.8	24.0	37.8	21.4
Lawn and garden equipment	100.0	11.2	43.6	34.4	10.8
Lawn and garden supplies	100.0	20.6	24.0	29.5	25.9
Living room chairs	100.0	16.1	19.9	35.0	28.9
Living room tables	100.0	14.2	25.5	28.9	31.4
Mattresses and springs	100.0	14.2	21.9	33.9	29.9
Outdoor equipment	100.0	13.6	22.6	45.7	18.0
Outdoor furniture	100.0	16.6	21.2	29.0	33.2
Plants and fresh flowers, indoor	100.0	26.8	25.4	25.7	22.1
Postage	100.0	21.0	21.9	34.8	22.3
Power tools	100.0	10.9	18.8	34.6	35.5
Sewing materials for household items	100.0	16.0	30.1	23.4	30.5
Sofas	100.0	15.7	17.6	34.0	32.6
Stationery, stationery supplies, giftwrap	100.0	26.3	24.1	26.8	22.9
Wall units, cabinets, and other furniture	100.0	18.7	18.9	33.5	28.9
Household services	100.0	17.9	21.3	35.6	25.1
Appliance repair, including service center	100.0	19.2	23.8	31.6	25.4
Babysitting and childcare in own or other home	100.0	21.4	23.2	30.1	25.3
Care for the elderly, invalids, handicapped, etc.	100.0	12.6	32.7	31.9	22.8
Day care centers, nursery schools, preschools	100.0	17.9	24.4	36.7	21.0
Gardening, lawn care service	100.0	19.9	18.2	36.0	26.0
Housekeeping services	100.0	20.1	18.0	33.1	28.8
Moving, storage, and freight express	100.0	9.8	15.0	34.5	40.6
Security system service fee	100.0	16.1	15.5	48.1	20.3
Termite and pest control services	100.0	8.1	10.2	53.8	27.9

Note: Numbers may not add to total because of rounding.
Source: Calculations by New Strategist based on the Bureau of Labor Statistics' 2005 Consumer Expenditure Survey

Table 28. Household Furnishings, Services, and Supplies: Average spending by education, 2005

(average annual spending of consumer units (CU) on household furnishings, services, and supplies, by education of consumer unit reference person, 2005)

	total consumer units	less than high school graduate	high school graduate	some college	associate's degree	college graduate total	bachelor's degree	master's, professional, doctorate
Number of consumer units (in 000s)	117,356	18,028	30,389	25,285	11,592	32,062	20,231	11,831
Number of persons per CU	2.5	2.7	2.5	2.4	2.5	2.4	2.5	2.4
Average before-tax income of CU	$58,712.00	$30,643.00	$45,721.00	$52,233.00	$60,417.00	$91,300.00	$82,276.00	$106,732.00
Average spending of CU, total	46,408.80	27,435.43	38,162.07	43,861.34	49,708.65	65,542.30	61,378.81	72,826.82
Household furnishings and supplies	**1,879.74**	**953.87**	**1,413.00**	**1,710.43**	**2,090.15**	**2,863.63**	**2,542.77**	**3,465.43**
Appliances, kitchen, small electric	$18.66	$11.86	$14.70	$17.84	$19.12	$26.71	$24.75	$30.07
Appliances, major	223.33	114.35	179.99	238.52	231.04	309.56	276.18	373.80
Bathroom linens	21.86	17.50	17.57	14.59	21.67	33.64	35.41	30.14
Bedroom furniture, excl. mattresses and springs	93.86	46.53	76.17	87.30	122.26	132.15	126.08	142.54
Bedroom linens	65.03	31.12	64.30	52.68	67.30	91.02	88.94	95.15
Cleansing and toilet tissue, paper towels, and napkins	94.91	91.06	90.05	84.62	89.27	110.90	109.59	113.50
Closet and storage items	14.34	7.58	8.89	9.54	24.10	23.50	25.58	19.40
Curtains and draperies	18.61	6.94	13.41	17.34	21.95	29.89	23.13	41.45
Decorative items for the home	189.76	44.97	111.04	119.95	169.23	394.45	264.56	651.29
Floor coverings	56.20	14.82	30.10	42.60	58.76	114.00	94.83	146.77
Floor coverings, nonpermanent	29.87	4.70	8.58	23.29	20.30	72.83	54.67	103.88
Wall-to-wall carpeting	26.34	10.11	21.52	19.31	38.46	41.17	40.16	42.89
Housewares	80.36	39.97	63.40	67.79	89.91	123.00	121.80	125.08
Infants' equipment	13.99	8.44	7.03	8.70	17.28	26.31	24.73	29.45
Infants' furniture	8.30	4.11	4.73	6.70	11.86	14.02	13.49	14.93
Kitchen and dining room furniture	50.19	30.07	25.60	52.37	55.06	81.35	71.37	98.41
Kitchen and dining room linens	8.63	2.63	7.77	7.43	7.15	13.74	13.96	13.32
Lamps and lighting fixtures	19.67	7.67	9.60	18.66	15.90	38.11	30.92	50.40
Laundry and cleaning equipment	16.47	11.18	14.27	13.86	16.80	23.01	21.97	25.07
Laundry and cleaning supplies	134.13	125.56	131.16	127.77	140.16	144.13	145.27	141.86
Lawn and garden equipment	50.96	29.02	62.07	41.70	114.81	36.98	29.58	49.64
Lawn and garden supplies	94.26	25.53	72.00	72.05	122.01	157.45	162.61	147.25
Living room chairs	52.57	30.99	35.77	50.12	64.36	78.29	72.86	87.56
Living room tables	17.81	9.92	11.17	18.34	12.12	30.18	24.76	39.46
Mattresses and springs	57.86	31.97	32.61	60.83	72.33	88.78	84.16	96.66
Outdoor equipment	28.69	12.38	8.98	32.71	43.62	47.80	34.19	74.72
Outdoor furniture	18.02	4.74	8.93	18.91	18.66	33.16	20.89	54.14
Plants and fresh flowers, indoor	45.53	14.59	33.92	40.93	43.24	78.37	64.60	101.90
Postage	67.89	35.95	58.03	66.22	67.59	94.27	82.16	118.22
Power tools	53.67	19.33	28.49	49.88	83.51	88.20	92.63	79.43
Sewing materials for household items	10.09	2.90	7.31	11.65	10.77	15.28	13.52	18.30
Sofas	106.91	62.26	74.03	122.26	133.61	141.41	143.58	137.69
Stationery, stationery supplies, giftwrap	85.27	31.80	67.19	67.90	71.47	145.96	121.08	195.15
Wall units, cabinets, and other furniture	61.91	26.13	42.72	68.67	53.23	98.01	83.59	122.68
Household services	**593.11**	**208.13**	**363.90**	**524.60**	**604.23**	**1,076.85**	**917.11**	**1,349.98**
Appliance repair, including service center	14.47	7.69	11.22	15.73	16.05	19.78	17.62	23.48
Babysitting and childcare in own or other home	70.25	43.34	49.13	46.32	67.21	125.36	109.90	151.78
Care for the elderly, invalids, handicapped, etc.	24.79	23.75	11.23	37.19	12.55	32.87	29.16	39.21
Day care centers, nursery schools, preschools	225.01	65.82	137.94	218.65	290.13	378.54	346.41	433.48
Gardening, lawn care service	95.73	33.17	60.89	76.40	87.97	181.98	144.73	245.68
Housekeeping services	92.14	17.42	43.80	56.88	58.90	219.80	161.19	320.02
Moving, storage, and freight express	36.44	7.87	27.54	45.73	30.42	55.81	51.23	63.65
Security system service fee	16.48	3.88	10.89	13.33	19.92	30.11	26.49	36.29
Termite and pest control services	17.80	5.19	11.26	14.37	21.08	32.60	30.38	36.39

Note: Numbers will not add to total because not all categories are shown.
Source: Bureau of Labor Statistics, unpublished data from the 2005 Consumer Expenditure Survey

Table 29. Household Furnishings, Services, and Supplies: Indexed spending by education, 2005

(indexed average annual spending of consumer units (CU) on household furnishings, services, and supplies by education of consumer unit reference person, 2005; index definition: an index of 100 is the average for all consumer units; an index of 132 means that spending by consumer units in that group is 32 percent above the average for all consumer units; an index of 68 indicates spending that is 32 percent below the average for all consumer units)

	total consumer units	less than high school graduate	high school graduate	some college	associate's degree	college graduate total	bachelor's degree	master's, professional, doctorate
Average spending of CU, total	$46,409	$27,435	$38,162	$43,861	$49,709	$65,542	$61,379	$72,827
Average spending of CU, index	100	59	82	95	107	141	132	157
Household furnishings and supplies	**100**	**51**	**75**	**91**	**111**	**152**	**135**	**184**
Appliances, kitchen, small electric	100	64	79	96	102	143	133	161
Appliances, major	100	51	81	107	103	139	124	167
Bathroom linens	100	80	80	67	99	154	162	138
Bedroom furniture, excl. mattresses and springs	100	50	81	93	130	141	134	152
Bedroom linens	100	48	99	81	103	140	137	146
Cleansing and toilet tissue, paper towels, and napkins	100	96	95	89	94	117	115	120
Closet and storage items	100	53	62	67	168	164	178	135
Curtains and draperies	100	37	72	93	118	161	124	223
Decorative items for the home	100	24	59	63	89	208	139	343
Floor coverings	100	26	54	76	105	203	169	261
Floor coverings, nonpermanent	100	16	29	78	68	244	183	348
Wall-to-wall carpeting	100	38	82	73	146	156	152	163
Housewares	100	50	79	84	112	153	152	156
Infants' equipment	100	60	50	62	124	188	177	211
Infants' furniture	100	50	57	81	143	169	163	180
Kitchen and dining room furniture	100	60	51	104	110	162	142	196
Kitchen and dining room linens	100	30	90	86	83	159	162	154
Lamps and lighting fixtures	100	39	49	95	81	194	157	256
Laundry and cleaning equipment	100	68	87	84	102	140	133	152
Laundry and cleaning supplies	100	94	98	95	104	107	108	106
Lawn and garden equipment	100	57	122	82	225	73	58	97
Lawn and garden supplies	100	27	76	76	129	167	173	156
Living room chairs	100	59	68	95	122	149	139	167
Living room tables	100	56	63	103	68	169	139	222
Mattresses and springs	100	55	56	105	125	153	145	167
Outdoor equipment	100	43	31	114	152	167	119	260
Outdoor furniture	100	26	50	105	104	184	116	300
Plants and fresh flowers, indoor	100	32	75	90	95	172	142	224
Postage	100	53	85	98	100	139	121	174
Power tools	100	36	53	93	156	164	173	148
Sewing materials for household items	100	29	72	115	107	151	134	181
Sofas	100	58	69	114	125	132	134	129
Stationery, stationery supplies, giftwrap	100	37	79	80	84	171	142	229
Wall units, cabinets, and other furniture	100	42	69	111	86	158	135	198
Household services	**100**	**35**	**61**	**88**	**102**	**182**	**155**	**228**
Appliance repair, including service center	100	53	78	109	111	137	122	162
Babysitting and childcare in own or other home	100	62	70	66	96	178	156	216
Care for the elderly, invalids, handicapped, etc.	100	96	45	150	51	133	118	158
Day care centers, nursery schools, preschools	100	29	61	97	129	168	154	193
Gardening, lawn care service	100	35	64	80	92	190	151	257
Housekeeping services	100	19	48	62	64	239	175	347
Moving, storage, and freight express	100	22	76	125	83	153	141	175
Security system service fee	100	24	66	81	121	183	161	220
Termite and pest control services	100	29	63	81	118	183	171	204

Source: Calculations by New Strategist based on the Bureau of Labor Statistics' 2005 Consumer Expenditure Survey

Table 30. Household Furnishings, Services, and Supplies: Total spending by education, 2005

(total annual spending on household furnishings, services, and supplies, by consumer unit (CU) educational attainment group, 2005; consumer units and dollars in thousands)

	total consumer units	less than high school graduate	high school graduate	some college	associate's degree	college graduate total	bachelor's degree	master's, professional, doctorate
Number of consumer units	117,356	18,028	30,389	25,285	11,592	32,062	20,231	11,831
Total spending of all CUs	$5,446,351,133	$494,605,932	$1,159,707,145	$1,109,033,982	$576,222,671	$2,101,417,223	$1,241,754,705	$861,614,107
Household furnishings and supplies	**220,598,767**	**17,196,368**	**42,939,657**	**43,248,223**	**24,229,019**	**91,813,705**	**51,442,780**	**40,999,502**
Appliances, kitchen, small electric	2,189,863	213,812	446,718	451,084	221,639	856,376	500,717	355,758
Appliances, major	26,209,115	2,061,502	5,469,716	6,030,978	2,678,216	9,925,113	5,587,398	4,422,428
Bathroom linens	2,565,402	315,490	533,935	368,908	251,199	1,078,566	716,380	356,586
Bedroom furniture, excl. mattresses and springs	11,015,034	838,843	2,314,730	2,207,381	1,417,238	4,236,993	2,550,724	1,686,391
Bedroom linens	7,631,661	561,031	1,954,013	1,332,014	780,142	2,918,283	1,799,345	1,125,720
Cleansing and toilet tissue, paper towels, and napkins	11,138,258	1,641,630	2,736,529	2,139,617	1,034,818	3,555,676	2,217,115	1,342,819
Closet and storage items	1,682,885	136,652	270,158	241,219	279,367	753,457	517,509	229,521
Curtains and draperies	2,183,995	125,114	407,516	438,442	254,444	958,333	467,943	490,395
Decorative items for the home	22,269,475	810,719	3,374,395	3,032,936	1,961,714	12,646,856	5,352,313	7,705,412
Floor coverings	6,595,407	267,175	914,709	1,077,141	681,146	3,655,068	1,918,506	1,736,436
Floor coverings, nonpermanent	3,505,424	84,732	260,738	588,888	235,318	2,335,075	1,106,029	1,229,004
Wall-to-wall carpeting	3,091,157	182,263	653,971	488,253	445,828	1,319,993	812,477	507,432
Housewares	9,430,728	720,579	1,926,663	1,714,070	1,042,237	3,943,626	2,464,136	1,479,821
Infants' equipment	1,641,810	152,156	213,635	219,980	200,310	843,551	500,313	348,423
Infants' furniture	974,055	74,095	143,740	169,410	137,481	449,509	272,916	176,637
Kitchen and dining room furniture	5,890,098	542,102	777,958	1,324,175	638,256	2,608,244	1,443,886	1,164,289
Kitchen and dining room linens	1,012,782	47,414	236,123	187,868	82,883	440,532	282,425	157,589
Lamps and lighting fixtures	2,308,393	138,275	291,734	471,818	184,313	1,221,883	625,543	596,282
Laundry and cleaning equipment	1,932,853	201,543	433,651	350,450	194,746	737,747	444,475	296,603
Laundry and cleaning supplies	15,740,960	2,263,596	3,985,821	3,230,664	1,624,735	4,621,096	2,938,957	1,678,346
Lawn and garden equipment	5,980,462	523,173	1,886,245	1,054,385	1,330,878	1,185,653	598,433	587,291
Lawn and garden supplies	11,061,977	460,255	2,188,008	1,821,784	1,414,340	5,048,162	3,289,763	1,742,115
Living room chairs	6,169,405	558,688	1,087,015	1,267,284	746,061	2,510,134	1,474,031	1,035,922
Living room tables	2,090,110	178,838	339,445	463,727	140,495	967,631	500,920	466,851
Mattresses and springs	6,790,218	576,355	990,985	1,538,087	838,449	2,846,464	1,702,641	1,143,584
Outdoor equipment	3,366,944	223,187	272,893	827,072	505,643	1,532,564	691,698	884,012
Outdoor furniture	2,114,755	85,453	271,374	478,139	216,307	1,063,176	422,626	640,530
Plants and fresh flowers, indoor	5,343,219	263,029	1,030,795	1,034,915	501,238	2,512,699	1,306,923	1,205,579
Postage	7,967,299	648,107	1,763,474	1,674,373	783,503	3,022,485	1,662,179	1,398,661
Power tools	6,298,497	348,481	865,783	1,261,216	968,048	2,827,868	1,873,998	939,736
Sewing materials for household items	1,184,122	52,281	222,144	294,570	124,846	489,907	273,523	216,507
Sofas	12,546,530	1,122,423	2,249,698	3,091,344	1,548,807	4,533,887	2,904,767	1,629,010
Stationery, stationery supplies, giftwrap	10,006,946	573,290	2,041,837	1,716,852	828,480	4,679,770	2,449,569	2,308,820
Wall units, cabinets, and other furniture	7,265,510	471,072	1,298,218	1,736,321	617,042	3,142,397	1,691,109	1,451,427
Household services	**69,605,017**	**3,752,168**	**11,058,557**	**13,264,511**	**7,004,234**	**34,525,965**	**18,554,052**	**15,971,613**
Appliance repair, incl. service center	1,698,141	138,635	340,965	397,733	186,052	634,186	356,470	277,792
Babysitting and childcare in own or other home	8,244,259	781,334	1,493,012	1,171,201	779,098	4,019,292	2,223,387	1,795,709
Care for the elderly, invalids, handicapped, etc.	2,909,255	428,165	341,268	940,349	145,480	1,053,878	589,936	463,894
Day care centers, nursery schools, preschools	26,406,274	1,186,603	4,191,859	5,528,565	3,363,187	12,136,749	7,008,221	5,128,502
Gardening, lawn care service	11,234,490	597,989	1,850,386	1,931,774	1,019,748	5,834,643	2,928,033	2,906,640
Housekeeping services	10,813,182	314,048	1,331,038	1,438,211	682,769	7,047,228	3,261,035	3,786,157
Moving, storage, and freight express	4,276,453	141,880	836,913	1,156,283	352,629	1,789,380	1,036,434	753,043
Security system service fee	1,934,027	69,949	330,936	337,049	230,913	965,387	535,919	429,347
Termite and pest control services	2,088,937	93,565	342,180	363,345	244,359	1,045,221	614,618	430,530

Note: Numbers will not add to total because not all categories are shown and because of rounding.
Source: Calculations by New Strategist based on the Bureau of Labor Statistics' 2005 Consumer Expenditure Survey

Table 31. Household Furnishings, Services, and Supplies: Market shares by education, 2005

(percentage of total annual spending on household furnishings, services, and supplies accounted for by consumer unit educational attainment groups, 2005)

	total consumer units	less than high school graduate	high school graduate	some college	associate's degree	college graduate total	bachelor's degree	master's, professional, doctorate
Share of total consumer units	100.0%	15.4%	25.9%	21.5%	9.9%	27.3%	17.2%	10.1%
Share of total before-tax income	100.0	8.0	20.2	19.2	10.2	42.5	24.2	18.3
Share of total spending	100.0	9.1	21.3	20.4	10.6	38.6	22.8	15.8
Household furnishings and supplies	**100.0**	**7.8**	**19.5**	**19.6**	**11.0**	**41.6**	**23.3**	**18.6**
Appliances, kitchen, small electric	100.0	9.8	20.4	20.6	10.1	39.1	22.9	16.2
Appliances, major	100.0	7.9	20.9	23.0	10.2	37.9	21.3	16.9
Bathroom linens	100.0	12.3	20.8	14.4	9.8	42.0	27.9	13.9
Bedroom furniture, excl. mattresses and springs	100.0	7.6	21.0	20.0	12.9	38.5	23.2	15.3
Bedroom linens	100.0	7.4	25.6	17.5	10.2	38.2	23.6	14.8
Cleansing and toilet tissue, paper towels, and napkins	100.0	14.7	24.6	19.2	9.3	31.9	19.9	12.1
Closet and storage items	100.0	8.1	16.1	14.3	16.6	44.8	30.8	13.6
Curtains and draperies	100.0	5.7	18.7	20.1	11.7	43.9	21.4	22.5
Decorative items for the home	100.0	3.6	15.2	13.6	8.8	56.8	24.0	34.6
Floor coverings	100.0	4.1	13.9	16.3	10.3	55.4	29.1	26.3
Floor coverings, nonpermanent	100.0	2.4	7.4	16.8	6.7	66.6	31.6	35.1
Wall-to-wall carpeting	100.0	5.9	21.2	15.8	14.4	42.7	26.3	16.4
Housewares	100.0	7.6	20.4	18.2	11.1	41.8	26.1	15.7
Infants' equipment	100.0	9.3	13.0	13.4	12.2	51.4	30.5	21.2
Infants' furniture	100.0	7.6	14.8	17.4	14.1	46.1	28.0	18.1
Kitchen and dining room furniture	100.0	9.2	13.2	22.5	10.8	44.3	24.5	19.8
Kitchen and dining room linens	100.0	4.7	23.3	18.5	8.2	43.5	27.9	15.6
Lamps and lighting fixtures	100.0	6.0	12.6	20.4	8.0	52.9	27.1	25.8
Laundry and cleaning equipment	100.0	10.4	22.4	18.1	10.1	38.2	23.0	15.3
Laundry and cleaning supplies	100.0	14.4	25.3	20.5	10.3	29.4	18.7	10.7
Lawn and garden equipment	100.0	8.7	31.5	17.6	22.3	19.8	10.0	9.8
Lawn and garden supplies	100.0	4.2	19.8	16.5	12.8	45.6	29.7	15.7
Living room chairs	100.0	9.1	17.6	20.5	12.1	40.7	23.9	16.8
Living room tables	100.0	8.6	16.2	22.2	6.7	46.3	24.0	22.3
Mattresses and springs	100.0	8.5	14.6	22.7	12.3	41.9	25.1	16.8
Outdoor equipment	100.0	6.6	8.1	24.6	15.0	45.5	20.5	26.3
Outdoor furniture	100.0	4.0	12.8	22.6	10.2	50.3	20.0	30.3
Plants and fresh flowers, indoor	100.0	4.9	19.3	19.4	9.4	47.0	24.5	22.6
Postage	100.0	8.1	22.1	21.0	9.8	37.9	20.9	17.6
Power tools	100.0	5.5	13.7	20.0	15.4	44.9	29.8	14.9
Sewing materials for household items	100.0	4.4	18.8	24.9	10.5	41.4	23.1	18.3
Sofas	100.0	8.9	17.9	24.6	12.3	36.1	23.2	13.0
Stationery, stationery supplies, giftwrap	100.0	5.7	20.4	17.2	8.3	46.8	24.5	23.1
Wall units, cabinets, and other furniture	100.0	6.5	17.9	23.9	8.5	43.3	23.3	20.0
Household services	**100.0**	**5.4**	**15.9**	**19.1**	**10.1**	**49.6**	**26.7**	**22.9**
Appliance repair, including service center	100.0	8.2	20.1	23.4	11.0	37.3	21.0	16.4
Babysitting and childcare in own or other home	100.0	9.5	18.1	14.2	9.5	48.8	27.0	21.8
Care for the elderly, invalids, handicapped, etc.	100.0	14.7	11.7	32.3	5.0	36.2	20.3	15.9
Day care centers, nursery schools, preschools	100.0	4.5	15.9	20.9	12.7	46.0	26.5	19.4
Gardening, lawn care service	100.0	5.3	16.5	17.2	9.1	51.9	26.1	25.9
Housekeeping services	100.0	2.9	12.3	13.3	6.3	65.2	30.2	35.0
Moving, storage, and freight express	100.0	3.3	19.6	27.0	8.2	41.8	24.2	17.6
Security system service fee	100.0	3.6	17.1	17.4	11.9	49.9	27.7	22.2
Termite and pest control services	100.0	4.5	16.4	17.4	11.7	50.0	29.4	20.6

Note: Numbers may not add to total because of rounding.
Source: Calculations by New Strategist based on the Bureau of Labor Statistics' 2005 Consumer Expenditure Survey

Appliance Repair, including Service Center

Best customers: Householders aged 45 or older
                            Married couples

Customer trends: Average household spending on appliance repair may decline as it becomes
                            increasingly cost effective to buy new appliances rather than repair old ones.

The best customers of appliance repair are older householders and married couples. Not only do older householders have older appliances, but their appliances are often of higher quality, making it costlier to replace rather than repair. Householders aged 45 or older spend 9 to 35 percent more than the average household on appliance repair, controlling 67 percent of spending in this market. Married couples spend 40 percent more than average on this item, with spending peaking at 80 percent above average among couples with adult children at home.

Average household spending on appliance repair rose by a substantial 27 percent between 2000 and 2005, after adjusting for inflation. Behind the trend is the aging of the large baby-boom generation into the best-customer age groups. Average household spending on appliance repair may decline as it becomes increasingly cost effective to buy new appliances rather than repair old ones.

Table 32. Appliance repair, including service center

Total household spending $1,698,141,320.00
Average household spends   14.47

	AVERAGE HOUSEHOLD SPENDING	BEST CUSTOMERS (index)	BIGGEST CUSTOMERS (market share)
AGE OF HOUSEHOLDER			
Average household	**$14.47**	**100**	**100.0%**
Under age 25	1.88	13	0.9
Aged 25 to 34	10.02	69	11.6
Aged 35 to 44	14.47	100	20.3
Aged 45 to 54	16.94	117	24.3
Aged 55 to 64	17.83	123	19.0
Aged 65 to 74	19.60	135	13.3
Aged 75 or older	15.74	109	10.5

	AVERAGE HOUSEHOLD SPENDING	BEST CUSTOMERS (index)	BIGGEST CUSTOMERS (market share)
HOUSEHOLD INCOME			
Average household	**$14.47**	**100**	**100.0%**
Under $20,000	5.71	39	9.0
$20,000 to $39,999	9.82	68	16.6
$40,000 to $49,999	7.95	55	5.4
$50,000 to $69,999	16.11	111	16.1
$70,000 to $79,999	16.51	114	6.5
$80,000 to $99,999	23.29	161	13.0
$100,000 or more	32.92	228	33.4
HOUSEHOLD TYPE			
Average household	**14.47**	**100**	**100.0**
Married couples	20.72	143	72.4
Married couples, no children	20.19	140	30.1
Married couples, with children	21.17	146	36.8
Oldest child under 6	16.92	117	5.6
Oldest child 6 to 17	20.11	139	18.3
Oldest child 18 or older	26.00	180	12.9
Single parent with child under 18	6.39	44	2.6
Single person	6.61	46	13.4
RACE AND HISPANIC ORIGIN			
Average household	**14.47**	**100**	**100.0**
Asian	11.56	80	2.9
Black	5.90	41	4.9
Hispanic	7.77	54	5.7
Non-Hispanic white and other	16.68	115	89.4
REGION			
Average household	**14.47**	**100**	**100.0**
Northeast	14.55	101	19.2
Midwest	14.96	103	23.8
South	12.75	88	31.6
West	16.68	115	25.4
EDUCATION			
Average household	**14.47**	**100**	**100.0**
Less than high school graduate	7.69	53	8.2
High school graduate	11.22	78	20.1
Some college	15.73	109	23.4
Associate's degree	16.05	111	11.0
College graduate	19.78	137	37.3
Bachelor's degree	17.62	122	21.0
Master's, professional, doctoral degree	23.48	162	16.4

Note: Market shares may not sum to 100.0 because of rounding and missing categories by household type. "Asian" and "black" include Hispanics and non-Hispanics who identify themselves as being of the respective race alone. "Hispanic" includes people of any race who identify themselves as Hispanic. "Other" includes people who identify themselves as non-Hispanic and as Alaska Native, American Indian, Asian (who are also included in the "Asian" row), Native Hawaiian or other Pacific Islander, as well as non-Hispanics reporting more than one race.
Source: Calculations by New Strategist based on the Bureau of Labor Statistics' 2005 Consumer Expenditure Survey

Appliances, Major

Best customers:	Householders aged 35 to 64
	Married couples without children at home
	Married couples with school-aged or older children
Customer trends:	Average household spending on major appliances may fall as growth in homeownership slows and the small generation X moves into the peak-spending age group.

The biggest spenders on major appliances are married couples outfitting their home for expanding families or upgrading appliances after their children leave home. This explains why householders ranging in age from 35 to 64 spend 7 to 33 percent more than average on this item, accounting for 65 percent of the market. Married couples without children at home (most of them empty-nesters) spend 37 percent more than average on major appliances. Couples with school-aged or older children at home spend 37 to 79 percent more than average on this item.

Average household spending on major appliances rose 4 percent between 2000 and 2005, after adjusting for inflation. Behind the increase was the baby-boom generation solidly in the best-customer lifestage. Average household spending on major appliances may fall in the years ahead as growth in homeownership slows and the small generation X enters the best-customer age group.

Table 33. Appliances, major

Total household spending	$26,209,115,480.00
Average household spends	223.33

	AVERAGE HOUSEHOLD SPENDING	BEST CUSTOMERS (index)	BIGGEST CUSTOMERS (market share)
AGE OF HOUSEHOLDER			
Average household	**$223.33**	**100**	**100.0%**
Under age 25	95.29	43	3.1
Aged 25 to 34	183.93	82	13.8
Aged 35 to 44	247.01	111	22.5
Aged 45 to 54	239.38	107	22.3
Aged 55 to 64	298.03	133	20.6
Aged 65 to 74	216.54	97	9.5
Aged 75 or older	191.75	86	8.3

	AVERAGE HOUSEHOLD SPENDING	BEST CUSTOMERS (index)	BIGGEST CUSTOMERS (market share)
HOUSEHOLD INCOME			
Average household	**$223.33**	**100**	**100.0%**
Under $20,000	74.47	33	7.6
$20,000 to $39,999	125.70	56	13.7
$40,000 to $49,999	175.37	79	7.7
$50,000 to $69,999	232.38	104	15.0
$70,000 to $79,999	242.60	109	6.2
$80,000 to $99,999	317.13	142	11.4
$100,000 or more	579.81	260	38.2
HOUSEHOLD TYPE			
Average household	**223.33**	**100**	**100.0**
Married couples	316.59	142	71.7
Married couples, no children	305.79	137	29.5
Married couples, with children	333.20	149	37.5
Oldest child under 6	186.53	84	4.0
Oldest child 6 to 17	399.43	179	23.6
Oldest child 18 or older	306.58	137	9.8
Single parent with child under 18	71.68	32	1.9
Single person	103.67	46	13.6
RACE AND HISPANIC ORIGIN			
Average household	**223.33**	**100**	**100.0**
Asian	376.74	169	6.2
Black	143.42	64	7.7
Hispanic	170.82	76	8.1
Non-Hispanic white and other	242.34	109	84.1
REGION			
Average household	**223.33**	**100**	**100.0**
Northeast	209.73	94	17.9
Midwest	209.78	94	21.6
South	214.33	96	34.4
West	264.10	118	26.1
EDUCATION			
Average household	**223.33**	**100**	**100.0**
Less than high school graduate	114.35	51	7.9
High school graduate	179.99	81	20.9
Some college	238.52	107	23.0
Associate's degree	231.04	103	10.2
College graduate	309.56	139	37.9
Bachelor's degree	276.18	124	21.3
Master's, professional, doctoral degree	373.80	167	16.9

Note: Market shares may not sum to 100.0 because of rounding and missing categories by household type. "Asian" and "black" include Hispanics and non-Hispanics who identify themselves as being of the respective race alone. "Hispanic" includes people of any race who identify themselves as Hispanic. "Other" includes people who identify themselves as non-Hispanic and as Alaska Native, American Indian, Asian (who are also included in the "Asian" row), Native Hawaiian or other Pacific Islander, as well as non-Hispanics reporting more than one race.
Source: Calculations by New Strategist based on the Bureau of Labor Statistics' 2005 Consumer Expenditure Survey

Babysitting and Child Care in Own or Other Home

Best customers:
Householders aged 25 to 44
Married couples with children under age 18
Single parents
Asians and Hispanics

Customer trends:
Average household spending on babysitting may rise as the large millennial generation has children.

Child care is one of the largest expenses faced by parents. Those who spend the most on babysitting (including everything from hiring a teen to be with the kids on a Saturday night to a live-in nanny) are married couples with preschoolers. This household type spends nearly seven times the average on babysitting. Couples with school-aged children spend more than twice the average on this item, as do single parents. Householders aged 25 to 34, many with children, spend 95 percent more than average on babysitting. Householders aged 35 to 44 spend more than twice the average. Asians and Hispanics, who have relatively large families, spend 28 to 62 percent more than average on babysitting.

Average household spending on babysitting fell 4 percent between 2000 and 2005, after adjusting for inflation. One reason for the decline is the entry of the small generation X into the childrearing lifestage. Another factor may be parents' growing preference for day care centers over babysitters. In the years ahead, spending on babysitting could rise as the large millennial generation has children.

Table 34. Babysitting and child care in own or other home

Total household spending $8,244,259,000.00
Average household spends   70.25

	AVERAGE HOUSEHOLD SPENDING	BEST CUSTOMERS (index)	BIGGEST CUSTOMERS (market share)
AGE OF HOUSEHOLDER			
Average household	**$70.25**	**100**	**100.0%**
Under age 25	84.34	120	8.7
Aged 25 to 34	136.98	195	32.6
Aged 35 to 44	165.50	236	47.8
Aged 45 to 54	32.17	46	9.5
Aged 55 to 64	3.97	6	0.9
Aged 65 to 74	1.62	2	0.2
Aged 75 or older	1.21	2	0.2

	AVERAGE HOUSEHOLD SPENDING	BEST CUSTOMERS (index)	BIGGEST CUSTOMERS (market share)
HOUSEHOLD INCOME			
Average household	**$70.25**	**100**	**100.0%**
Under $20,000	14.69	21	4.8
$20,000 to $39,999	34.47	49	12.0
$40,000 to $49,999	56.68	81	7.9
$50,000 to $69,999	58.10	83	11.9
$70,000 to $79,999	101.33	144	8.3
$80,000 to $99,999	118.75	169	13.6
$100,000 or more	198.53	283	41.5
HOUSEHOLD TYPE			
Average household	**70.25**	**100**	**100.0**
Married couples	104.83	149	75.5
Married couples, no children	1.58	2	0.5
Married couples, with children	190.66	271	68.3
Oldest child under 6	489.56	697	33.6
Oldest child 6 to 17	179.32	255	33.7
Oldest child 18 or older	10.08	14	1.0
Single parent with child under 18	156.19	222	13.1
Single person	1.29	2	0.5
RACE AND HISPANIC ORIGIN			
Average household	**70.25**	**100**	**100.0**
Asian	89.64	128	4.7
Black	50.83	72	8.7
Hispanic	113.75	162	17.2
Non-Hispanic white and other	67.17	96	74.1
REGION			
Average household	**70.25**	**100**	**100.0**
Northeast	78.99	112	21.4
Midwest	70.94	101	23.2
South	58.88	84	30.1
West	80.50	115	25.3
EDUCATION			
Average household	**70.25**	**100**	**100.0**
Less than high school graduate	43.34	62	9.5
High school graduate	49.13	70	18.1
Some college	46.32	66	14.2
Associate's degree	67.21	96	9.5
College graduate	125.36	178	48.8
Bachelor's degree	109.90	156	27.0
Master's, professional, doctoral degree	151.78	216	21.8

Note: Market shares may not sum to 100.0 because of rounding and missing categories by household type. "Asian" and "black" include Hispanics and non-Hispanics who identify themselves as being of the respective race alone. "Hispanic" includes people of any race who identify themselves as Hispanic. "Other" includes people who identify themselves as non-Hispanic and as Alaska Native, American Indian, Asian (who are also included in the "Asian" row), Native Hawaiian or other Pacific Islander, as well as non-Hispanics reporting more than one race.
Source: Calculations by New Strategist based on the Bureau of Labor Statistics' 2005 Consumer Expenditure Survey

Bathroom Linens

Best customers: Householders aged 35 to 54
Married couples with children at home

Customer trends: Average household spending on bathroom linens may decline as boomers become empty-nesters.

The biggest spenders on bathroom linens are households with children. Married couples with children at home spend 40 percent more than the average household on this item. Single parents spend 34 percent more. Householders aged 35 to 54, most with children at home, spend 21 to 44 percent more than average on this item.

Average household spending on bathroom linens rose by 10 percent between 2000 and 2005, after adjusting for inflation. One factor behind the spending increase is the large baby-boom generation in the best-customer lifestage. As boomers become empty-nesters, average household spending on bathroom linens may decline.

Table 35. Bathroom linens

Total household spending	$2,565,402,160.00
Average household spends	21.86

	AVERAGE HOUSEHOLD SPENDING	BEST CUSTOMERS (index)	BIGGEST CUSTOMERS (market share)
AGE OF HOUSEHOLDER			
Average household	**$21.86**	**100**	**100.0%**
Under age 25	10.76	49	3.6
Aged 25 to 34	23.37	107	17.9
Aged 35 to 44	26.40	121	24.5
Aged 45 to 54	31.41	144	29.9
Aged 55 to 64	18.75	86	13.2
Aged 65 to 74	15.76	72	7.1
Aged 75 or older	8.99	41	4.0

	AVERAGE HOUSEHOLD SPENDING	BEST CUSTOMERS (index)	BIGGEST CUSTOMERS (market share)
HOUSEHOLD INCOME			
Average household	**$21.86**	**100**	**100.0%**
Under $20,000	12.52	57	13.1
$20,000 to $39,999	13.06	60	14.6
$40,000 to $49,999	20.74	95	9.3
$50,000 to $69,999	23.70	108	15.7
$70,000 to $79,999	33.67	154	8.8
$80,000 to $99,999	38.97	178	14.4
$100,000 or more	32.22	147	21.7
HOUSEHOLD TYPE			
Average household	**21.86**	**100**	**100.0**
Married couples	25.17	115	58.2
Married couples, no children	16.44	75	16.2
Married couples, with children	30.56	140	35.2
Oldest child under 6	25.78	118	5.7
Oldest child 6 to 17	29.25	134	17.6
Oldest child 18 or older	36.64	168	12.0
Single parent with child under 18	29.29	134	7.9
Single person	12.04	55	16.1
RACE AND HISPANIC ORIGIN			
Average household	**21.86**	**100**	**100.0**
Asian	16.64	76	2.8
Black	24.13	110	13.2
Hispanic	25.95	119	12.6
Non-Hispanic white and other	20.95	96	74.3
REGION			
Average household	**21.86**	**100**	**100.0**
Northeast	24.65	113	21.5
Midwest	23.26	106	24.5
South	20.69	95	34.0
West	19.97	91	20.1
EDUCATION			
Average household	**21.86**	**100**	**100.0**
Less than high school graduate	17.50	80	12.3
High school graduate	17.57	80	20.8
Some college	14.59	67	14.4
Associate's degree	21.67	99	9.8
College graduate	33.64	154	42.0
Bachelor's degree	35.41	162	27.9
Master's, professional, doctoral degree	30.14	138	13.9

Note: Market shares may not sum to 100.0 because of rounding and missing categories by household type. "Asian" and "black" include Hispanics and non-Hispanics who identify themselves as being of the respective race alone. "Hispanic" includes people of any race who identify themselves as Hispanic. "Other" includes people who identify themselves as non-Hispanic and as Alaska Native, American Indian, Asian (who are also included in the "Asian" row), Native Hawaiian or other Pacific Islander, as well as non-Hispanics reporting more than one race.
Source: Calculations by New Strategist based on the Bureau of Labor Statistics' 2005 Consumer Expenditure Survey

Bedroom Furniture (except Mattresses and Springs)

Best customers:
Householders aged 25 to 44
Married couples with children under age 18
Single parents

Customer trends:
Average household spending on bedroom furniture could decline as the small generation X fills the best-customer lifestage.

The best customers of bedroom furniture (excl. mattresses and springs) are households with children, outfitting their homes for their expanding families. Married couples with preschoolers spend more than twice the average on this item. Couples with school-aged children spend 51 percent more, and single parents spend 25 percent more than average on bedroom furniture. Householders aged 25 to 44, most with children at home, spend 38 to 53 percent more than average on this item and account for 54 percent of the market.

Average household spending on bedroom furniture (excl. mattresses and springs) rose 20 percent between 2000 and 2005, after adjusting for inflation. Average household spending on bedroom furniture could decline in the years ahead as the small generation X fills the best-customer lifestage.

Table 36. Bedroom furniture (except mattresses and springs)

Total household spending $11,015,034,160.00
Average household spends   93.86

	AVERAGE HOUSEHOLD SPENDING	BEST CUSTOMERS (index)	BIGGEST CUSTOMERS (market share)
AGE OF HOUSEHOLDER			
Average household	**$93.86**	**100**	**100.0%**
Under age 25	78.17	83	6.1
Aged 25 to 34	143.45	153	25.6
Aged 35 to 44	129.25	138	28.0
Aged 45 to 54	70.16	75	15.5
Aged 55 to 64	85.99	92	14.1
Aged 65 to 74	80.48	86	8.4
Aged 75 or older	22.57	24	2.3

	AVERAGE HOUSEHOLD SPENDING	BEST CUSTOMERS (index)	BIGGEST CUSTOMERS (market share)
HOUSEHOLD INCOME			
Average household	**$93.86**	**100**	**100.0%**
Under $20,000	43.00	46	10.5
$20,000 to $39,999	63.63	68	16.5
$40,000 to $49,999	96.28	103	10.0
$50,000 to $69,999	88.98	95	13.7
$70,000 to $79,999	150.84	161	9.2
$80,000 to $99,999	149.65	159	12.8
$100,000 or more	173.77	185	27.2
HOUSEHOLD TYPE			
Average household	**93.86**	**100**	**100.0**
Married couples	126.86	135	68.3
Married couples, no children	104.39	111	24.0
Married couples, with children	147.97	158	39.7
Oldest child under 6	230.20	245	11.8
Oldest child 6 to 17	141.33	151	19.9
Oldest child 18 or older	104.79	112	8.0
Single parent with child under 18	117.47	125	7.4
Single person	44.98	48	14.0
RACE AND HISPANIC ORIGIN			
Average household	**93.86**	**100**	**100.0**
Asian	119.18	127	4.6
Black	90.58	97	11.5
Hispanic	108.59	116	12.3
Non-Hispanic white and other	92.38	98	76.3
REGION			
Average household	**93.86**	**100**	**100.0**
Northeast	70.18	75	14.2
Midwest	73.21	78	17.9
South	111.86	119	42.8
West	106.57	114	25.0
EDUCATION			
Average household	**93.86**	**100**	**100.0**
Less than high school graduate	46.53	50	7.6
High school graduate	76.17	81	21.0
Some college	87.30	93	20.0
Associate's degree	122.26	130	12.9
College graduate	132.15	141	38.5
Bachelor's degree	126.08	134	23.2
Master's, professional, doctoral degree	142.54	152	15.3

Note: Market shares may not sum to 100.0 because of rounding and missing categories by household type. "Asian" and "black" include Hispanics and non-Hispanics who identify themselves as being of the respective race alone. "Hispanic" includes people of any race who identify themselves as Hispanic. "Other" includes people who identify themselves as non-Hispanic and as Alaska Native, American Indian, Asian (who are also included in the "Asian" row), Native Hawaiian or other Pacific Islander, as well as non-Hispanics reporting more than one race.
Source: Calculations by New Strategist based on the Bureau of Labor Statistics' 2005 Consumer Expenditure Survey

Bedroom Linens

Best customers:	**Householders aged 25 to 54**
	Married couples without children at home
	Married couples with children at home
	Asians
Customer trends:	**Average household spending on bedroom linens may continue to grow as boomers become empty-nesters and redecorate their homes.**

The biggest spenders on bedroom linens are married couples. Couples without children at home spend 13 percent more than average on this item, many upgrading their linens after their children leave home. Couples with children at home spend 53 percent more than the average on bedroom linens. Householders ranging in age from 25 to 54, many with children, spend 14 to 29 percent more than average on this item. Asians spend 47 percent more than average on bedroom linens.

Average household spending on bedroom linens rose 29 percent between 2000 and 2005, after adjusting for inflation. Behind the increase is the baby-boom generation in the best-customer lifestage. As millions of boomers become empty-nesters and redecorate their homes, average household spending on bedroom linens may continue to grow.

Table 37. Bedroom linens

Total household spending	$7,631,660,680.00
Average household spends	65.03

	AVERAGE HOUSEHOLD SPENDING	BEST CUSTOMERS (index)	BIGGEST CUSTOMERS (market share)
AGE OF HOUSEHOLDER			
Average household	**$65.03**	**100**	**100.0%**
Under age 25	30.72	47	3.4
Aged 25 to 34	73.87	114	19.0
Aged 35 to 44	79.05	122	24.7
Aged 45 to 54	84.09	129	26.9
Aged 55 to 64	64.00	98	15.2
Aged 65 to 74	44.88	69	6.8
Aged 75 or older	28.21	43	4.2

	AVERAGE HOUSEHOLD SPENDING	BEST CUSTOMERS (index)	BIGGEST CUSTOMERS (market share)
HOUSEHOLD INCOME			
Average household	**$65.03**	**100**	**100.0%**
Under $20,000	14.37	22	5.1
$20,000 to $39,999	60.27	93	22.6
$40,000 to $49,999	69.66	107	10.5
$50,000 to $69,999	78.56	121	17.5
$70,000 to $79,999	67.97	105	6.0
$80,000 to $99,999	101.57	156	12.6
$100,000 or more	106.24	163	24.0
HOUSEHOLD TYPE			
Average household	**65.03**	**100**	**100.0**
Married couples	85.44	131	66.4
Married couples, no children	73.73	113	24.4
Married couples, with children	99.56	153	38.5
Oldest child under 6	82.72	127	6.1
Oldest child 6 to 17	110.66	170	22.4
Oldest child 18 or older	89.78	138	9.9
Single parent with child under 18	64.23	99	5.8
Single person	29.28	45	13.2
RACE AND HISPANIC ORIGIN			
Average household	**65.03**	**100**	**100.0**
Asian	95.84	147	5.4
Black	48.14	74	8.9
Hispanic	40.44	62	6.6
Non-Hispanic white and other	70.73	109	84.3
REGION			
Average household	**65.03**	**100**	**100.0**
Northeast	60.49	93	17.7
Midwest	73.38	113	26.0
South	67.56	104	37.3
West	56.47	87	19.1
EDUCATION			
Average household	**65.03**	**100**	**100.0**
Less than high school graduate	31.12	48	7.4
High school graduate	64.30	99	25.6
Some college	52.68	81	17.5
Associate's degree	67.30	103	10.2
College graduate	91.02	140	38.2
Bachelor's degree	88.94	137	23.6
Master's, professional, doctoral degree	95.15	146	14.8

Note: Market shares may not sum to 100.0 because of rounding and missing categories by household type. "Asian" and "black" include Hispanics and non-Hispanics who identify themselves as being of the respective race alone. "Hispanic" includes people of any race who identify themselves as Hispanic. "Other" includes people who identify themselves as non-Hispanic and as Alaska Native, American Indian, Asian (who are also included in the "Asian" row), Native Hawaiian or other Pacific Islander, as well as non-Hispanics reporting more than one race.
Source: Calculations by New Strategist based on the Bureau of Labor Statistics' 2005 Consumer Expenditure Survey

Cleansing and Toilet Tissue, Paper Towels, and Napkins

Best customers: Householders aged 35 to 74
                               Married couples
                               Hispanics

Customer trends: Average household spending is likely to fall as household size declines with the
                               aging of the baby-boom generation.

Because everyone buys cleansing and toilet tissue, paper towels, and napkins, there are few differences in spending on this item by demographic characteristic. Householders ranging in age from 35 to 74 spend 9 to 17 percent more than average on this item. Married couples spend 31 percent more. Hispanics, who have the largest families, spend 15 percent more than average on cleansing and toilet tissue, paper towels, and napkins.

Average household spending on cleansing and toilet tissue, paper towels, and napkins rose 22 percent between 2000 and 2005, after adjusting for inflation. One factor behind the increase is the rapidly growing Hispanic population. Average household spending on this item could fall in the years ahead as boomers age and average household size resumes its long-term decline.

Table 38. Cleansing and toilet tissue, paper towels, and napkins

Total household spending $11,138,257,960.00
Average household spends   94.91

AGE OF HOUSEHOLDER	AVERAGE HOUSEHOLD SPENDING	BEST CUSTOMERS (index)	BIGGEST CUSTOMERS (market share)
Average household	$94.91	100	100.0%
Under age 25	48.95	52	3.8
Aged 25 to 34	76.35	80	13.5
Aged 35 to 44	110.96	117	23.7
Aged 45 to 54	104.82	110	23.0
Aged 55 to 64	109.44	115	17.8
Aged 65 to 74	102.98	109	10.6
Aged 75 or older	78.33	83	8.0

	AVERAGE HOUSEHOLD SPENDING	BEST CUSTOMERS (index)	BIGGEST CUSTOMERS (market share)
HOUSEHOLD INCOME			
Average household	**$94.91**	**100**	**100.0%**
Under $20,000	65.11	69	15.7
$20,000 to $39,999	71.20	75	18.3
$40,000 to $49,999	83.05	88	8.5
$50,000 to $69,999	104.95	111	16.0
$70,000 to $79,999	112.90	119	6.8
$80,000 to $99,999	120.50	127	10.2
$100,000 or more	149.51	158	23.2
HOUSEHOLD TYPE			
Average household	**94.91**	**100**	**100.0**
Married couples	124.48	131	66.3
Married couples, no children	109.24	115	24.8
Married couples, with children	133.57	141	35.4
Oldest child under 6	107.50	113	5.5
Oldest child 6 to 17	131.00	138	18.2
Oldest child 18 or older	157.65	166	11.9
Single parent with child under 18	76.87	81	4.8
Single person	48.16	51	14.8
RACE AND HISPANIC ORIGIN			
Average household	**94.91**	**100**	**100.0**
Asian	85.59	90	3.3
Black	67.83	71	8.6
Hispanic	108.92	115	12.2
Non-Hispanic white and other	96.95	102	79.2
REGION			
Average household	**94.91**	**100**	**100.0**
Northeast	95.54	101	19.2
Midwest	89.94	95	21.8
South	95.01	100	35.9
West	99.20	105	23.0
EDUCATION			
Average household	**94.91**	**100**	**100.0**
Less than high school graduate	91.06	96	14.7
High school graduate	90.05	95	24.6
Some college	84.62	89	19.2
Associate's degree	89.27	94	9.3
College graduate	110.90	117	31.9
Bachelor's degree	109.59	115	19.9
Master's, professional, doctoral degree	113.50	120	12.1

Note: Market shares may not sum to 100.0 because of rounding and missing categories by household type. "Asian" and "black" include Hispanics and non-Hispanics who identify themselves as being of the respective race alone. "Hispanic" includes people of any race who identify themselves as Hispanic. "Other" includes people who identify themselves as non-Hispanic and as Alaska Native, American Indian, Asian (who are also included in the "Asian" row), Native Hawaiian or other Pacific Islander, as well as non-Hispanics reporting more than one race.
Source: Calculations by New Strategist based on the Bureau of Labor Statistics' 2005 Consumer Expenditure Survey

Closet and Storage Items

Best customers: Householders aged 35 to 44
Married couples with children at home
Asians

Customer trends: Average household spending on closet and storage items could decline as the small generation X enters the best-customer age group.

Parents are most in need of closet and storage items, giving them a place to stash their children's burgeoning toys, clothes, and electronic gear. This explains why householders aged 35 to 44, most with children at home, spend 98 percent more than average on this item. Married couples with children at home spend more than twice the average on this item. Asians spend 62 percent more than average on closet and storage items.

Average household spending on closet and storage items increased 57 percent from 2000 to 2005, after adjusting for inflation. Average household spending on closet and storage items could fall in the years ahead as boomers become empty-nesters and the small generation X enters the best-customer age group.

Table 39. Closet and storage items

Total household spending $1,682,885,040.00
Average household spends   14.34

	AVERAGE HOUSEHOLD SPENDING	BEST CUSTOMERS (index)	BIGGEST CUSTOMERS (market share)
AGE OF HOUSEHOLDER			
Average household	**$14.34**	**100**	**100.0%**
Under age 25	5.02	35	2.5
Aged 25 to 34	11.55	81	13.5
Aged 35 to 44	28.46	198	40.3
Aged 45 to 54	16.71	117	24.2
Aged 55 to 64	10.71	75	11.5
Aged 65 to 74	8.39	59	5.7
Aged 75 or older	3.46	24	2.3

	AVERAGE HOUSEHOLD SPENDING	BEST CUSTOMERS (index)	BIGGEST CUSTOMERS (market share)
HOUSEHOLD INCOME			
Average household	**$14.34**	**100**	**100.0%**
Under $20,000	2.97	21	4.7
$20,000 to $39,999	7.34	51	12.5
$40,000 to $49,999	6.43	45	4.4
$50,000 to $69,999	23.66	165	23.8
$70,000 to $79,999	12.15	85	4.9
$80,000 to $99,999	15.34	107	8.6
$100,000 or more	37.57	262	38.5
HOUSEHOLD TYPE			
Average household	**14.34**	**100**	**100.0**
Married couples	22.07	154	77.8
Married couples, no children	14.96	104	22.5
Married couples, with children	29.50	206	51.8
Oldest child under 6	30.93	216	10.4
Oldest child 6 to 17	27.46	191	25.3
Oldest child 18 or older	32.53	227	16.2
Single parent with child under 18	12.00	84	4.9
Single person	3.53	25	7.2
RACE AND HISPANIC ORIGIN			
Average household	**14.34**	**100**	**100.0**
Asian	23.19	162	5.9
Black	4.07	28	3.4
Hispanic	9.58	67	7.1
Non-Hispanic white and other	16.49	115	89.2
REGION			
Average household	**14.34**	**100**	**100.0**
Northeast	14.91	104	19.8
Midwest	14.73	103	23.6
South	13.44	94	33.6
West	14.94	104	23.0
EDUCATION			
Average household	**14.34**	**100**	**100.0**
Less than high school graduate	7.58	53	8.1
High school graduate	8.89	62	16.1
Some college	9.54	67	14.3
Associate's degree	24.10	168	16.6
College graduate	23.50	164	44.8
Bachelor's degree	25.58	178	30.8
Master's, professional, doctoral degree	19.40	135	13.6

Note: Market shares may not sum to 100.0 because of rounding and missing categories by household type. "Asian" and "black" include Hispanics and non-Hispanics who identify themselves as being of the respective race alone. "Hispanic" includes people of any race who identify themselves as Hispanic. "Other" includes people who identify themselves as non-Hispanic and as Alaska Native, American Indian, Asian (who are also included in the "Asian" row), Native Hawaiian or other Pacific Islander, as well as non-Hispanics reporting more than one race.
Source: Calculations by New Strategist based on the Bureau of Labor Statistics' 2005 Consumer Expenditure Survey

Curtains and Draperies

Best customers:	Householders aged 35 to 44 and 55 to 74
	Married couples without children at home
	Married couples with children under age 18
	Asians
Customer trends:	Average household spending on curtains and draperies could rise as boomers become empty-nesters and redecorate their homes.

The best customers of curtains and draperies are married couples with children under age 18. Couples with school-aged children spend more than twice the average on curtains and draperies, while those with preschoolers spend 44 percent more. Couples without children at home (most of them empty-nesters) spend 10 percent more than average on this item, redecorating after their children leave home. Householders aged 35 to 44, most with children, spend 40 percent more than average on this item. Householders aged 55 to 74 spend 22 to 28 percent more on curtains and draperies. Asians spend 86 percent more than average on this item.

Average household spending on curtains and draperies fell 22 percent between 2000 and 2005, after adjusting for inflation. Behind the spending decline was the exit of the baby-boom generation from the crowded-nest lifestage. Average household spending on curtains and draperies could rise in the years ahead as aging boomers redecorate their homes once their children leave home.

Table 40. Curtains and draperies

Total household spending $2,183,995,160.00
Average household spends 18.61

	AVERAGE HOUSEHOLD SPENDING	BEST CUSTOMERS (index)	BIGGEST CUSTOMERS (market share)
AGE OF HOUSEHOLDER			
Average household	**$18.61**	**100**	**100.0%**
Under age 25	7.41	40	2.9
Aged 25 to 34	19.71	106	17.7
Aged 35 to 44	25.97	140	28.3
Aged 45 to 54	14.30	77	16.0
Aged 55 to 64	23.89	128	19.8
Aged 65 to 74	22.74	122	12.0
Aged 75 or older	6.31	34	3.3

	AVERAGE HOUSEHOLD SPENDING	BEST CUSTOMERS (index)	BIGGEST CUSTOMERS (market share)
HOUSEHOLD INCOME			
Average household	**$18.61**	**100**	**100.0%**
Under $20,000	8.19	44	10.1
$20,000 to $39,999	8.75	47	11.5
$40,000 to $49,999	16.17	87	8.5
$50,000 to $69,999	18.31	98	14.2
$70,000 to $79,999	43.07	231	13.3
$80,000 to $99,999	22.15	119	9.6
$100,000 or more	41.65	224	32.9
HOUSEHOLD TYPE			
Average household	**18.61**	**100**	**100.0**
Married couples	26.23	141	71.3
Married couples, no children	20.47	110	23.7
Married couples, with children	31.12	167	42.1
Oldest child under 6	26.84	144	7.0
Oldest child 6 to 17	41.77	224	29.6
Oldest child 18 or older	14.38	77	5.5
Single parent with child under 18	10.12	54	3.2
Single person	10.21	55	16.1
RACE AND HISPANIC ORIGIN			
Average household	**18.61**	**100**	**100.0**
Asian	34.64	186	6.8
Black	8.59	46	5.5
Hispanic	14.92	80	8.5
Non-Hispanic white and other	20.63	111	86.0
REGION			
Average household	**18.61**	**100**	**100.0**
Northeast	18.38	99	18.8
Midwest	21.06	113	26.0
South	16.48	89	31.8
West	19.71	106	23.4
EDUCATION			
Average household	**18.61**	**100**	**100.0**
Less than high school graduate	6.94	37	5.7
High school graduate	13.41	72	18.7
Some college	17.34	93	20.1
Associate's degree	21.95	118	11.7
College graduate	29.89	161	43.9
Bachelor's degree	23.13	124	21.4
Master's, professional, doctoral degree	41.45	223	22.5

Note: Market shares may not sum to 100.0 because of rounding and missing categories by household type. "Asian" and "black" include Hispanics and non-Hispanics who identify themselves as being of the respective race alone. "Hispanic" includes people of any race who identify themselves as Hispanic. "Other" includes people who identify themselves as non-Hispanic and as Alaska Native, American Indian, Asian (who are also included in the "Asian" row), Native Hawaiian or other Pacific Islander, as well as non-Hispanics reporting more than one race.
Source: Calculations by New Strategist based on the Bureau of Labor Statistics' 2005 Consumer Expenditure Survey

Day Care Centers, Nursery Schools, Preschools

Best customers:

Householders aged 25 to 44
Married couples with children under age 18
Single parents
Asians

Customer trends:

Average household spending on day care centers should rise when the large millennial generation has children.

The best customers of day care centers are married couples whose oldest child is under age 6. This household type spends more than eight times the average on day care centers. Married couples whose oldest child is aged 6 to 17 spend more than twice the average on this item, while single parents spend nearly two times the average. Householders aged 25 to 44, most of them parents, spend more than twice the average on day care centers. Asians spend 58 percent more.

Average household spending on day care centers fell by 5 percent between 2000 and 2005, after adjusting for inflation. This decline occurred because a smaller proportion of households needed day care services as the baby-boom generation aged out of the childrearing lifestage. Average household spending on day care centers could rise in the years ahead when the large millennial generation has children.

Table 41. Day care centers, nursery schools, preschools

Total household spending $26,406,273,560.00
Average household spends   225.01

	AVERAGE HOUSEHOLD SPENDING	BEST CUSTOMERS (index)	BIGGEST CUSTOMERS (market share)
AGE OF HOUSEHOLDER			
Average household	**$225.01**	**100**	**100.0%**
Under age 25	151.75	67	4.9
Aged 25 to 34	513.40	228	38.2
Aged 35 to 44	496.51	221	44.8
Aged 45 to 54	91.28	41	8.4
Aged 55 to 64	40.01	18	2.7
Aged 65 to 74	10.60	5	0.5
Aged 75 or older	10.81	5	0.5

	AVERAGE HOUSEHOLD SPENDING	BEST CUSTOMERS (index)	BIGGEST CUSTOMERS (market share)
HOUSEHOLD INCOME			
Average household	**$225.01**	**100**	**100.0%**
Under $20,000	43.33	19	4.4
$20,000 to $39,999	96.31	43	10.4
$40,000 to $49,999	157.29	70	6.8
$50,000 to $69,999	233.48	104	15.0
$70,000 to $79,999	295.24	131	7.5
$80,000 to $99,999	512.71	228	18.3
$100,000 or more	573.63	255	37.5
HOUSEHOLD TYPE			
Average household	**225.01**	**100**	**100.0**
Married couples	350.85	156	78.8
Married couples, no children	10.98	5	1.1
Married couples, with children	638.08	284	71.4
Oldest child under 6	1,823.55	810	39.1
Oldest child 6 to 17	530.54	236	31.1
Oldest child 18 or older	37.11	16	1.2
Single parent with child under 18	441.14	196	11.5
Single person	7.31	3	1.0
RACE AND HISPANIC ORIGIN			
Average household	**225.01**	**100**	**100.0**
Asian	356.16	158	5.8
Black	224.32	100	11.9
Hispanic	216.66	96	10.2
Non-Hispanic white and other	226.16	101	77.9
REGION			
Average household	**225.01**	**100**	**100.0**
Northeast	211.10	94	17.9
Midwest	238.51	106	24.4
South	230.21	102	36.7
West	214.50	95	21.0
EDUCATION			
Average household	**225.01**	**100**	**100.0**
Less than high school graduate	65.82	29	4.5
High school graduate	137.94	61	15.9
Some college	218.65	97	20.9
Associate's degree	290.13	129	12.7
College graduate	378.54	168	46.0
Bachelor's degree	346.41	154	26.5
Master's, professional, doctoral degree	433.48	193	19.4

Note: Market shares may not sum to 100.0 because of rounding and missing categories by household type. "Asian" and "black" include Hispanics and non-Hispanics who identify themselves as being of the respective race alone. "Hispanic" includes people of any race who identify themselves as Hispanic. "Other" includes people who identify themselves as non-Hispanic and as Alaska Native, American Indian, Asian (who are also included in the "Asian" row), Native Hawaiian or other Pacific Islander, as well as non-Hispanics reporting more than one race.
Source: Calculations by New Strategist based on the Bureau of Labor Statistics' 2005 Consumer Expenditure Survey

Decorative Items for the Home

Best customers: Householders aged 55 to 64
                             Married couples with adult children at home

Customer trends: Average household spending on decorative items is likely to rise as empty-nest
                             boomers redecorate their homes.

Decorative items for the home—a category that includes the many whimsical items of home decor—are the second-largest expense within the home furnishings and equipment category, behind only major appliances. The biggest spenders on decorative items for the home are older householders and married couples with adult children at home. Householders aged 55 to 64 spend 81 percent more than the average household on this item. Married couples with adult children at home spend nearly three times the average on decorative items.

Average household spending on decorative items for the home fell 6 percent between 2000 and 2005, after adjusting for inflation. Average household spending on decorative items should rise in the years ahead as boomers fill the best-customer age groups, but only if discretionary income grows.

Table 42. Decorative items for the home

Total household spending $22,269,474,560.00
Average household spends   189.76

AGE OF HOUSEHOLDER	AVERAGE HOUSEHOLD SPENDING	BEST CUSTOMERS (index)	BIGGEST CUSTOMERS (market share)
Average household	$189.76	100	100.0%
Under age 25	92.63	49	3.6
Aged 25 to 34	120.16	63	10.6
Aged 35 to 44	209.17	110	22.4
Aged 45 to 54	206.54	109	22.6
Aged 55 to 64	343.73	181	27.9
Aged 65 to 74	219.97	116	11.4
Aged 75 or older	44.86	24	2.3

	AVERAGE HOUSEHOLD SPENDING	BEST CUSTOMERS (index)	BIGGEST CUSTOMERS (market share)
HOUSEHOLD INCOME			
Average household	**$189.76**	**100**	**100.0%**
Under $20,000	50.99	27	6.2
$20,000 to $39,999	86.17	45	11.1
$40,000 to $49,999	170.64	90	8.8
$50,000 to $69,999	152.91	81	11.6
$70,000 to $79,999	185.51	98	5.6
$80,000 to $99,999	321.51	169	13.6
$100,000 or more	530.50	280	41.1
HOUSEHOLD TYPE			
Average household	**189.76**	**100**	**100.0**
Married couples	260.69	137	69.5
Married couples, no children	186.95	99	21.2
Married couples, with children	329.74	174	43.7
Oldest child under 6	241.79	127	6.1
Oldest child 6 to 17	247.90	131	17.2
Oldest child 18 or older	556.40	293	21.0
Single parent with child under 18	71.03	37	2.2
Single person	105.92	56	16.3
RACE AND HISPANIC ORIGIN			
Average household	**189.76**	**100**	**100.0**
Asian	84.07	44	1.6
Black	114.88	61	7.2
Hispanic	105.48	56	5.9
Non-Hispanic white and other	212.25	112	86.7
REGION			
Average household	**189.76**	**100**	**100.0**
Northeast	146.52	77	14.7
Midwest	173.06	91	21.0
South	150.17	79	28.4
West	307.59	162	35.7
EDUCATION			
Average household	**189.76**	**100**	**100.0**
Less than high school graduate	44.97	24	3.6
High school graduate	111.04	59	15.2
Some college	119.95	63	13.6
Associate's degree	169.23	89	8.8
College graduate	394.45	208	56.8
Bachelor's degree	264.56	139	24.0
Master's, professional, doctoral degree	651.29	343	34.6

Note: Market shares may not sum to 100.0 because of rounding and missing categories by household type. "Asian" and "black" include Hispanics and non-Hispanics who identify themselves as being of the respective race alone. "Hispanic" includes people of any race who identify themselves as Hispanic. "Other" includes people who identify themselves as non-Hispanic and as Alaska Native, American Indian, Asian (who are also included in the "Asian" row), Native Hawaiian or other Pacific Islander, as well as non-Hispanics reporting more than one race.
Source: Calculations by New Strategist based on the Bureau of Labor Statistics' 2005 Consumer Expenditure Survey

Floor Coverings, Nonpermanent

Best customers:	Householders aged 45 to 64
	High-income households
	Married couples without children at home
	Married couples with children under age 18
	Asians
	College graduates

Customer trends:	Average household spending on rugs should continue to rise as empty-nest boomers redecorate their homes.

The best customers of rugs are affluent, older householders. Those aged 45 to 54 spend more than two times the average on this item. Householders aged 55 to 64 spend 29 percent more. Together, these two age groups account for 64 percent of the market. Married couples without children at home (most of them empty-nesters) spend 26 percent more than average on rugs. Couples with school-aged children spend nearly three times the average, while those with preschoolers spend 66 percent more. Households with incomes of $100,000 or more spend more than four times the average on rugs, accounting for 60 percent of the market. Asians and college graduates spend more than twice the average on this item.

Average household spending on rugs rose by a substantial 73 percent between 2000 and 2005, after adjusting for inflation. Behind the spending increase was the aging of the baby-boom generation. Average household spending on rugs should continue to rise in the years ahead as boomers fill the best-customer age groups.

Table 43. Floor coverings, nonpermanent

Total household spending $3,505,423,720.00
Average household spends   29.87

	AVERAGE HOUSEHOLD SPENDING	BEST CUSTOMERS (index)	BIGGEST CUSTOMERS (market share)
AGE OF HOUSEHOLDER			
Average household	**$29.87**	**100**	**100.0%**
Under age 25	6.02	20	1.5
Aged 25 to 34	20.47	69	11.5
Aged 35 to 44	20.46	68	13.9
Aged 45 to 54	63.70	213	44.3
Aged 55 to 64	38.51	129	19.9
Aged 65 to 74	21.68	73	7.1
Aged 75 or older	5.61	19	1.8

	AVERAGE HOUSEHOLD SPENDING	BEST CUSTOMERS (index)	BIGGEST CUSTOMERS (market share)
HOUSEHOLD INCOME			
Average household	**$29.87**	**100**	**100.0%**
Under $20,000	4.82	16	3.7
$20,000 to $39,999	8.31	28	6.8
$40,000 to $49,999	13.72	46	4.5
$50,000 to $69,999	28.84	97	14.0
$70,000 to $79,999	24.70	83	4.7
$80,000 to $99,999	24.77	83	6.7
$100,000 or more	121.24	406	59.7
HOUSEHOLD TYPE			
Average household	**29.87**	**100**	**100.0**
Married couples	47.51	159	80.4
Married couples, no children	37.56	126	27.1
Married couples, with children	61.11	205	51.5
Oldest child under 6	49.70	166	8.0
Oldest child 6 to 17	80.60	270	35.6
Oldest child 18 or older	32.87	110	7.9
Single parent with child under 18	10.29	34	2.0
Single person	8.43	28	8.3
RACE AND HISPANIC ORIGIN			
Average household	**29.87**	**100**	**100.0**
Asian	63.78	214	7.8
Black	9.13	31	3.7
Hispanic	9.44	32	3.4
Non-Hispanic white and other	35.82	120	93.0
REGION			
Average household	**29.87**	**100**	**100.0**
Northeast	27.06	91	17.3
Midwest	23.06	77	17.8
South	36.19	121	43.5
West	29.10	97	21.5
EDUCATION			
Average household	**29.87**	**100**	**100.0**
Less than high school graduate	4.70	16	2.4
High school graduate	8.58	29	7.4
Some college	23.29	78	16.8
Associate's degree	20.30	68	6.7
College graduate	72.83	244	66.6
Bachelor's degree	54.67	183	31.6
Master's, professional, doctoral degree	103.88	348	35.1

Note: Market shares may not sum to 100.0 because of rounding and missing categories by household type. "Asian" and "black" include Hispanics and non-Hispanics who identify themselves as being of the respective race alone. "Hispanic" includes people of any race who identify themselves as Hispanic. "Other" includes people who identify themselves as non-Hispanic and as Alaska Native, American Indian, Asian (who are also included in the "Asian" row), Native Hawaiian or other Pacific Islander, as well as non-Hispanics reporting more than one race.
Source: Calculations by New Strategist based on the Bureau of Labor Statistics' 2005 Consumer Expenditure Survey

Floor Coverings, Wall-to-Wall

Best customers: Householders aged 35 to 44 and 55 to 64
Married couples

Customer trends: Average household spending on wall-to-wall carpeting is likely to rise as empty-nest boomers redecorate their homes, but only if discretionary income rebounds.

The best customers of wall-to-wall floor coverings are married couples adding carpeting to their homes or renewing worn carpets. Householders aged 35 to 44 spend 29 percent more than average on wall-to-wall carpeting. Those aged 55 to 56 spend 67 percent more. Together, these two age groups account for more than half the market. Married couples without children at home (most of them empty-nesters) spend 46 percent more than average on this item. Couples with children at home spend 40 percent more than average on wall-to-wall floor coverings.

Average household spending on wall-to-wall floor coverings fell 20 percent between 2000 and 2005, after adjusting for inflation. Average household spending on wall-to-wall carpeting could rise in the years ahead as boomers fill the best-customer lifestage.

Table 44. Floor coverings, wall-to-wall

Total household spending	$3,091,157,040.00
Average household spends	26.34

	AVERAGE HOUSEHOLD SPENDING	BEST CUSTOMERS (index)	BIGGEST CUSTOMERS (market share)
AGE OF HOUSEHOLDER			
Average household	**$26.34**	**100**	**100.0%**
Under age 25	11.29	43	3.1
Aged 25 to 34	20.71	79	13.2
Aged 35 to 44	34.08	129	26.3
Aged 45 to 54	27.09	103	21.4
Aged 55 to 64	44.06	167	25.8
Aged 65 to 74	12.03	46	4.5
Aged 75 or older	15.69	60	5.8

	AVERAGE HOUSEHOLD SPENDING	BEST CUSTOMERS (index)	BIGGEST CUSTOMERS (market share)
HOUSEHOLD INCOME			
Average household	**$26.34**	**100**	**100.0%**
Under $20,000	11.48	44	10.0
$20,000 to $39,999	13.54	51	12.5
$40,000 to $49,999	26.70	101	9.9
$50,000 to $69,999	19.45	74	10.7
$70,000 to $79,999	24.52	93	5.3
$80,000 to $99,999	41.51	158	12.7
$100,000 or more	69.64	264	38.9
HOUSEHOLD TYPE			
Average household	**26.34**	**100**	**100.0**
Married couples	35.91	136	68.9
Married couples, no children	38.33	146	31.4
Married couples, with children	36.77	140	35.1
Oldest child under 6	36.24	138	6.6
Oldest child 6 to 17	38.49	146	19.3
Oldest child 18 or older	33.96	129	9.2
Single parent with child under 18	14.92	57	3.3
Single person	16.77	64	18.6
RACE AND HISPANIC ORIGIN			
Average household	**26.34**	**100**	**100.0**
Asian	32.92	125	4.6
Black	7.10	27	3.2
Hispanic	10.64	40	4.3
Non-Hispanic white and other	31.41	119	92.5
REGION			
Average household	**26.34**	**100**	**100.0**
Northeast	30.84	117	22.3
Midwest	32.85	125	28.7
South	19.83	75	27.0
West	26.22	100	21.9
EDUCATION			
Average household	**26.34**	**100**	**100.0**
Less than high school graduate	10.11	38	5.9
High school graduate	21.52	82	21.2
Some college	19.31	73	15.8
Associate's degree	38.46	146	14.4
College graduate	41.17	156	42.7
Bachelor's degree	40.16	152	26.3
Master's, professional, doctoral degree	42.89	163	16.4

Note: Market shares may not sum to 100.0 because of rounding and missing categories by household type. "Asian" and "black" include Hispanics and non-Hispanics who identify themselves as being of the respective race alone. "Hispanic" includes people of any race who identify themselves as Hispanic. "Other" includes people who identify themselves as non-Hispanic and as Alaska Native, American Indian, Asian (who are also included in the "Asian" row), Native Hawaiian or other Pacific Islander, as well as non-Hispanics reporting more than one race.
Source: Calculations by New Strategist based on the Bureau of Labor Statistics' 2005 Consumer Expenditure Survey

Gardening and Lawn Care Services

Best customers: **Householders aged 55 or older**

                                 Married couples without children at home

Customer trends: **Average household spending on gardening and lawn care services will rise as the population ages.**

Older householders are most likely to spend on gardening and lawn care services. Householders aged 55 or older, many of whom need help maintaining their lawns, spend 44 to 94 percent more than average on this item and control 57 percent of the market. Married couples without children at home (most of them older) spend 47 percent more than average on gardening and lawn care services

Average household spending on gardening and lawn care services fell 4 percent between 2000 and 2005, after adjusting for inflation. This category should grow with the aging of the baby-boom generation into the best-customer age groups.

Table 45. Gardening and lawn care services

Total household spending   **$11,234,489,880.00**
Average household spends   **95.73**

	AVERAGE HOUSEHOLD SPENDING	BEST CUSTOMERS (index)	BIGGEST CUSTOMERS (market share)
AGE OF HOUSEHOLDER			
Average household	**$95.73**	**100**	**100.0%**
Under age 25	12.90	13	1.0
Aged 25 to 34	36.87	39	6.4
Aged 35 to 44	72.54	76	15.4
Aged 45 to 54	93.62	98	20.3
Aged 55 to 64	148.93	156	24.0
Aged 65 to 74	138.24	144	14.2
Aged 75 or older	185.25	194	18.7

	AVERAGE HOUSEHOLD SPENDING	BEST CUSTOMERS (index)	BIGGEST CUSTOMERS (market share)
HOUSEHOLD INCOME			
Average household	**$95.73**	**100**	**100.0%**
Under $20,000	45.56	48	10.9
$20,000 to $39,999	60.48	63	15.4
$40,000 to $49,999	62.62	65	6.4
$50,000 to $69,999	71.68	75	10.8
$70,000 to $79,999	82.51	86	4.9
$80,000 to $99,999	117.78	123	9.9
$100,000 or more	271.16	283	41.6
HOUSEHOLD TYPE			
Average household	**95.73**	**100**	**100.0**
Married couples	116.03	121	61.3
Married couples, no children	140.53	147	31.6
Married couples, with children	99.49	104	26.1
Oldest child under 6	84.16	88	4.2
Oldest child 6 to 17	110.10	115	15.2
Oldest child 18 or older	90.27	94	6.7
Single parent with child under 18	33.44	35	2.1
Single person	85.80	90	26.2
RACE AND HISPANIC ORIGIN			
Average household	**95.73**	**100**	**100.0**
Asian	126.04	132	4.8
Black	46.71	49	5.8
Hispanic	50.42	53	5.6
Non-Hispanic white and other	109.41	114	88.6
REGION			
Average household	**95.73**	**100**	**100.0**
Northeast	99.84	104	19.9
Midwest	75.53	79	18.2
South	95.93	100	36.0
West	112.94	118	26.0
EDUCATION			
Average household	**95.73**	**100**	**100.0**
Less than high school graduate	33.17	35	5.3
High school graduate	60.89	64	16.5
Some college	76.40	80	17.2
Associate's degree	87.97	92	9.1
College graduate	181.98	190	51.9
Bachelor's degree	144.73	151	26.1
Master's, professional, doctoral degree	245.68	257	25.9

Note: Market shares may not sum to 100.0 because of rounding and missing categories by household type. "Asian" and "black" include Hispanics and non-Hispanics who identify themselves as being of the respective race alone. "Hispanic" includes people of any race who identify themselves as Hispanic. "Other" includes people who identify themselves as non-Hispanic and as Alaska Native, American Indian, Asian (who are also included in the "Asian" row), Native Hawaiian or other Pacific Islander, as well as non-Hispanics reporting more than one race.
Source: Calculations by New Strategist based on the Bureau of Labor Statistics' 2005 Consumer Expenditure Survey

Housekeeping Services

Best customers:	**Householders aged 45 or older**
	High-income households
	Married couples without children at home
	Married couples with children under age 18
	College graduates
Customer trends:	**Average household spending on housekeeping services will rise as the population ages, but only if discretionary income grows.**

The best customers of housekeeping services are older people and the affluent—the first group often needs such services, while the second group can afford them. Householders aged 45 or older spend 8 to 49 percent more than average on housekeeping services. High-income households spend nearly four times the average and control 57 percent of the market. Married couples without children at home, most of them older, spend 57 percent more than average on housekeeping services. Those with children under age 18 (the busiest households) spend 39 to 46 percent more. College graduates, who dominate the nation's affluent, spend more than twice the average on housekeeping services and control 65 percent of the market.

Average household spending on housekeeping services rose a modest 4 percent between 2000 and 2005, after adjusting for inflation. Behind the increase was the aging of the baby-boom generation into the best-customer age groups. Spending on housekeeping services should rise in the years ahead along with the aging of the population—but only if discretionary income grows.

Table 46. Housekeeping services

Total household spending	$10,813,181,840.00
Average household spends	92.14

	AVERAGE HOUSEHOLD SPENDING	BEST CUSTOMERS (index)	BIGGEST CUSTOMERS (market share)
AGE OF HOUSEHOLDER			
Average household	**$92.14**	**100**	**100.0%**
Under age 25	2.80	3	0.2
Aged 25 to 34	56.77	62	10.3
Aged 35 to 44	88.78	96	19.6
Aged 45 to 54	99.58	108	22.5
Aged 55 to 64	130.36	141	21.8
Aged 65 to 74	104.97	114	11.2
Aged 75 or older	137.68	149	14.4

	AVERAGE HOUSEHOLD SPENDING	BEST CUSTOMERS (index)	BIGGEST CUSTOMERS (market share)
HOUSEHOLD INCOME			
Average household	**$92.14**	**100**	**100.0%**
Under $20,000	34.17	37	8.5
$20,000 to $39,999	29.58	32	7.8
$40,000 to $49,999	37.31	40	4.0
$50,000 to $69,999	54.28	59	8.5
$70,000 to $79,999	64.94	70	4.0
$80,000 to $99,999	117.82	128	10.3
$100,000 or more	356.53	387	56.9
HOUSEHOLD TYPE			
Average household	**92.14**	**100**	**100.0**
Married couples	126.97	138	69.7
Married couples, no children	144.96	157	33.9
Married couples, with children	118.73	129	32.4
Oldest child under 6	128.38	139	6.7
Oldest child 6 to 17	134.30	146	19.2
Oldest child 18 or older	83.49	91	6.5
Single parent with child under 18	37.86	41	2.4
Single person	67.58	73	21.5
RACE AND HISPANIC ORIGIN			
Average household	**92.14**	**100**	**100.0**
Asian	62.80	68	2.5
Black	11.53	13	1.5
Hispanic	39.35	43	4.5
Non-Hispanic white and other	111.66	121	94.0
REGION			
Average household	**92.14**	**100**	**100.0**
Northeast	97.23	106	20.1
Midwest	72.05	78	18.0
South	84.86	92	33.1
West	120.56	131	28.8
EDUCATION			
Average household	**92.14**	**100**	**100.0**
Less than high school graduate	17.42	19	2.9
High school graduate	43.80	48	12.3
Some college	56.88	62	13.3
Associate's degree	58.90	64	6.3
College graduate	219.80	239	65.2
Bachelor's degree	161.19	175	30.2
Master's, professional, doctoral degree	320.02	347	35.0

Note: Market shares may not sum to 100.0 because of rounding and missing categories by household type. "Asian" and "black" include Hispanics and non-Hispanics who identify themselves as being of the respective race alone. "Hispanic" includes people of any race who identify themselves as Hispanic. "Other" includes people who identify themselves as non-Hispanic and as Alaska Native, American Indian, Asian (who are also included in the "Asian" row), Native Hawaiian or other Pacific Islander, as well as non-Hispanics reporting more than one race.
Source: Calculations by New Strategist based on the Bureau of Labor Statistics' 2005 Consumer Expenditure Survey

Housewares

Best customers: **Householders aged 45 to 64**
                             Married couples

Customer trends: **Average household spending on housewares will continue to rise as boomers help their grown children outfit their homes.**

Housewares is a category that includes dishes, glassware, flatware, and non-electric cookware—all the things that fill our kitchen cupboards. The best customers of housewares are middle-aged and older householders. Those aged 45 to 64 spend 21 to 33 percent more than average on housewares. Married couples spend 33 percent more than average on this item, with the figure peaking at 57 percent above average among couples with adult children at home. Many are helping children outfit apartments.

Average household spending on housewares rose 9 percent between 2000 and 2005, after adjusting for inflation. The entry of millions of boomers into the best-customer age groups was behind the rise. Average household spending on housewares should climb in the years ahead as boomers upgrade their kitchens and help grown children outfit their homes.

Table 47. Housewares

Total household spending	$9,430,728,160.00		
Average household spends	80.36		
	AVERAGE HOUSEHOLD SPENDING	**BEST CUSTOMERS (index)**	**BIGGEST CUSTOMERS (market share)**
AGE OF HOUSEHOLDER			
Average household	**$80.36**	**100**	**100.0%**
Under age 25	53.21	66	4.8
Aged 25 to 34	66.27	82	13.8
Aged 35 to 44	74.46	93	18.8
Aged 45 to 54	96.94	121	25.1
Aged 55 to 64	107.01	133	20.5
Aged 65 to 74	89.83	112	11.0
Aged 75 or older	53.11	66	6.4

	AVERAGE HOUSEHOLD SPENDING	BEST CUSTOMERS (index)	BIGGEST CUSTOMERS (market share)
HOUSEHOLD INCOME			
Average household	**$80.36**	**100**	**100.0%**
Under $20,000	35.11	44	10.0
$20,000 to $39,999	42.95	53	13.0
$40,000 to $49,999	44.09	55	5.4
$50,000 to $69,999	74.73	93	13.4
$70,000 to $79,999	125.76	156	9.0
$80,000 to $99,999	141.42	176	14.2
$100,000 or more	179.95	224	32.9
HOUSEHOLD TYPE			
Average household	**80.36**	**100**	**100.0**
Married couples	107.20	133	67.4
Married couples, no children	109.62	136	29.4
Married couples, with children	106.99	133	33.5
Oldest child under 6	120.97	151	7.3
Oldest child 6 to 17	92.42	115	15.2
Oldest child 18 or older	125.77	157	11.2
Single parent with child under 18	56.89	71	4.2
Single person	45.79	57	16.7
RACE AND HISPANIC ORIGIN			
Average household	**80.36**	**100**	**100.0**
Asian	70.28	87	3.2
Black	32.75	41	4.9
Hispanic	63.20	79	8.4
Non-Hispanic white and other	89.72	112	86.6
REGION			
Average household	**80.36**	**100**	**100.0**
Northeast	74.53	93	17.7
Midwest	81.85	102	23.4
South	66.97	83	29.9
West	105.53	131	29.0
EDUCATION			
Average household	**80.36**	**100**	**100.0**
Less than high school graduate	39.97	50	7.6
High school graduate	63.40	79	20.4
Some college	67.79	84	18.2
Associate's degree	89.91	112	11.1
College graduate	123.00	153	41.8
Bachelor's degree	121.80	152	26.1
Master's, professional, doctoral degree	125.08	156	15.7

Note: Market shares may not sum to 100.0 because of rounding and missing categories by household type. "Asian" and "black" include Hispanics and non-Hispanics who identify themselves as being of the respective race alone. "Hispanic" includes people of any race who identify themselves as Hispanic. "Other" includes people who identify themselves as non-Hispanic and as Alaska Native, American Indian, Asian (who are also included in the "Asian" row), Native Hawaiian or other Pacific Islander, as well as non-Hispanics reporting more than one race.
Source: Calculations by New Strategist based on the Bureau of Labor Statistics' 2005 Consumer Expenditure Survey

Infants' Equipment and Furniture

Best customers: Householders aged 25 to 34 and 55 to 64
Married couples with preschoolers
Married couples with adult children at home
Hispanics
Households in the West

Customer trends: Average household spending on infants' equipment and furniture should
continue to increase as the large millennial generation has children.

The best customers of infants' equipment and furniture are young married couples with preschoolers. Married couples with preschoolers spend more than six times the average on this item. Householders aged 25 to 34 spend nearly twice the average on infants' equipment and furniture. Householders aged 55 to 64 spend 14 percent more than average as they buy infants' equipment and furniture for grandchildren. This also explains why couples with adult children at home spend 60 percent more than average on this item. Hispanics, who have the largest families, spend 48 percent more than average on infants' equipment and furniture. Households in the West, where many Hispanics live, spend 35 percent more than average on this item.

Average household spending on infants' equipment and furniture increased 38 percent between 2000 and 2005, after adjusting for inflation. Behind the increase was the growing Hispanic population. Spending on infants' equipment and furniture is likely to continue to rise as the large millennial generation has children.

Table 48. Infants' equipment and furniture

Total household spending $2,615,865,240.00
Average household spends   22.29

	AVERAGE HOUSEHOLD SPENDING	BEST CUSTOMERS (index)	BIGGEST CUSTOMERS (market share)
AGE OF HOUSEHOLDER			
Average household	**$22.29**	**100**	**100.0%**
Under age 25	27.83	125	9.1
Aged 25 to 34	43.88	197	32.9
Aged 35 to 44	25.10	113	22.9
Aged 45 to 54	16.05	72	15.0
Aged 55 to 64	25.42	114	17.6
Aged 65 to 74	3.81	17	1.7
Aged 75 or older	1.81	8	0.8

	AVERAGE HOUSEHOLD SPENDING	BEST CUSTOMERS (index)	BIGGEST CUSTOMERS (market share)
HOUSEHOLD INCOME			
Average household	**$22.29**	**100**	**100.0%**
Under $20,000	5.39	24	5.5
$20,000 to $39,999	16.44	74	18.0
$40,000 to $49,999	25.32	114	11.1
$50,000 to $69,999	15.30	69	9.9
$70,000 to $79,999	29.58	133	7.6
$80,000 to $99,999	35.77	160	12.9
$100,000 or more	51.28	230	33.8
HOUSEHOLD TYPE			
Average household	**22.29**	**100**	**100.0**
Married couples	34.35	154	77.9
Married couples, no children	20.99	94	20.3
Married couples, with children	45.62	205	51.5
Oldest child under 6	148.03	664	32.0
Oldest child 6 to 17	13.58	61	8.0
Oldest child 18 or older	35.57	160	11.4
Single parent with child under 18	8.40	38	2.2
Single person	7.30	33	9.6
RACE AND HISPANIC ORIGIN			
Average household	**22.29**	**100**	**100.0**
Asian	20.12	90	3.3
Black	17.55	79	9.4
Hispanic	33.04	148	15.7
Non-Hispanic white and other	21.52	97	74.9
REGION			
Average household	**22.29**	**100**	**100.0**
Northeast	19.15	86	16.4
Midwest	23.86	107	24.6
South	18.22	82	29.3
West	30.00	135	29.7
EDUCATION			
Average household	**22.29**	**100**	**100.0**
Less than high school graduate	12.55	56	8.6
High school graduate	11.76	53	13.7
Some college	15.40	69	14.9
Associate's degree	29.14	131	12.9
College graduate	40.33	181	49.4
Bachelor's degree	38.22	171	29.6
Master's, professional, doctoral degree	44.38	199	20.1

Note: Market shares may not sum to 100.0 because of rounding and missing categories by household type. "Asian" and "black" include Hispanics and non-Hispanics who identify themselves as being of the respective race alone. "Hispanic" includes people of any race who identify themselves as Hispanic. "Other" includes people who identify themselves as non-Hispanic and as Alaska Native, American Indian, Asian (who are also included in the "Asian" row), Native Hawaiian or other Pacific Islander, as well as non-Hispanics reporting more than one race.
Source: Calculations by New Strategist based on the Bureau of Labor Statistics' 2005 Consumer Expenditure Survey

Kitchen and Dining Room Furniture

Best customers:
Householders aged 25 to 44 and 55 to 64
Married couples with children under age 18
Asians and Hispanics

Customer trends:
Average household spending on kitchen and dining room furniture should stabilize when the large millennial generation has children.

The best customers of kitchen and dining room furniture are married couples outfitting their homes as their families expand or empty-nesters redecorating after their children leave home. Householders aged 25 to 44 spend 19 to 51 percent more than average on this item, while those aged 55 to 64 spend 15 percent more. Married couples with children under age 18 spend more than twice the average on this item. Asians and Hispanics, who have relatively large families, spend 37 to 70 percent more on kitchen and dining room furniture.

Average household spending on kitchen and dining room furniture fell 5 percent between 2000 and 2005, after adjusting for inflation. Behind the decline was the baby-boom's exit from the family formation lifestage. Average household spending on kitchen and dining room furniture should stabilize when the large millennial generation has children.

Table 49. Kitchen and dining room furniture

Total household spending $5,890,097,640.00
Average household spends   50.19

	AVERAGE HOUSEHOLD SPENDING	BEST CUSTOMERS (index)	BIGGEST CUSTOMERS (market share)
AGE OF HOUSEHOLDER			
Average household	**$50.19**	**100**	**100.0%**
Under age 25	22.75	45	3.3
Aged 25 to 34	59.75	119	19.9
Aged 35 to 44	75.88	151	30.7
Aged 45 to 54	48.22	96	20.0
Aged 55 to 64	57.74	115	17.7
Aged 65 to 74	33.17	66	6.5
Aged 75 or older	9.82	20	1.9

	AVERAGE HOUSEHOLD SPENDING	BEST CUSTOMERS (index)	BIGGEST CUSTOMERS (market share)
HOUSEHOLD INCOME			
Average household	**$50.19**	**100**	**100.0%**
Under $20,000	11.74	23	5.4
$20,000 to $39,999	22.72	45	11.0
$40,000 to $49,999	37.50	75	7.3
$50,000 to $69,999	43.22	86	12.4
$70,000 to $79,999	81.94	163	9.4
$80,000 to $99,999	72.16	144	11.6
$100,000 or more	146.63	292	42.9
HOUSEHOLD TYPE			
Average household	**50.19**	**100**	**100.0**
Married couples	75.08	150	75.6
Married couples, no children	47.53	95	20.4
Married couples, with children	95.17	190	47.7
Oldest child under 6	110.89	221	10.7
Oldest child 6 to 17	119.95	239	31.5
Oldest child 18 or older	38.89	77	5.5
Single parent with child under 18	39.92	80	4.7
Single person	19.52	39	11.4
RACE AND HISPANIC ORIGIN			
Average household	**50.19**	**100**	**100.0**
Asian	85.35	170	6.2
Black	21.65	43	5.2
Hispanic	68.55	137	14.5
Non-Hispanic white and other	52.08	104	80.5
REGION			
Average household	**50.19**	**100**	**100.0**
Northeast	39.42	79	15.0
Midwest	43.93	88	20.1
South	50.16	100	35.9
West	66.10	132	29.0
EDUCATION			
Average household	**50.19**	**100**	**100.0**
Less than high school graduate	30.07	60	9.2
High school graduate	25.60	51	13.2
Some college	52.37	104	22.5
Associate's degree	55.06	110	10.8
College graduate	81.35	162	44.3
Bachelor's degree	71.37	142	24.5
Master's, professional, doctoral degree	98.41	196	19.8

Note: Market shares may not sum to 100.0 because of rounding and missing categories by household type. Asian and black include Hispanics and non-Hispanics who identify themselves as being of the respective race alone. Hispanic includes people of any race who identify themselves as Hispanic. Other includes people who identify themselves as non-Hispanic and as Alaska Native, American Indian, Asian (who are also included in the Asian row), Native Hawaiian or other Pacific Islander, as well as non-Hispanics reporting more than one race.
Source: Calculations by New Strategist based on the Bureau of Labor Statistics' 2005 Consumer Expenditure Survey

Kitchen and Dining Room Linens

Best customers: Householders aged 55 to 74
                           Married couples without children at home

Customer trends: Average household spending on kitchen and dining room linens may rise as the
                           large baby-boom generation fills the best customer age groups.

The best customers of kitchen and dining room linens are older married couples outfitting their children's homes for expanding families or replenishing their linen supply after their children leave home. Householders aged 55 to 74 spend 23 to 73 percent more than average on this item. Married couples without children at home (most of them empty-nesters) spend more than twice the average.

Average household spending on kitchen and dining room linens fell 18 percent between 2000 and 2005, after adjusting for inflation. Behind the decline was price discounting as cheaper imports lowered costs. Average household spending on kitchen and dining room linens could climb as boomers fill the best-customer lifestage.

Table 50. Kitchen and dining room linens

Total household spending $1,012,782,280.00
Average household spends   8.63

	AVERAGE HOUSEHOLD SPENDING	BEST CUSTOMERS (index)	BIGGEST CUSTOMERS (market share)
AGE OF HOUSEHOLDER			
Average household	**$8.63**	**100**	**100.0%**
Under age 25	2.71	31	2.3
Aged 25 to 34	5.37	62	10.4
Aged 35 to 44	8.45	98	19.9
Aged 45 to 54	8.86	103	21.3
Aged 55 to 64	10.62	123	19.0
Aged 65 to 74	14.90	173	16.9
Aged 75 or older	9.38	109	10.5

	AVERAGE HOUSEHOLD SPENDING	BEST CUSTOMERS (index)	BIGGEST CUSTOMERS (market share)
HOUSEHOLD INCOME			
Average household	**$8.63**	**100**	**100.0%**
Under $20,000	3.16	37	8.4
$20,000 to $39,999	5.26	61	14.9
$40,000 to $49,999	5.07	59	5.7
$50,000 to $69,999	11.44	133	19.2
$70,000 to $79,999	10.76	125	7.1
$80,000 to $99,999	12.35	143 .	11.5
$100,000 or more	18.07	209	30.8
HOUSEHOLD TYPE			
Average household	**8.63**	**100**	**100.0**
Married couples	11.79	137	69.1
Married couples, no children	18.64	216	46.6
Married couples, with children	6.79	79	19.8
Oldest child under 6	5.14	60	2.9
Oldest child 6 to 17	6.97	81	10.7
Oldest child 18 or older	7.61	88	6.3
Single parent with child under 18	4.43	51	3.0
Single person	4.28	50	14.5
RACE AND HISPANIC ORIGIN			
Average household	**8.63**	**100**	**100.0**
Asian	7.18	83	3.0
Black	1.21	14	1.7
Hispanic	5.59	65	6.9
Non-Hispanic white and other	10.12	117	90.9
REGION			
Average household	**8.63**	**100**	**100.0**
Northeast	13.24	153	29.2
Midwest	7.44	86	19.8
South	7.41	86	30.8
West	7.83	91	20.0
EDUCATION			
Average household	**8.63**	**100**	**100.0**
Less than high school graduate	2.63	30	4.7
High school graduate	7.77	90	23.3
Some college	7.43	86	18.5
Associate's degree	7.15	83	8.2
College graduate	13.74	159	43.5
Bachelor's degree	13.96	162	27.9
Master's, professional, doctoral degree	13.32	154	15.6

Note: Market shares may not sum to 100.0 because of rounding and missing categories by household type. "Asian" and "black" include Hispanics and non-Hispanics who identify themselves as being of the respective race alone. "Hispanic" includes people of any race who identify themselves as Hispanic. "Other" includes people who identify themselves as non-Hispanic and as Alaska Native, American Indian, Asian (who are also included in the "Asian" row), Native Hawaiian or other Pacific Islander, as well as non-Hispanics reporting more than one race.
Source: Calculations by New Strategist based on the Bureau of Labor Statistics' 2005 Consumer Expenditure Survey

Kitchen Appliances, Small Electric

Best customers:
Householders aged 35 to 64
Married couples

Customer trends:
Average household spending on small electric kitchen appliances will rise as boomers fill the best-customer age group, but price competition from discounters will limit the increase.

The category small electric kitchen appliances includes coffee makers, food processors, bread makers, and so on. The best customers of small electric kitchen appliances are middle-aged and older married couples. Householders ranging in age from aged 35 to 64 spend 7 to 12 percent more than average on this item. Married couples spend 24 percent more than average on small electric kitchen appliances, some helping grown children outfit their first homes.

Average household spending on small electric kitchen appliances fell 3 percent between 2000 and 2005, after adjusting for inflation. Falling prices were behind the decline as discounters offered less-expensive imports. Average household spending on small electric kitchen appliances should climb in the next few years as boomers fill the best-customer age groups. But price competition from discounters could limit the gains.

Table 51. Kitchen appliances, small electric

Total household spending: $2,189,862,960.00
Average household spends: 18.66

AGE OF HOUSEHOLDER	AVERAGE HOUSEHOLD SPENDING	BEST CUSTOMERS (index)	BIGGEST CUSTOMERS (market share)
Average household	$18.66	100	100.0%
Under age 25	12.26	66	4.8
Aged 25 to 34	19.40	104	17.4
Aged 35 to 44	20.83	112	22.7
Aged 45 to 54	19.93	107	22.2
Aged 55 to 64	20.29	109	16.8
Aged 65 to 74	18.13	97	9.5
Aged 75 or older	12.86	69	6.7

	AVERAGE HOUSEHOLD SPENDING	BEST CUSTOMERS (index)	BIGGEST CUSTOMERS (market share)
HOUSEHOLD INCOME			
Average household	**$18.66**	**100**	**100.0%**
Under $20,000	8.94	48	11.0
$20,000 to $39,999	14.14	76	18.5
$40,000 to $49,999	21.81	117	11.4
$50,000 to $69,999	20.74	111	16.1
$70,000 to $79,999	20.83	112	6.4
$80,000 to $99,999	23.04	123	9.9
$100,000 or more	33.93	182	26.7
HOUSEHOLD TYPE			
Average household	**18.66**	**100**	**100.0**
Married couples	23.22	124	62.9
Married couples, no children	23.25	125	26.9
Married couples, with children	23.20	124	31.3
Oldest child under 6	22.93	123	5.9
Oldest child 6 to 17	23.73	127	16.8
Oldest child 18 or older	22.41	120	8.6
Single parent with child under 18	10.48	56	3.3
Single person	12.81	69	20.1
RACE AND HISPANIC ORIGIN			
Average household	**18.66**	**100**	**100.0**
Asian	20.07	108	3.9
Black	9.91	53	6.4
Hispanic	16.75	90	9.5
Non-Hispanic white and other	20.29	109	84.3
REGION			
Average household	**18.66**	**100**	**100.0**
Northeast	16.70	89	17.0
Midwest	20.08	108	24.8
South	16.24	87	31.2
West	22.82	122	27.0
EDUCATION			
Average household	**18.66**	**100**	**100.0**
Less than high school graduate	11.86	64	9.8
High school graduate	14.70	79	20.4
Some college	17.84	96	20.6
Associate's degree	19.12	102	10.1
College graduate	26.71	143	39.1
Bachelor's degree	24.75	133	22.9
Master's, professional, doctoral degree	30.07	161	16.2

Note: Market shares may not sum to 100.0 because of rounding and missing categories by household type. "Asian" and "black" include Hispanics and non-Hispanics who identify themselves as being of the respective race alone. "Hispanic" includes people of any race who identify themselves as Hispanic. "Other" includes people who identify themselves as non-Hispanic and as Alaska Native, American Indian, Asian (who are also included in the "Asian" row), Native Hawaiian or other Pacific Islander, as well as non-Hispanics reporting more than one race.
Source: Calculations by New Strategist based on the Bureau of Labor Statistics' 2005 Consumer Expenditure Survey

Lamps and Lighting Fixtures

Best customers: Householders aged 25 to 44
High-income households
Married couples without children at home
Married couples with school-aged or older children

Customer trends: Average household spending on lamps and lighting fixtures could continue to rise as empty-nest boomers redecorate their homes.

The best customers of lamps and lighting fixtures are affluent, young and middle-aged married couples. Householders aged 25 to 44 spend 33 to 37 percent more than the average on lamps and lighting fixtures. Households with incomes of $100,000 or more spend nearly four times the average on this item, controlling more than half the market. Married couples without children at home (most of them empty-nesters) spend 22 percent more than average on lamps, while those adult children at home spend 29 percent more than average Couples with school-aged children spend more than twice the average on lamps.

Average household spending on lamps and lighting fixtures rose by 61 percent between 2000 and 2005, after adjusting for inflation. Average household spending on lamps and lighting fixtures could continue to rise in the years ahead as boomers become empty-nesters.

Table 52. Lamps and lighting fixtures

Total household spending $2,308,392,520.00
Average household spends   19.67

AGE OF HOUSEHOLDER	AVERAGE HOUSEHOLD SPENDING	BEST CUSTOMERS (index)	BIGGEST CUSTOMERS (market share)
Average household	$19.67	100	100.0%
Under age 25	5.05	26	1.9
Aged 25 to 34	26.96	137	22.9
Aged 35 to 44	26.20	133	27.1
Aged 45 to 54	18.52	94	19.6
Aged 55 to 64	19.37	98	15.2
Aged 65 to 74	18.73	95	9.3
Aged 75 or older	8.21	42	4.0

	AVERAGE HOUSEHOLD SPENDING	BEST CUSTOMERS (index)	BIGGEST CUSTOMERS (market share)
HOUSEHOLD INCOME			
Average household	**$19.67**	**100**	**100.0%**
Under $20,000	4.28	22	5.0
$20,000 to $39,999	8.21	42	10.2
$40,000 to $49,999	12.18	62	6.0
$50,000 to $69,999	13.07	66	9.6
$70,000 to $79,999	19.33	98	5.6
$80,000 to $99,999	18.44	94	7.5
$100,000 or more	74.91	381	56.0
HOUSEHOLD TYPE			
Average household	**19.67**	**100**	**100.0**
Married couples	29.33	149	75.4
Married couples, no children	24.01	122	26.3
Married couples, with children	35.31	180	45.2
Oldest child under 6	14.66	75	3.6
Oldest child 6 to 17	48.21	245	32.3
Oldest child 18 or older	25.47	129	9.3
Single parent with child under 18	6.32	32	1.9
Single person	8.56	44	12.7
RACE AND HISPANIC ORIGIN			
Average household	**19.67**	**100**	**100.0**
Asian	19.04	97	3.5
Black	5.76	29	3.5
Hispanic	10.98	56	5.9
Non-Hispanic white and other	22.98	117	90.6
REGION			
Average household	**19.67**	**100**	**100.0**
Northeast	18.48	94	17.9
Midwest	18.51	94	21.7
South	19.68	100	35.9
West	21.88	111	24.5
EDUCATION			
Average household	**19.67**	**100**	**100.0**
Less than high school graduate	7.67	39	6.0
High school graduate	9.60	49	12.6
Some college	18.66	95	20.4
Associate's degree	15.90	81	8.0
College graduate	38.11	194	52.9
Bachelor's degree	30.92	157	27.1
Master's, professional, doctoral degree	50.40	256	25.8

Note: Market shares may not sum to 100.0 because of rounding and missing categories by household type. "Asian" and "black" include Hispanics and non-Hispanics who identify themselves as being of the respective race alone. "Hispanic" includes people of any race who identify themselves as Hispanic. "Other" includes people who identify themselves as non-Hispanic and as Alaska Native, American Indian, Asian (who are also included in the "Asian" row), Native Hawaiian or other Pacific Islander, as well as non-Hispanics reporting more than one race.
Source: Calculations by New Strategist based on the Bureau of Labor Statistics' 2005 Consumer Expenditure Survey

Laundry Equipment

Best customers: Householders aged 35 to 64
Married couples

Customer trends: Average household spending on laundry equipment should continue to rise as boomers fill the best-customer age groups.

The best customers of laundry equipment are middle-aged married couples. Householders ranging in age from 45 to 64 spend 14 to 28 percent more than average on this item. Married couples without children at home spend 36 percent more than average on laundry equipment. Married couples with children at home spend 25 percent more than the average household on laundry equipment, with the figure peaking at 60 percent among couples with adult children at home.

Average household spending on laundry equipment rose 44 percent between 2000 and 2005, after adjusting for inflation. Average household spending on laundry equipment should continue to rise as boomers fill the best-customer age groups.

Table 53. Laundry equipment

Total household spending $1,932,853,320.00
Average household spends   16.47

	AVERAGE HOUSEHOLD SPENDING	BEST CUSTOMERS (index)	BIGGEST CUSTOMERS (market share)
AGE OF HOUSEHOLDER			
Average household	**$16.47**	**100**	**100.0%**
Under age 25	8.80	53	3.9
Aged 25 to 34	13.43	82	13.6
Aged 35 to 44	18.78	114	23.2
Aged 45 to 54	21.05	128	26.6
Aged 55 to 64	21.06	128	19.7
Aged 65 to 74	12.60	77	7.5
Aged 75 or older	10.25	62	6.0

	AVERAGE HOUSEHOLD SPENDING	BEST CUSTOMERS (index)	BIGGEST CUSTOMERS (market share)
HOUSEHOLD INCOME			
Average household	**$16.47**	**100**	**100.0%**
Under $20,000	7.85	48	10.9
$20,000 to $39,999	12.09	73	17.9
$40,000 to $49,999	13.49	82	8.0
$50,000 to $69,999	18.41	112	16.2
$70,000 to $79,999	23.70	144	8.2
$80,000 to $99,999	13.74	83	6.7
$100,000 or more	34.61	210	30.9
HOUSEHOLD TYPE			
Average household	**16.47**	**100**	**100.0**
Married couples	21.08	128	64.7
Married couples, no children	22.44	136	29.4
Married couples, with children	20.55	125	31.4
Oldest child under 6	25.33	154	7.4
Oldest child 6 to 17	15.91	97	12.7
Oldest child 18 or older	26.29	160	11.4
Single parent with child under 18	8.09	49	2.9
Single person	10.37	63	18.4
RACE AND HISPANIC ORIGIN			
Average household	**16.47**	**100**	**100.0**
Asian	14.94	91	3.3
Black	5.95	36	4.3
Hispanic	13.17	80	8.5
Non-Hispanic white and other	18.45	112	86.9
REGION			
Average household	**16.47**	**100**	**100.0**
Northeast	13.42	81	15.5
Midwest	16.36	99	22.9
South	14.92	91	32.5
West	21.70	132	29.0
EDUCATION			
Average household	**16.47**	**100**	**100.0**
Less than high school graduate	11.18	68	10.4
High school graduate	14.27	87	22.4
Some college	13.86	84	18.1
Associate's degree	16.80	102	10.1
College graduate	23.01	140	38.2
Bachelor's degree	21.97	133	23.0
Master's, professional, doctoral degree	25.07	152	15.3

Note: Market shares may not sum to 100.0 because of rounding and missing categories by household type. "Asian" and "black" include Hispanics and non-Hispanics who identify themselves as being of the respective race alone. "Hispanic" includes people of any race who identify themselves as Hispanic. "Other" includes people who identify themselves as non-Hispanic and as Alaska Native, American Indian, Asian (who are also included in the "Asian" row), Native Hawaiian or other Pacific Islander, as well as non-Hispanics reporting more than one race.
Source: Calculations by New Strategist based on the Bureau of Labor Statistics' 2005 Consumer Expenditure Survey

Laundry and Cleaning Supplies

Best customers: Householders aged 35 to 64
Married couples with children at home
Hispanics

Customer trends: Average household spending on laundry and cleaning supplies is likely to fall as the population ages.

Households with children spend the most on laundry and cleaning supplies. Householders ranging in age from 35 to 64, many with children at home, spend 12 to 20 percent more than average on this item. Married couples with children at home spend 46 percent more than average on laundry and cleaning supplies. Hispanics, who have the largest families, spend 17 percent more than average on this item.

Average household spending on laundry and cleaning supplies fell 10 percent between 2000 and 2005, after adjusting for inflation. Behind the decline was the baby-boom generation's exit from the crowded nest lifestage. Average household spending on this item is likely to continue to fall as boomers age and the much smaller generation X enters the best-customer lifestage.

Table 54. Laundry and cleaning supplies			
Total household spending	$15,740,960,280.00		
Average household spends	134.13		
	AVERAGE HOUSEHOLD SPENDING	BEST CUSTOMERS (index)	BIGGEST CUSTOMERS (market share)
AGE OF HOUSEHOLDER			
Average household	**$134.13**	**100**	**100.0%**
Under age 25	63.31	47	3.4
Aged 25 to 34	127.33	95	15.9
Aged 35 to 44	161.23	120	24.4
Aged 45 to 54	154.45	115	23.9
Aged 55 to 64	149.58	112	17.2
Aged 65 to 74	122.37	91	8.9
Aged 75 or older	89.42	67	6.4

	AVERAGE HOUSEHOLD SPENDING	BEST CUSTOMERS (index)	BIGGEST CUSTOMERS (market share)
HOUSEHOLD INCOME			
Average household	**$134.13**	**100**	**100.0%**
Under $20,000	81.11	60	13.9
$20,000 to $39,999	107.27	80	19.5
$40,000 to $49,999	140.84	105	10.2
$50,000 to $69,999	156.31	117	16.8
$70,000 to $79,999	154.57	115	6.6
$80,000 to $99,999	163.57	122	9.8
$100,000 or more	198.07	148	21.7
HOUSEHOLD TYPE			
Average household	**134.13**	**100**	**100.0**
Married couples	172.53	129	65.0
Married couples, no children	140.10	104	22.5
Married couples, with children	195.18	146	36.6
Oldest child under 6	182.22	136	6.6
Oldest child 6 to 17	194.21	145	19.1
Oldest child 18 or older	206.56	154	11.0
Single parent with child under 18	136.86	102	6.0
Single person	65.67	49	14.3
RACE AND HISPANIC ORIGIN			
Average household	**134.13**	**100**	**100.0**
Asian	90.76	68	2.5
Black	119.18	89	10.6
Hispanic	156.28	117	12.4
Non-Hispanic white and other	133.28	99	77.0
REGION			
Average household	**134.13**	**100**	**100.0**
Northeast	118.08	88	16.8
Midwest	140.04	104	24.0
South	141.27	105	37.8
West	130.39	97	21.4
EDUCATION			
Average household	**134.13**	**100**	**100.0**
Less than high school graduate	125.56	94	14.4
High school graduate	131.16	98	25.3
Some college	127.77	95	20.5
Associate's degree	140.16	104	10.3
College graduate	144.13	107	29.4
Bachelor's degree	145.27	108	18.7
Master's, professional, doctoral degree	141.86	106	10.7

Note: Market shares may not sum to 100.0 because of rounding and missing categories by household type. "Asian" and "black" include Hispanics and non-Hispanics who identify themselves as being of the respective race alone. "Hispanic" includes people of any race who identify themselves as Hispanic. "Other" includes people who identify themselves as non-Hispanic and as Alaska Native, American Indian, Asian (who are also included in the "Asian" row), Native Hawaiian or other Pacific Islander, as well as non-Hispanics reporting more than one race.
Source: Calculations by New Strategist based on the Bureau of Labor Statistics' 2005 Consumer Expenditure Survey

Lawn and Garden Equipment

Best customers: Householders aged 35 to 44 and 55 to 74
                             Married couples without children at home
                             Married couples with school-aged children
                             Households in the Midwest

Customer trends: Average household spending on lawn and garden equipment should rise along
                             with homeownership.

The best customers of lawn and garden equipment are homeowners with grass to mow and gardens to tend. Householders aged 35 to 44 spend 20 percent more than average on mowers and other lawn and garden equipment, while those ranging in age from 55 to 74 spend 32 to 98 percent more than the average. Married couples without children at home spend 53 percent more than average on lawn and garden equipment. Those with school-aged children spend 29 percent more. Households in the Midwest, where grass is king, spend 89 percent more than average on lawn and garden equipment.

Average household spending on lawn and garden equipment fell 4 percent between 2000 and 2005, after adjusting for inflation, despite the surge in homeownership. Average household spending on lawn and garden equipment should rise along with homeownership in the years ahead.

Table 55. Lawn and garden equipment

Total household spending $5,980,461,760.00
Average household spends   50.96

	AVERAGE HOUSEHOLD SPENDING	BEST CUSTOMERS (index)	BIGGEST CUSTOMERS (market share)
AGE OF HOUSEHOLDER			
Average household	**$50.96**	**100**	**100.0%**
Under age 25	15.02	29	2.1
Aged 25 to 34	17.94	35	5.9
Aged 35 to 44	61.02	120	24.3
Aged 45 to 54	44.67	88	18.2
Aged 55 to 64	100.94	198	30.6
Aged 65 to 74	67.13	132	12.9
Aged 75 or older	31.39	62	6.0

	AVERAGE HOUSEHOLD SPENDING	BEST CUSTOMERS (index)	BIGGEST CUSTOMERS (market share)
HOUSEHOLD INCOME			
Average household	**$50.96**	**100**	**100.0%**
Under $20,000	17.73	35	8.0
$20,000 to $39,999	37.35	73	17.9
$40,000 to $49,999	42.90	84	8.2
$50,000 to $69,999	55.40	109	15.7
$70,000 to $79,999	45.05	88	5.1
$80,000 to $99,999	53.41	105	8.4
$100,000 or more	127.31	250	36.7
HOUSEHOLD TYPE			
Average household	**50.96**	**100**	**100.0**
Married couples	62.95	124	62.5
Married couples, no children	77.76	153	32.9
Married couples, with children	54.12	106	26.7
Oldest child under 6	27.67	54	2.6
Oldest child 6 to 17	65.92	129	17.1
Oldest child 18 or older	50.22	99	7.0
Single parent with child under 18	27.07	53	3.1
Single person	22.12	43	12.7
RACE AND HISPANIC ORIGIN			
Average household	**50.96**	**100**	**100.0**
Asian	3.52	7	0.3
Black	24.00	47	5.6
Hispanic	17.45	34	3.6
Non-Hispanic white and other	59.65	117	90.8
REGION			
Average household	**50.96**	**100**	**100.0**
Northeast	30.01	59	11.2
Midwest	96.49	189	43.6
South	48.85	96	34.4
West	24.98	49	10.8
EDUCATION			
Average household	**50.96**	**100**	**100.0**
Less than high school graduate	29.02	57	8.7
High school graduate	62.07	122	31.5
Some college	41.70	82	17.6
Associate's degree	114.81	225	22.3
College graduate	36.98	73	19.8
Bachelor's degree	29.58	58	10.0
Master's, professional, doctoral degree	49.64	97	9.8

Note: Market shares may not sum to 100.0 because of rounding and missing categories by household type. "Asian" and "black" include Hispanics and non-Hispanics who identify themselves as being of the respective race alone. "Hispanic" includes people of any race who identify themselves as Hispanic. "Other" includes people who identify themselves as non-Hispanic and as Alaska Native, American Indian, Asian (who are also included in the "Asian" row), Native Hawaiian or other Pacific Islander, as well as non-Hispanics reporting more than one race.
Source: Calculations by New Strategist based on the Bureau of Labor Statistics' 2005 Consumer Expenditure Survey

Lawn and Garden Supplies

Best customers:	**Householders aged 35 to 64**
	Married couples
Customer trends:	**Average household spending on lawn and garden supplies should continue to rise as boomers enter the empty-nest lifestage.**

The best customers of lawn and garden supplies are middle-aged married couples, most of whom are homeowners with lawns and gardens to tend. Householders ranging in age from 35 to 64 spend 15 to 46 percent more than the average household on lawn and garden supplies. Married couples spend 43 percent more than average on lawn and garden supplies.

Average household spending on lawn and garden supplies increased by 24 percent between 2000 and 2005, after adjusting for inflation. Behind the rise was the entry of the baby-boom generation into the empty-nest lifestage. As millions of boomers become empty-nesters over the next few years, spending on lawn and garden supplies should continue to rise.

Table 56. Lawn and garden supplies

Total household spending	$11,061,976,560.00
Average household spends	94.26

	AVERAGE HOUSEHOLD SPENDING	BEST CUSTOMERS (index)	BIGGEST CUSTOMERS (market share)
AGE OF HOUSEHOLDER			
Average household	**$94.26**	**100**	**100.0%**
Under age 25	15.33	16	1.2
Aged 25 to 34	58.82	62	10.4
Aged 35 to 44	108.30	115	23.3
Aged 45 to 54	137.24	146	30.3
Aged 55 to 64	122.57	130	20.1
Aged 65 to 74	90.15	96	9.4
Aged 75 or older	59.32	63	6.1

	AVERAGE HOUSEHOLD SPENDING	BEST CUSTOMERS (index)	BIGGEST CUSTOMERS (market share)
HOUSEHOLD INCOME			
Average household	**$94.26**	**100**	**100.0%**
Under $20,000	42.94	46	10.4
$20,000 to $39,999	46.47	49	12.0
$40,000 to $49,999	69.13	73	7.2
$50,000 to $69,999	84.05	89	12.9
$70,000 to $79,999	98.96	105	6.0
$80,000 to $99,999	111.65	118	9.5
$100,000 or more	258.57	274	40.3
HOUSEHOLD TYPE			
Average household	**94.26**	**100**	**100.0**
Married couples	134.89	143	72.4
Married couples, no children	128.11	136	29.3
Married couples, with children	145.67	155	38.9
Oldest child under 6	182.24	193	9.3
Oldest child 6 to 17	138.18	147	19.3
Oldest child 18 or older	133.91	142	10.2
Single parent with child under 18	30.97	33	1.9
Single person	51.74	55	16.1
RACE AND HISPANIC ORIGIN			
Average household	**94.26**	**100**	**100.0**
Asian	62.41	66	2.4
Black	23.38	25	3.0
Hispanic	18.79	20	2.1
Non-Hispanic white and other	114.79	122	94.4
REGION			
Average household	**94.26**	**100**	**100.0**
Northeast	101.99	108	20.6
Midwest	98.34	104	24.0
South	77.40	82	29.5
West	110.82	118	25.9
EDUCATION			
Average household	**94.26**	**100**	**100.0**
Less than high school graduate	25.53	27	4.2
High school graduate	72.00	76	19.8
Some college	72.05	76	16.5
Associate's degree	122.01	129	12.8
College graduate	157.45	167	45.6
Bachelor's degree	162.61	173	29.7
Master's, professional, doctoral degree	147.25	156	15.7

Note: Market shares may not sum to 100.0 because of rounding and missing categories by household type. "Asian" and "black" include Hispanics and non-Hispanics who identify themselves as being of the respective race alone. "Hispanic" includes people of any race who identify themselves as Hispanic. "Other" includes people who identify themselves as non-Hispanic and as Alaska Native, American Indian, Asian (who are also included in the "Asian" row), Native Hawaiian or other Pacific Islander, as well as non-Hispanics reporting more than one race.
Source: Calculations by New Strategist based on the Bureau of Labor Statistics' 2005 Consumer Expenditure Survey

Living Room Chairs

Best customers: Householders aged 35 to 44 and 55 to 74

High-income households

Married couples

Customer trends: Average household spending on living room chairs should rise as empty-nest

boomers redecorate their homes.

The best customers of living room chairs are affluent married couples setting up a first home or redecorating after the children leave home. Householders aged 35 to 44 spend 24 percent more than average on living room chairs while those aged 55 to 74 spend 43 to 52 percent more than average. Married couples without children at home (most of them empty-nesters) spend 76 percent more than average on living room chairs. Couples with children at home spend 35 percent more on this item.

Average household spending on living room chairs increased by 6 percent between 2000 and 2006, after adjusting for inflation. Average household spending on living room chairs should rise in the years ahead as millions of boomers become empty-nesters and redecorate their homes.

Table 57. Living room chairs

| Total household spending | $6,169,404,920.00 |
| Average household spends | 52.57 |

AGE OF HOUSEHOLDER	AVERAGE HOUSEHOLD SPENDING	BEST CUSTOMERS (index)	BIGGEST CUSTOMERS (market share)
Average household	**$52.57**	**100**	**100.0%**
Under age 25	18.52	35	2.6
Aged 25 to 34	31.01	59	9.9
Aged 35 to 44	65.01	124	25.1
Aged 45 to 54	44.32	84	17.5
Aged 55 to 64	79.79	152	23.4
Aged 65 to 74	75.07	143	14.0
Aged 75 or older	40.83	78	7.5

	AVERAGE HOUSEHOLD SPENDING	BEST CUSTOMERS (index)	BIGGEST CUSTOMERS (market share)
HOUSEHOLD INCOME			
Average household	**$52.57**	**100**	**100.0%**
Under $20,000	24.04	46	10.5
$20,000 to $39,999	24.96	47	11.6
$40,000 to $49,999	42.85	82	8.0
$50,000 to $69,999	37.70	72	10.4
$70,000 to $79,999	43.36	82	4.7
$80,000 to $99,999	54.88	104	8.4
$100,000 or more	166.27	316	46.5
HOUSEHOLD TYPE			
Average household	**52.57**	**100**	**100.0**
Married couples	78.17	149	75.2
Married couples, no children	92.30	176	37.8
Married couples, with children	70.98	135	34.0
Oldest child under 6	67.86	129	6.2
Oldest child 6 to 17	73.33	139	18.4
Oldest child 18 or older	68.77	131	9.4
Single parent with child under 18	19.95	38	2.2
Single person	24.35	46	13.6
RACE AND HISPANIC ORIGIN			
Average household	**52.57**	**100**	**100.0**
Asian	29.07	55	2.0
Black	26.86	51	6.1
Hispanic	33.84	64	6.8
Non-Hispanic white and other	59.02	112	87.1
REGION			
Average household	**52.57**	**100**	**100.0**
Northeast	44.50	85	16.1
Midwest	45.49	87	19.9
South	51.29	98	35.0
West	69.01	131	28.9
EDUCATION			
Average household	**52.57**	**100**	**100.0**
Less than high school graduate	30.99	59	9.1
High school graduate	35.77	68	17.6
Some college	50.12	95	20.5
Associate's degree	64.36	122	12.1
College graduate	78.29	149	40.7
Bachelor's degree	72.86	139	23.9
Master's, professional, doctoral degree	87.56	167	16.8

Note: Market shares may not sum to 100.0 because of rounding and missing categories by household type. "Asian" and "black" include Hispanics and non-Hispanics who identify themselves as being of the respective race alone. "Hispanic" includes people of any race who identify themselves as Hispanic. "Other" includes people who identify themselves as non-Hispanic and as Alaska Native, American Indian, Asian (who are also included in the "Asian" row), Native Hawaiian or other Pacific Islander, as well as non-Hispanics reporting more than one race.
Source: Calculations by New Strategist based on the Bureau of Labor Statistics' 2005 Consumer Expenditure Survey

Living Room Tables

Best customers:
Householders aged 25 to 44 and 65 to 74
High-income households
Married couples without children at home
Married couples with children under age 18

Customer trends:
Average household spending on living room tables should rise as empty-nest boomers redecorate their homes.

The best customers of living room tables are affluent married couples. Married couples without children at home (most of them empty-nesters) spend 21 percent more than average on living room tables, while those with children under age 18 at home spend 22 to 52 percent more than average on this item. Households with incomes of $100,000 or more spend fully three times more than average on living room tables. Householders aged 25 to 44 spend 27 to 53 percent more than average on living room tables, furnishing their first homes. Householders aged 65 to 74 spend 26 percent more than average, redecorating as empty-nesters.

Average household spending on living room tables fell 9 percent between 2000 and 2005, after adjusting for inflation. Average household spending on living room tables could rise in the next few years as boomers become empty-nesters and redecorate their homes.

Table 58. Living room tables

Total household spending $2,090,110,360.00
Average household spends 17.81

	AVERAGE HOUSEHOLD SPENDING	BEST CUSTOMERS (index)	BIGGEST CUSTOMERS (market share)
AGE OF HOUSEHOLDER			
Average household	**$17.81**	**100**	**100.0%**
Under age 25	8.05	45	3.3
Aged 25 to 34	22.59	127	21.2
Aged 35 to 44	27.32	153	31.2
Aged 45 to 54	12.89	72	15.0
Aged 55 to 64	16.80	94	14.6
Aged 65 to 74	22.39	126	12.3
Aged 75 or older	4.47	25	2.4

	AVERAGE HOUSEHOLD SPENDING	BEST CUSTOMERS (index)	BIGGEST CUSTOMERS (market share)
HOUSEHOLD INCOME			
Average household	**$17.81**	**100**	**100.0%**
Under $20,000	4.44	25	5.7
$20,000 to $39,999	10.47	59	14.3
$40,000 to $49,999	12.79	72	7.0
$50,000 to $69,999	13.85	78	11.2
$70,000 to $79,999	28.29	159	9.1
$80,000 to $99,999	18.78	105	8.5
$100,000 or more	53.46	300	44.1
HOUSEHOLD TYPE			
Average household	**17.81**	**100**	**100.0**
Married couples	23.29	131	66.1
Married couples, no children	21.53	121	26.1
Married couples, with children	23.32	131	32.9
Oldest child under 6	21.64	122	5.9
Oldest child 6 to 17	27.12	152	20.1
Oldest child 18 or older	17.44	98	7.0
Single parent with child under 18	13.85	78	4.6
Single person	10.41	58	17.1
RACE AND HISPANIC ORIGIN			
Average household	**17.81**	**100**	**100.0**
Asian	12.88	72	2.6
Black	11.75	66	7.9
Hispanic	16.75	94	10.0
Non-Hispanic white and other	18.89	106	82.2
REGION			
Average household	**17.81**	**100**	**100.0**
Northeast	13.31	75	14.2
Midwest	19.73	111	25.5
South	14.33	80	28.9
West	25.37	142	31.4
EDUCATION			
Average household	**17.81**	**100**	**100.0**
Less than high school graduate	9.92	56	8.6
High school graduate	11.17	63	16.2
Some college	18.34	103	22.2
Associate's degree	12.12	68	6.7
College graduate	30.18	169	46.3
Bachelor's degree	24.76	139	24.0
Master's, professional, doctoral degree	39.46	222	22.3

Note: Market shares may not sum to 100.0 because of rounding and missing categories by household type. "Asian" and "black" include Hispanics and non-Hispanics who identify themselves as being of the respective race alone. "Hispanic" includes people of any race who identify themselves as Hispanic. "Other" includes people who identify themselves as non-Hispanic and as Alaska Native, American Indian, Asian (who are also included in the "Asian" row), Native Hawaiian or other Pacific Islander, as well as non-Hispanics reporting more than one race.
Source: Calculations by New Strategist based on the Bureau of Labor Statistics' 2005 Consumer Expenditure Survey

Mattresses and Springs

Best customers:	Householders aged 25 to 44 and 55 to 64
	Married couples without children at home
	Married couples with school-aged or older children
Customer trends:	Average household spending on mattresses and springs should stabilize in the next few years as boomers fill the best-customer lifestage.

The best customers of mattresses and springs are married couples, some purchasing mattresses for expanding families and others upgrading their mattresses after their children leave home. Householders aged 25 to 44 spend 18 to 20 percent more than average on mattresses and springs. Those aged 55 to 64 spend 16 percent more than average on this item. Married couples without children at home (most of them empty-nesters) spend 29 percent more than average on mattresses. Those with school-aged or adult children at home—who have the largest households—spend 25 to 43 percent more than average.

Average household spending on mattresses and springs fell 4 percent between 2000 and 2005, after adjusting for inflation. Average household spending on mattresses and springs could rise in the next few years as boomers fill the best-customer lifestage.

Table 59. Mattresses and springs

Total household spending	$6,790,218,160.00
Average household spends	57.86

	AVERAGE HOUSEHOLD SPENDING	BEST CUSTOMERS (index)	BIGGEST CUSTOMERS (market share)
AGE OF HOUSEHOLDER			
Average household	**$57.86**	**100**	**100.0%**
Under age 25	38.07	66	4.8
Aged 25 to 34	69.32	120	20.0
Aged 35 to 44	68.20	118	23.9
Aged 45 to 54	54.28	94	19.5
Aged 55 to 64	67.18	116	17.9
Aged 65 to 74	54.75	95	9.3
Aged 75 or older	27.18	47	4.5

	AVERAGE HOUSEHOLD SPENDING	BEST CUSTOMERS (index)	BIGGEST CUSTOMERS (market share)
HOUSEHOLD INCOME			
Average household	**$57.86**	**100**	**100.0%**
Under $20,000	25.46	44	10.1
$20,000 to $39,999	32.06	55	13.5
$40,000 to $49,999	47.57	82	8.0
$50,000 to $69,999	52.77	91	13.2
$70,000 to $79,999	86.44	149	8.6
$80,000 to $99,999	104.18	180	14.5
$100,000 or more	126.52	219	32.1
HOUSEHOLD TYPE			
Average household	**57.86**	**100**	**100.0**
Married couples	75.28	130	65.8
Married couples, no children	74.52	129	27.8
Married couples, with children	75.12	130	32.7
Oldest child under 6	59.00	102	4.9
Oldest child 6 to 17	82.67	143	18.8
Oldest child 18 or older	72.07	125	8.9
Single parent with child under 18	31.92	55	3.2
Single person	35.76	62	18.1
RACE AND HISPANIC ORIGIN			
Average household	**57.86**	**100**	**100.0**
Asian	62.87	109	4.0
Black	23.17	40	4.8
Hispanic	67.34	116	12.4
Non-Hispanic white and other	61.87	107	82.9
REGION			
Average household	**57.86**	**100**	**100.0**
Northeast	43.22	75	14.2
Midwest	55.15	95	21.9
South	54.67	94	33.9
West	78.54	136	29.9
EDUCATION			
Average household	**57.86**	**100**	**100.0**
Less than high school graduate	31.97	55	8.5
High school graduate	32.61	56	14.6
Some college	60.83	105	22.7
Associate's degree	72.33	125	12.3
College graduate	88.78	153	41.9
Bachelor's degree	84.16	145	25.1
Master's, professional, doctoral degree	96.66	167	16.8

Note: Market shares may not sum to 100.0 because of rounding and missing categories by household type. "Asian" and "black" include Hispanics and non-Hispanics who identify themselves as being of the respective race alone. "Hispanic" includes people of any race who identify themselves as Hispanic. "Other" includes people who identify themselves as non-Hispanic and as Alaska Native, American Indian, Asian (who are also included in the "Asian" row), Native Hawaiian or other Pacific Islander, as well as non-Hispanics reporting more than one race.
Source: Calculations by New Strategist based on the Bureau of Labor Statistics' 2005 Consumer Expenditure Survey

Moving, Storage, and Freight Express

Best customers: Householders aged 45 to 74
Married couples without children at home

Customer trends: Average household spending on moving, storage, and freight express may rise
as boomers enter the best-customer lifestage.

The biggest spenders on moving, storage, and freight express are households that can afford to pay for moving services or that need storage space. Householders aged 45 to 74 do not move much, but when they do many can afford to hire moving services. In addition, older householders have accumulated belongings over the years that may require additional storage space. These factors explain why householders aged 45 to 74 spend more than average on moving and storage services. Married couples without children at home, most of them empty-nesters, spend 83 percent more than average on this item.

Average household spending on moving, storage and freight express fell by less than 1 percent between 2000 and 2005, after adjusting for inflation. Average household spending on this item may rise in the years ahead as boomers enter the best-customer lifestage.

Table 60. Moving, storage, and freight express

Total household spending $4,276,452,640.00
Average household spends   36.44

AGE OF HOUSEHOLDER	AVERAGE HOUSEHOLD SPENDING	BEST CUSTOMERS (index)	BIGGEST CUSTOMERS (market share)
Average household	$36.44	100	100.0%
Under age 25	13.55	37	2.7
Aged 25 to 34	25.87	71	11.9
Aged 35 to 44	27.89	77	15.5
Aged 45 to 54	41.67	114	23.8
Aged 55 to 64	49.22	135	20.8
Aged 65 to 74	75.53	207	20.3
Aged 75 or older	18.69	51	5.0

	AVERAGE HOUSEHOLD SPENDING	BEST CUSTOMERS (index)	BIGGEST CUSTOMERS (market share)
HOUSEHOLD INCOME			
Average household	**$36.44**	**100**	**100.0%**
Under $20,000	14.05	39	8.8
$20,000 to $39,999	32.10	88	21.5
$40,000 to $49,999	38.38	105	10.3
$50,000 to $69,999	34.33	94	13.6
$70,000 to $79,999	54.32	149	8.5
$80,000 to $99,999	30.79	84	6.8
$100,000 or more	75.49	207	30.4
HOUSEHOLD TYPE			
Average household	**36.44**	**100**	**100.0**
Married couples	47.07	129	65.3
Married couples, no children	66.83	183	39.5
Married couples, with children	30.08	83	20.8
Oldest child under 6	31.62	87	4.2
Oldest child 6 to 17	30.70	84	11.1
Oldest child 18 or older	27.91	77	5.5
Single parent with child under 18	17.19	47	2.8
Single person	25.43	70	20.4
RACE AND HISPANIC ORIGIN			
Average household	**36.44**	**100**	**100.0**
Asian	24.17	66	2.4
Black	26.48	73	8.7
Hispanic	16.85	46	4.9
Non-Hispanic white and other	40.61	111	86.4
REGION			
Average household	**36.44**	**100**	**100.0**
Northeast	18.83	52	9.8
Midwest	23.74	65	15.0
South	35.07	96	34.5
West	67.16	184	40.6
EDUCATION			
Average household	**36.44**	**100**	**100.0**
Less than high school graduate	7.87	22	3.3
High school graduate	27.54	76	19.6
Some college	45.73	125	27.0
Associate's degree	30.42	83	8.2
College graduate	55.81	153	41.8
Bachelor's degree	51.23	141	24.2
Master's, professional, doctoral degree	63.65	175	17.6

Note: Market shares may not sum to 100.0 because of rounding and missing categories by household type. "Asian" and "black" include Hispanics and non-Hispanics who identify themselves as being of the respective race alone. "Hispanic" includes people of any race who identify themselves as Hispanic. "Other" includes people who identify themselves as non-Hispanic and as Alaska Native, American Indian, Asian (who are also included in the "Asian" row), Native Hawaiian or other Pacific Islander, as well as non-Hispanics reporting more than one race.
Source: Calculations by New Strategist based on the Bureau of Labor Statistics' 2005 Consumer Expenditure Survey

Outdoor Equipment

Best customers:	**Householders aged 45 to 64**
	Married couples with school-aged children
	Households in the South
Customer trends:	**Average household spending on outdoor equipment should stabilize as boomers become empty-nesters.**

The best customers of outdoor equipment (such as grills) are middle-aged married couples. Householders aged 45 to 64 spend 39 to 84 percent more than the average household on outdoor equipment. Married couples without children at home, most of them empty-nesters, spend 22 percent more than average on this item. Couples with school-aged children spend 46 percent more than the average. With the warmer year round climate, households in the South spend 27 percent more than average on outdoor equipment.

Average household spending on outdoor equipment rose by a substantial 38 percent between 2000 and 2005, after adjusting for inflation. The surge in homeownership is one factor behind the spending increase. Average household spending on outdoor equipment should stabilize as boomers become empty-nesters.

Table 61. Outdoor equipment

Total household spending $3,366,943,640.00
Average household spends 28.69

	AVERAGE HOUSEHOLD SPENDING	BEST CUSTOMERS (index)	BIGGEST CUSTOMERS (market share)
AGE OF HOUSEHOLDER			
Average household	**$28.69**	**100**	**100.0%**
Under age 25	3.59	13	0.9
Aged 25 to 34	19.83	69	11.6
Aged 35 to 44	23.49	82	16.6
Aged 45 to 54	52.81	184	38.3
Aged 55 to 64	39.99	139	21.5
Aged 65 to 74	15.49	54	5.3
Aged 75 or older	20.48	71	6.9

	AVERAGE HOUSEHOLD SPENDING	BEST CUSTOMERS (index)	BIGGEST CUSTOMERS (market share)
HOUSEHOLD INCOME			
Average household	**$28.69**	**100**	**100.0%**
Under $20,000	2.68	9	2.1
$20,000 to $39,999	13.40	47	11.4
$40,000 to $49,999	26.54	93	9.0
$50,000 to $69,999	34.36	120	17.3
$70,000 to $79,999	54.99	192	11.0
$80,000 to $99,999	27.86	97	7.8
$100,000 or more	75.74	264	38.8
HOUSEHOLD TYPE			
Average household	**28.69**	**100**	**100.0**
Married couples	33.37	116	58.8
Married couples, no children	35.09	122	26.4
Married couples, with children	32.95	115	28.9
Oldest child under 6	17.95	63	3.0
Oldest child 6 to 17	41.99	146	19.3
Oldest child 18 or older	25.92	90	6.5
Single parent with child under 18	–	–	–
Single person	5.35	19	5.5
RACE AND HISPANIC ORIGIN			
Average household	**28.69**	**100**	**100.0**
Asian	41.97	146	5.3
Black	9.95	35	4.1
Hispanic	23.46	82	8.7
Non-Hispanic white and other	32.13	112	86.8
REGION			
Average household	**28.69**	**100**	**100.0**
Northeast	20.47	71	13.6
Midwest	28.23	98	22.6
South	36.55	127	45.7
West	23.47	82	18.0
EDUCATION			
Average household	**28.69**	**100**	**100.0**
Less than high school graduate	12.38	43	6.6
High school graduate	8.98	31	8.1
Some college	32.71	114	24.6
Associate's degree	43.62	152	15.0
College graduate	47.80	167	45.5
Bachelor's degree	34.19	119	20.5
Master's, professional, doctoral degree	74.72	260	26.3

Note: Market shares may not sum to 100.0 because of rounding and missing categories by household type. "Asian" and "black" include Hispanics and non-Hispanics who identify themselves as being of the respective race alone. "Hispanic" includes people of any race who identify themselves as Hispanic. "Other" includes people who identify themselves as non-Hispanic and as Alaska Native, American Indian, Asian (who are also included in the "Asian" row), Native Hawaiian or other Pacific Islander, as well as non-Hispanics reporting more than one race. – means sample is too small to make a reliable estimate.
Source: Calculations by New Strategist based on the Bureau of Labor Statistics' 2005 Consumer Expenditure Survey

Outdoor Furniture

Best customers:	**Householders aged 35 to 44 and 55 to 64**
	High-income households
	Married couples
Customer trends:	**Average household spending on outdoor furniture should rise as boomers**
	become empty-nesters and upgrade their outdoor furniture.

The best customers of outdoor furniture are affluent, middle-aged, married couples. Householders aged 35 to 44 and 55 to 64 spend 26 to 86 percent more than average on this item. Households with incomes of $100,000 or more spend more than four times the average and account for 62 percent of the market. Married couples without children at home (most of them empty-nesters) spend 46 percent more than average on outdoor furniture. Those with children spend 84 percent more than average on this item.

Average household spending on outdoor furniture rose 5 percent between 2000 and 2005, after adjusting for inflation. Average household spending on outdoor furniture should continue to rise as boomers become empty-nesters and upgrade their outdoor tables and chairs.

Table 62. Outdoor furniture

Total household spending	$2,114,755,120.00
Average household spends	18.02

	AVERAGE HOUSEHOLD SPENDING	BEST CUSTOMERS (index)	BIGGEST CUSTOMERS (market share)
AGE OF HOUSEHOLDER			
Average household	**$18.02**	**100**	**100.0%**
Under age 25	1.98	11	0.8
Aged 25 to 34	10.23	57	9.5
Aged 35 to 44	33.58	186	37.8
Aged 45 to 54	19.12	106	22.1
Aged 55 to 64	22.67	126	19.4
Aged 65 to 74	13.07	73	7.1
Aged 75 or older	6.10	34	3.3

	AVERAGE HOUSEHOLD SPENDING	BEST CUSTOMERS (index)	BIGGEST CUSTOMERS (market share)
HOUSEHOLD INCOME			
Average household	**$18.02**	**100**	**100.0%**
Under $20,000	1.20	7	1.5
$20,000 to $39,999	5.76	32	7.8
$40,000 to $49,999	5.24	29	2.8
$50,000 to $69,999	11.70	65	9.4
$70,000 to $79,999	13.48	75	4.3
$80,000 to $99,999	27.02	150	12.1
$100,000 or more	76.09	422	62.1
HOUSEHOLD TYPE			
Average household	**18.02**	**100**	**100.0**
Married couples	29.23	162	82.0
Married couples, no children	26.38	146	31.6
Married couples, with children	33.08	184	46.2
Oldest child under 6	29.37	163	7.9
Oldest child 6 to 17	40.68	226	29.8
Oldest child 18 or older	21.56	120	8.6
Single parent with child under 18	4.23	23	1.4
Single person	5.50	31	8.9
RACE AND HISPANIC ORIGIN			
Average household	**18.02**	**100**	**100.0**
Asian	3.83	21	0.8
Black	5.45	30	3.6
Hispanic	10.76	60	6.3
Non-Hispanic white and other	20.92	116	90.0
REGION			
Average household	**18.02**	**100**	**100.0**
Northeast	15.70	87	16.6
Midwest	16.62	92	21.2
South	14.54	81	29.0
West	27.14	151	33.2
EDUCATION			
Average household	**18.02**	**100**	**100.0**
Less than high school graduate	4.74	26	4.0
High school graduate	8.93	50	12.8
Some college	18.91	105	22.6
Associate's degree	18.66	104	10.2
College graduate	33.16	184	50.3
Bachelor's degree	20.89	116	20.0
Master's, professional, doctoral degree	54.14	300	30.3

Note: Market shares may not sum to 100.0 because of rounding and missing categories by household type. "Asian" and "black" include Hispanics and non-Hispanics who identify themselves as being of the respective race alone. "Hispanic" includes people of any race who identify themselves as Hispanic. "Other" includes people who identify themselves as non-Hispanic and as Alaska Native, American Indian, Asian (who are also included in the "Asian" row), Native Hawaiian or other Pacific Islander, as well as non-Hispanics reporting more than one race.
Source: Calculations by New Strategist based on the Bureau of Labor Statistics' 2005 Consumer Expenditure Survey

Plants and Fresh Flowers, Indoor

Best customers: Householders aged 35 to 74
                         Married couples without children at home
                         Married couples with school-aged or older children

Customer trends: Average household spending on indoor plants and fresh flowers should rise as
                         the large baby-boom generation fills the best-customer lifestage.

The best customers of indoor plants and fresh flowers are middle-aged married couples. Many are buying flowers for anniversaries or for ailing friends and relatives. Householders aged 35 to 74 spend 16 to 31 percent more than average on this item. Married couples without children at home (most of them empty-nesters) spend 58 percent more than average on indoor plants and fresh flowers. Those with school-aged or older children at home spend 37 percent more.

Average household spending on indoor plants and fresh flowers fell 30 percent between 2000 and 2005, after adjusting for inflation. The lackluster recovery following the recession of 2001 and the subsequent loss of discretionary income are behind the decline. Average household spending on indoor plants and fresh flowers should rise in the next few years as boomers fill the best-customer lifestage, but only if discretionary income rebounds.

Table 63. Plants and fresh flowers, indoor

Total household spending $5,343,218,680.00
Average household spends   45.53

	AVERAGE HOUSEHOLD SPENDING	BEST CUSTOMERS (index)	BIGGEST CUSTOMERS (market share)
AGE OF HOUSEHOLDER			
Average household	**$45.53**	**100**	**100.0%**
Under age 25	18.71	41	3.0
Aged 25 to 34	31.02	68	11.4
Aged 35 to 44	52.77	116	23.5
Aged 45 to 54	52.77	116	24.1
Aged 55 to 64	59.79	131	20.3
Aged 65 to 74	54.12	119	11.7
Aged 75 or older	28.54	63	6.1

	AVERAGE HOUSEHOLD SPENDING	BEST CUSTOMERS (index)	BIGGEST CUSTOMERS (market share)
HOUSEHOLD INCOME			
Average household	**$45.53**	**100**	**100.0%**
Under $20,000	15.34	34	7.7
$20,000 to $39,999	28.65	63	15.4
$40,000 to $49,999	28.82	63	6.2
$50,000 to $69,999	42.76	94	13.6
$70,000 to $79,999	47.04	103	5.9
$80,000 to $99,999	68.26	150	12.1
$100,000 or more	121.37	267	39.2
HOUSEHOLD TYPE			
Average household	**45.53**	**100**	**100.0**
Married couples	61.92	136	68.8
Married couples, no children	72.01	158	34.1
Married couples, with children	56.70	125	31.3
Oldest child under 6	38.54	85	4.1
Oldest child 6 to 17	60.25	132	17.5
Oldest child 18 or older	62.41	137	9.8
Single parent with child under 18	19.89	44	2.6
Single person	29.47	65	18.9
RACE AND HISPANIC ORIGIN			
Average household	**45.53**	**100**	**100.0**
Asian	37.96	83	3.0
Black	14.53	32	3.8
Hispanic	19.40	43	4.5
Non-Hispanic white and other	53.83	118	91.7
REGION			
Average household	**45.53**	**100**	**100.0**
Northeast	64.14	141	26.8
Midwest	50.23	110	25.4
South	32.61	72	25.7
West	45.57	100	22.1
EDUCATION			
Average household	**45.53**	**100**	**100.0**
Less than high school graduate	14.59	32	4.9
High school graduate	33.92	75	19.3
Some college	40.93	90	19.4
Associate's degree	43.24	95	9.4
College graduate	78.37	172	47.0
Bachelor's degree	64.60	142	24.5
Master's, professional, doctoral degree	101.90	224	22.6

Note: Market shares may not sum to 100.0 because of rounding and missing categories by household type. "Asian" and "black" include Hispanics and non-Hispanics who identify themselves as being of the respective race alone. "Hispanic" includes people of any race who identify themselves as Hispanic. "Other" includes people who identify themselves as non-Hispanic and as Alaska Native, American Indian, Asian (who are also included in the "Asian" row), Native Hawaiian or other Pacific Islander, as well as non-Hispanics reporting more than one race.
Source: Calculations by New Strategist based on the Bureau of Labor Statistics' 2005 Consumer Expenditure Survey

Postage

Best customers: Householders aged 55 to 74
Married couples without children at home

Customer trends: Average household spending on postage will decline as younger, wired
Americans replace older, off-line generations.

Older Americans are the biggest spenders on postage. Householders aged
55 to 74 spend 35 to 55 percent more than average on this item. Married
couples without children at home (most of them older, empty-nesters) spend
45 percent more than average on postage.

Average household spending on postage fell 1 percent between 2000
and 2005, after adjusting for inflation. Behind the stability is the hike in the
cost of postage as well as the popularity of the U.S. Postal Service's priority
mail options. Spending on postage in the years ahead will depend in part
on how successful the Postal Service is in the competition with FedEx and
UPS. It's likely, however, that average household spending on postage will
decline as the wired generations move into the older age groups.

Table 64. Postage

Total household spending $7,967,298,840.00
Average household spends   67.89

AGE OF HOUSEHOLDER	AVERAGE HOUSEHOLD SPENDING	BEST CUSTOMERS (index)	BIGGEST CUSTOMERS (market share)
Average household	**$67.89**	**100**	**100.0%**
Under age 25	30.93	46	3.3
Aged 25 to 34	39.13	58	9.6
Aged 35 to 44	62.03	91	18.6
Aged 45 to 54	73.53	108	22.5
Aged 55 to 64	91.94	135	20.9
Aged 65 to 74	105.16	155	15.2
Aged 75 or older	73.12	108	10.4

	AVERAGE HOUSEHOLD SPENDING	BEST CUSTOMERS (index)	BIGGEST CUSTOMERS (market share)
HOUSEHOLD INCOME			
Average household	**$67.89**	**100**	**100.0%**
Under $20,000	36.37	54	12.3
$20,000 to $39,999	57.51	85	20.7
$40,000 to $49,999	66.30	98	9.5
$50,000 to $69,999	67.71	100	14.4
$70,000 to $79,999	83.16	122	7.0
$80,000 to $99,999	98.54	145	11.7
$100,000 or more	105.96	156	22.9
HOUSEHOLD TYPE			
Average household	**67.89**	**100**	**100.0**
Married couples	84.50	124	62.9
Married couples, no children	98.27	145	31.2
Married couples, with children	75.55	111	28.0
Oldest child under 6	73.25	108	5.2
Oldest child 6 to 17	78.61	116	15.3
Oldest child 18 or older	71.12	105	7.5
Single parent with child under 18	32.93	49	2.9
Single person	52.17	77	22.5
RACE AND HISPANIC ORIGIN			
Average household	**67.89**	**100**	**100.0**
Asian	51.86	76	2.8
Black	35.48	52	6.3
Hispanic	42.80	63	6.7
Non-Hispanic white and other	76.05	112	86.9
REGION			
Average household	**67.89**	**100**	**100.0**
Northeast	74.92	110	21.0
Midwest	64.55	95	21.9
South	65.75	97	34.8
West	68.70	101	22.3
EDUCATION			
Average household	**67.89**	**100**	**100.0**
Less than high school graduate	35.95	53	8.1
High school graduate	58.03	85	22.1
Some college	66.22	98	21.0
Associate's degree	67.59	100	9.8
College graduate	94.27	139	37.9
Bachelor's degree	82.16	121	20.9
Master's, professional, doctoral degree	118.22	174	17.6

Note: Market shares may not sum to 100.0 because of rounding and missing categories by household type. "Asian" and "black" include Hispanics and non-Hispanics who identify themselves as being of the respective race alone. "Hispanic" includes people of any race who identify themselves as Hispanic. "Other" includes people who identify themselves as non-Hispanic and as Alaska Native, American Indian, Asian (who are also included in the "Asian" row), Native Hawaiian or other Pacific Islander, as well as non-Hispanics reporting more than one race.
Source: Calculations by New Strategist based on the Bureau of Labor Statistics' 2005 Consumer Expenditure Survey

Power Tools

Best customers: Householders aged 35 to 44

Customer trends: Average household spending on power tools should stabilize as boomers become empty-nesters.

The best customers of power tools are new homeowners tackling do-it-yourself projects. This explains why householders aged 35 to 44 spend more than twice the average on power tools. Many are recent homeowners who are taking on remodeling projects.

Average household spending on power tools more than doubled between 2000 and 2005, after adjusting for inflation. Record homeownership and innovative new tools are behind the increase. Spending should stabilize as boomers become empty-nesters.

Table 65. Power tools

Total household spending	$6,298,496,520.00
Average household spends	53.67

	AVERAGE HOUSEHOLD SPENDING	BEST CUSTOMERS (index)	BIGGEST CUSTOMERS (market share)
AGE OF HOUSEHOLDER			
Average household	**$53.67**	**100**	**100.0%**
Under age 25	27.88	52	3.8
Aged 25 to 34	23.93	45	7.5
Aged 35 to 44	121.54	226	46.0
Aged 45 to 54	41.13	77	15.9
Aged 55 to 64	55.14	103	15.8
Aged 65 to 74	22.74	42	4.2
Aged 75 or older	40.29	75	7.3

	AVERAGE HOUSEHOLD SPENDING	BEST CUSTOMERS (index)	BIGGEST CUSTOMERS (market share)
HOUSEHOLD INCOME			
Average household	**$53.67**	**100**	**100.0%**
Under $20,000	21.53	40	9.2
$20,000 to $39,999	70.96	132	32.3
$40,000 to $49,999	38.24	71	7.0
$50,000 to $69,999	26.62	50	7.2
$70,000 to $79,999	31.19	58	3.3
$80,000 to $99,999	81.14	151	12.2
$100,000 or more	111.76	208	30.6
HOUSEHOLD TYPE			
Average household	**53.67**	**100**	**100.0**
Married couples	53.32	99	50.2
Married couples, no children	59.03	110	23.7
Married couples, with children	51.85	97	24.3
Oldest child under 6	30.82	57	2.8
Oldest child 6 to 17	61.04	114	15.0
Oldest child 18 or older	48.90	91	6.5
Single parent with child under 18	16.30	30	1.8
Single person	57.68	107	31.4
RACE AND HISPANIC ORIGIN			
Average household	**53.67**	**100**	**100.0**
Asian	59.01	110	4.0
Black	12.52	23	2.8
Hispanic	26.26	49	5.2
Non-Hispanic white and other	63.61	119	91.9
REGION			
Average household	**53.67**	**100**	**100.0**
Northeast	30.64	57	10.9
Midwest	43.87	82	18.8
South	51.75	96	34.6
West	86.33	161	35.5
EDUCATION			
Average household	**53.67**	**100**	**100.0**
Less than high school graduate	19.33	36	5.5
High school graduate	28.49	53	13.7
Some college	49.88	93	20.0
Associate's degree	83.51	156	15.4
College graduate	88.20	164	44.9
Bachelor's degree	92.63	173	29.8
Master's, professional, doctoral degree	79.43	148	14.9

Note: Market shares may not sum to 100.0 because of rounding and missing categories by household type. "Asian" and "black" include Hispanics and non-Hispanics who identify themselves as being of the respective race alone. "Hispanic" includes people of any race who identify themselves as Hispanic. "Other" includes people who identify themselves as non-Hispanic and as Alaska Native, American Indian, Asian (who are also included in the "Asian" row), Native Hawaiian or other Pacific Islander, as well as non-Hispanics reporting more than one race.
Source: Calculations by New Strategist based on the Bureau of Labor Statistics' 2005 Consumer Expenditure Survey

Security System Service Fees

Best customers:

Householders aged 35 to 74
Married couples
Asians and Blacks
Households in the South

Customer trends:

Average household spending on home security system service fees should rise along with the aging of the population.

The best customers of home security system service fees are middle-aged or older married couples. Householders aged 35 to 74 spend 6 to 24 percent more than average on this item. Married couples spend 33 percent more than average on this item, with the figure peaking among couples with preschoolers at 89 percent above average. Asian households spend 36 percent more than average on home security system service fees, and blacks spend 15 percent more. Households in the South spend 34 percent more than average on this item.

Average household spending on home security system service fees fell 22 percent between 2000 and 2005, after adjusting for inflation. Average household spending on home security system service fees should rise along with the aging of the population.

Table 66. Security system service fees

Total household spending $1,934,026,880.00
Average household spends   16.48

AGE OF HOUSEHOLDER	AVERAGE HOUSEHOLD SPENDING	BEST CUSTOMERS (index)	BIGGEST CUSTOMERS (market share)
Average household	$16.48	100	100.0%
Under age 25	5.40	33	2.4
Aged 25 to 34	14.19	86	14.4
Aged 35 to 44	18.61	113	22.9
Aged 45 to 54	17.55	106	22.1
Aged 55 to 64	20.45	124	19.1
Aged 65 to 74	19.48	118	11.6
Aged 75 or older	12.65	77	7.4

	AVERAGE HOUSEHOLD SPENDING	BEST CUSTOMERS (index)	BIGGEST CUSTOMERS (market share)
HOUSEHOLD INCOME			
Average household	**$16.48**	**100**	**100.0%**
Under $20,000	4.89	30	6.8
$20,000 to $39,999	10.38	63	15.4
$40,000 to $49,999	14.47	88	8.6
$50,000 to $69,999	15.97	97	14.0
$70,000 to $79,999	14.58	88	5.1
$80,000 to $99,999	27.42	166	13.4
$100,000 or more	41.27	250	36.8
HOUSEHOLD TYPE			
Average household	**16.48**	**100**	**100.0**
Married couples	21.85	133	67.0
Married couples, no children	22.29	135	29.2
Married couples, with children	21.55	131	32.9
Oldest child under 6	31.10	189	9.1
Oldest child 6 to 17	19.39	118	15.5
Oldest child 18 or older	19.11	116	8.3
Single parent with child under 18	9.80	59	3.5
Single person	11.52	70	20.5
RACE AND HISPANIC ORIGIN			
Average household	**16.48**	**100**	**100.0**
Asian	22.36	136	5.0
Black	18.96	115	13.8
Hispanic	10.89	66	7.0
Non-Hispanic white and other	16.84	102	79.2
REGION			
Average household	**16.48**	**100**	**100.0**
Northeast	13.92	84	16.1
Midwest	11.09	67	15.5
South	22.07	134	48.1
West	15.21	92	20.3
EDUCATION			
Average household	**16.48**	**100**	**100.0**
Less than high school graduate	3.88	24	3.6
High school graduate	10.89	66	17.1
Some college	13.33	81	17.4
Associate's degree	19.92	121	11.9
College graduate	30.11	183	49.9
Bachelor's degree	26.49	161	27.7
Master's, professional, doctoral degree	36.29	220	22.2

Note: Market shares may not sum to 100.0 because of rounding and missing categories by household type. "Asian" and "black" include Hispanics and non-Hispanics who identify themselves as being of the respective race alone. "Hispanic" includes people of any race who identify themselves as Hispanic. "Other" includes people who identify themselves as non-Hispanic and as Alaska Native, American Indian, Asian (who are also included in the "Asian" row), Native Hawaiian or other Pacific Islander, as well as non-Hispanics reporting more than one race.
Source: Calculations by New Strategist based on the Bureau of Labor Statistics' 2005 Consumer Expenditure Survey

Sewing Materials for Household Items

Best customers:	**Householders aged 45 to 74** **Married couples without children at home** **Married couples with school-aged or older children**
Customer trends:	**Average household spending on sewing materials for household items may continue to fall as the baby-boom generation, with fewer sewing skills, enters the best-customer age groups.**

Sewing is becoming a lost art, with younger generations of women much less knowledgeable about sewing than older women. The best customers of sewing materials for household items—such as slipcovers and curtains—are householders aged 45 to 74. This age group spends 26 to 69 percent more than average on sewing materials for household items. Married couples without children at home (most of them empty-nesters) spend 84 percent more than average on sewing materials. Those with school-aged or older children at home spend 33 to 44 percent more than the average on this item.

Average household spending on sewing materials for household items fell 9 percent between 2000 and 2005, after adjusting for inflation. Average household spending on sewing materials for household items may continue to fall as boomers fill the best-customer age group.

Table 67. Sewing materials for household items

Total household spending	$1,184,122,040.00
Average household spends	10.09

	AVERAGE HOUSEHOLD SPENDING	BEST CUSTOMERS (index)	BIGGEST CUSTOMERS (market share)
AGE OF HOUSEHOLDER			
Average household	**$10.09**	**100**	**100.0%**
Under age 25	2.84	28	2.0
Aged 25 to 34	4.91	49	8.1
Aged 35 to 44	7.34	73	14.8
Aged 45 to 54	14.23	141	29.3
Aged 55 to 64	17.08	169	26.1
Aged 65 to 74	12.68	126	12.3
Aged 75 or older	7.60	75	7.3

	AVERAGE HOUSEHOLD SPENDING	BEST CUSTOMERS (index)	BIGGEST CUSTOMERS (market share)
HOUSEHOLD INCOME			
Average household	**$10.09**	**100**	**100.0%**
Under $20,000	4.96	49	11.3
$20,000 to $39,999	6.76	67	16.4
$40,000 to $49,999	7.57	75	7.3
$50,000 to $69,999	10.30	102	14.7
$70,000 to $79,999	11.80	117	6.7
$80,000 to $99,999	15.74	156	12.6
$100,000 or more	21.31	211	31.0
HOUSEHOLD TYPE			
Average household	**10.09**	**100**	**100.0**
Married couples	15.05	149	75.4
Married couples, no children	18.57	184	39.7
Married couples, with children	12.90	128	32.2
Oldest child under 6	7.81	77	3.7
Oldest child 6 to 17	14.49	144	18.9
Oldest child 18 or older	13.39	133	9.5
Single parent with child under 18	2.85	28	1.7
Single person	5.46	54	15.8
RACE AND HISPANIC ORIGIN			
Average household	**10.09**	**100**	**100.0**
Asian	8.36	83	3.0
Black	2.38	24	2.8
Hispanic	3.06	30	3.2
Non-Hispanic white and other	12.23	121	94.0
REGION			
Average household	**10.09**	**100**	**100.0**
Northeast	8.48	84	16.0
Midwest	13.22	131	30.1
South	6.57	65	23.4
West	13.94	138	30.5
EDUCATION			
Average household	**10.09**	**100**	**100.0**
Less than high school graduate	2.90	29	4.4
High school graduate	7.31	72	18.8
Some college	11.65	115	24.9
Associate's degree	10.77	107	10.5
College graduate	15.28	151	41.4
Bachelor's degree	13.52	134	23.1
Master's, professional, doctoral degree	18.30	181	18.3

Note: Market shares may not sum to 100.0 because of rounding and missing categories by household type. "Asian" and "black" include Hispanics and non-Hispanics who identify themselves as being of the respective race alone. "Hispanic" includes people of any race who identify themselves as Hispanic. "Other" includes people who identify themselves as non-Hispanic and as Alaska Native, American Indian, Asian (who are also included in the "Asian" row), Native Hawaiian or other Pacific Islander, as well as non-Hispanics reporting more than one race.
Source: Calculations by New Strategist based on the Bureau of Labor Statistics' 2005 Consumer Expenditure Survey

Sofas

Best customers: **Householders aged 25 to 44**
                          Married couples

Customer trends: **Average household spending on sofas may fall as boomers exit the best-customer lifestage unless empty-nesters boost their spending on redecorating their homes.**

Sofas are the fourth largest home furnishings expense for the average household, following only major appliances, decorative items, and laundry and cleaning supplies. The best customers of sofas are young and middle-aged married couples outfitting their home for expanding families. Householders aged 25 to 44 spend 15 to 28 percent more than average on sofas. Married couples spend 37 percent more, with spending peaking at 51 percent above average among couples with school-aged children.

Average household spending on sofas climbed 6 percent between 2000 and 2005, after adjusting for inflation. This increase occurred despite the large baby-boom generation's exit from the best-customer lifestage. Average household spending on sofas may fall in the years ahead unless empty-nest boomers decide to spend more on redecorating their homes.

Table 68. Sofas

Total household spending $12,546,529,960.00
Average household spends   106.91

AGE OF HOUSEHOLDER	AVERAGE HOUSEHOLD SPENDING	BEST CUSTOMERS (index)	BIGGEST CUSTOMERS (market share)
Average household	$106.91	100	100.0%
Under age 25	93.46	87	6.4
Aged 25 to 34	122.56	115	19.2
Aged 35 to 44	136.68	128	26.0
Aged 45 to 54	100.29	94	19.5
Aged 55 to 64	114.64	107	16.5
Aged 65 to 74	95.35	89	8.7
Aged 75 or older	40.96	38	3.7

	AVERAGE HOUSEHOLD SPENDING	BEST CUSTOMERS (index)	BIGGEST CUSTOMERS (market share)
HOUSEHOLD INCOME			
Average household	**$106.91**	**100**	**100.0%**
Under $20,000	38.25	36	8.2
$20,000 to $39,999	51.31	48	11.7
$40,000 to $49,999	94.63	89	8.6
$50,000 to $69,999	85.85	80	11.6
$70,000 to $79,999	110.28	103	5.9
$80,000 to $99,999	140.76	132	10.6
$100,000 or more	315.25	295	43.3
HOUSEHOLD TYPE			
Average household	**106.91**	**100**	**100.0**
Married couples	146.45	137	69.3
Married couples, no children	149.01	139	30.0
Married couples, with children	146.59	137	34.5
Oldest child under 6	138.80	130	6.3
Oldest child 6 to 17	161.21	151	19.9
Oldest child 18 or older	124.88	117	8.4
Single parent with child under 18	87.18	82	4.8
Single person	48.44	45	13.3
RACE AND HISPANIC ORIGIN			
Average household	**106.91**	**100**	**100.0**
Asian	125.52	117	4.3
Black	81.14	76	9.1
Hispanic	106.16	99	10.5
Non-Hispanic white and other	110.82	104	80.4
REGION			
Average household	**106.91**	**100**	**100.0**
Northeast	88.38	83	15.7
Midwest	81.99	77	17.6
South	101.37	95	34.0
West	157.93	148	32.6
EDUCATION			
Average household	**106.91**	**100**	**100.0**
Less than high school graduate	62.26	58	8.9
High school graduate	74.03	69	17.9
Some college	122.26	114	24.6
Associate's degree	133.61	125	12.3
College graduate	141.41	132	36.1
Bachelor's degree	143.58	134	23.2
Master's, professional, doctoral degree	137.69	129	13.0

Note: Market shares may not sum to 100.0 because of rounding and missing categories by household type. "Asian" and "black" include Hispanics and non-Hispanics who identify themselves as being of the respective race alone. "Hispanic" includes people of any race who identify themselves as Hispanic. "Other" includes people who identify themselves as non-Hispanic and as Alaska Native, American Indian, Asian (who are also included in the "Asian" row), Native Hawaiian or other Pacific Islander, as well as non-Hispanics reporting more than one race.
Source: Calculations by New Strategist based on the Bureau of Labor Statistics' 2005 Consumer Expenditure Survey

Stationery, Stationery Supplies, and Giftwrap

Best customers: Householders aged 35 to 64
Married couples

Customer trends: Average household spending on stationery and giftwrap is likely to stabilize in the years ahead as the small generation X enters the best-customer age groups.

The biggest spenders on the discretionary category of stationery, stationery supplies, and giftwrap are middle-aged married couples. These households are the best customers of giftwrap because of their extended families and large network of friends. Householders aged 35 to 64 spend 16 to 25 percent more than average on this item, controlling nearly 70 percent of the market. Married couples spend 35 percent more than average on this item, with spending peaking at 63 percent above average among couples with school-aged children.

Average household spending on stationery, stationery supplies, and giftwrap increased by 18 percent between 2000 and 2005, after adjusting for inflation. Average household spending on stationery and giftwrap is likely to stabilize in the years ahead as the small generation X enters the best-customer age groups.

Table 69. Stationery, stationery supplies, and giftwrap

Total household spending $10,006,946,120.00
Average household spends   85.27

	AVERAGE HOUSEHOLD SPENDING	BEST CUSTOMERS (index)	BIGGEST CUSTOMERS (market share)
AGE OF HOUSEHOLDER			
Average household	**$85.27**	**100**	**100.0%**
Under age 25	36.34	43	3.1
Aged 25 to 34	77.23	91	15.2
Aged 35 to 44	106.38	125	25.3
Aged 45 to 54	98.67	116	24.1
Aged 55 to 64	106.09	124	19.2
Aged 65 to 74	78.32	92	9.0
Aged 75 or older	39.74	47	4.5

	AVERAGE HOUSEHOLD SPENDING	BEST CUSTOMERS (index)	BIGGEST CUSTOMERS (market share)
HOUSEHOLD INCOME			
Average household	**$85.27**	**100**	**100.0%**
Under $20,000	29.61	35	8.0
$20,000 to $39,999	52.12	61	14.9
$40,000 to $49,999	68.79	81	7.9
$50,000 to $69,999	93.91	110	15.9
$70,000 to $79,999	86.25	101	5.8
$80,000 to $99,999	147.92	173	14.0
$100,000 or more	182.86	214	31.5
HOUSEHOLD TYPE			
Average household	**85.27**	**100**	**100.0**
Married couples	114.98	135	68.2
Married couples, no children	108.48	127	27.4
Married couples, with children	125.08	147	36.9
Oldest child under 6	123.72	145	7.0
Oldest child 6 to 17	139.39	163	21.6
Oldest child 18 or older	97.62	114	8.2
Single parent with child under 18	53.51	63	3.7
Single person	41.97	49	14.4
RACE AND HISPANIC ORIGIN			
Average household	**85.27**	**100**	**100.0**
Asian	62.34	73	2.7
Black	37.25	44	5.2
Hispanic	54.76	64	6.8
Non-Hispanic white and other	96.52	113	87.8
REGION			
Average household	**85.27**	**100**	**100.0**
Northeast	117.83	138	26.3
Midwest	89.23	105	24.1
South	63.57	75	26.8
West	88.51	104	22.9
EDUCATION			
Average household	**85.27**	**100**	**100.0**
Less than high school graduate	31.80	37	5.7
High school graduate	67.19	79	20.4
Some college	67.90	80	17.2
Associate's degree	71.47	84	8.3
College graduate	145.96	171	46.8
Bachelor's degree	121.08	142	24.5
Master's, professional, doctoral degree	195.15	229	23.1

Note: Market shares may not sum to 100.0 because of rounding and missing categories by household type. "Asian" and "black" include Hispanics and non-Hispanics who identify themselves as being of the respective race alone. "Hispanic" includes people of any race who identify themselves as Hispanic. "Other" includes people who identify themselves as non-Hispanic and as Alaska Native, American Indian, Asian (who are also included in the "Asian" row), Native Hawaiian or other Pacific Islander, as well as non-Hispanics reporting more than one race.
Source: Calculations by New Strategist based on the Bureau of Labor Statistics' 2005 Consumer Expenditure Survey

Termite and Pest Control Products and Services

Best customers: Householders aged 45 or older
                               Married couples without children at home
                               Married couples with school-aged or older children
                               Households in the South and West

Customer trends: Average household spending on termite and pest control will increase as the
                               Sunbelt population expands.

The best customers of termite and pest control products and services are older householders in the South, spending 50 percent more than average on this item and controlling 54 percent of the market. Households in the West spend 27 percent more. Insect problems are greater in the South and West than in the Midwest or Northeast because of the warmer climate. Householders aged 45 or older spend 8 to 42 percent more than average on this item. Married couples without children at home (most of them older) spend 59 percent more than average on termite and pest control, while those with school-aged or older children at home spend 56 to 74 percent more.

Average household spending on termite and pest control rose by a substantial 25 percent between 2000 and 2005, after adjusting for inflation. Behind the increase was the growing population of the South and West, where these services are often necessary. Spending on termite and pest control will continue to rise as the Sunbelt population grows.

Table 70. Termite and pest control products and services

Total household spending	$2,088,936,800.00
Average household spends	17.80

	AVERAGE HOUSEHOLD SPENDING	BEST CUSTOMERS (index)	BIGGEST CUSTOMERS (market share)
AGE OF HOUSEHOLDER			
Average household	**$17.80**	**100**	**100.0%**
Under age 25	2.67	15	1.1
Aged 25 to 34	11.43	64	10.7
Aged 35 to 44	17.20	97	19.6
Aged 45 to 54	20.94	118	24.5
Aged 55 to 64	25.32	142	21.9
Aged 65 to 74	21.26	119	11.7
Aged 75 or older	19.21	108	10.4

	AVERAGE HOUSEHOLD SPENDING	BEST CUSTOMERS (index)	BIGGEST CUSTOMERS (market share)
HOUSEHOLD INCOME			
Average household	**$17.80**	**100**	**100.0%**
Under $20,000	5.59	31	7.2
$20,000 to $39,999	10.93	61	15.0
$40,000 to $49,999	12.10	68	6.6
$50,000 to $69,999	16.73	94	13.6
$70,000 to $79,999	20.13	113	6.5
$80,000 to $99,999	31.44	177	14.2
$100,000 or more	44.66	251	36.9
HOUSEHOLD TYPE			
Average household	**17.80**	**100**	**100.0**
Married couples	26.36	148	74.9
Married couples, no children	28.26	159	34.2
Married couples, with children	27.25	153	38.5
Oldest child under 6	16.54	93	4.5
Oldest child 6 to 17	30.91	174	22.9
Oldest child 18 or older	27.73	156	11.1
Single parent with child under 18	6.21	35	2.1
Single person	9.26	52	15.2
RACE AND HISPANIC ORIGIN			
Average household	**17.80**	**100**	**100.0**
Asian	13.86	78	2.8
Black	7.31	41	4.9
Hispanic	9.50	53	5.7
Non-Hispanic white and other	20.52	115	89.4
REGION			
Average household	**17.80**	**100**	**100.0**
Northeast	7.56	42	8.1
Midwest	7.86	44	10.2
South	26.69	150	53.8
West	22.52	127	27.9
EDUCATION			
Average household	**17.80**	**100**	**100.0**
Less than high school graduate	5.19	29	4.5
High school graduate	11.26	63	16.4
Some college	14.37	81	17.4
Associate's degree	21.08	118	11.7
College graduate	32.60	183	50.0
Bachelor's degree	30.38	171	29.4
Master's, professional, doctoral degree	36.39	204	20.6

Note: Market shares may not sum to 100.0 because of rounding and missing categories by household type. "Asian" and "black" include Hispanics and non-Hispanics who identify themselves as being of the respective race alone. "Hispanic" includes people of any race who identify themselves as Hispanic. "Other" includes people who identify themselves as non-Hispanic and as Alaska Native, American Indian, Asian (who are also included in the "Asian" row), Native Hawaiian or other Pacific Islander, as well as non-Hispanics reporting more than one race.
Source: Calculations by New Strategist based on the Bureau of Labor Statistics' 2005 Consumer Expenditure Survey

Wall Units, Cabinets, and Other Furniture

Best customers:	**Householders aged 35 to 74**
	High-income households
	Married couples
Customer trends:	**Average household spending on wall units should continue to rise in the years ahead as boomers fill the best-customer age groups.**

The biggest spenders on wall units, cabinets, and other furniture are affluent, middle-aged married couples. Householders ranging in age from 35 to 74 spend 6 to 32 percent more than the average household on this item. Households with incomes of $100,000 or more spend more than three times the average on wall units, controlling 47 percent of the market. Married couples spend 45 percent more than average on wall units, with spending peaking at 93 percent above average among couples with school-aged children.

Average household spending on wall units, cabinets, and other furniture rose 8 percent between 2000 and 2005, after adjusting for inflation. Behind the gain was the purchasing of wall units to house new HDTVs. Average household spending on wall units should continue to rise in the years ahead as boomers fill the best-customer age groups.

Table 71. Wall units, cabinets, and other furniture

Total household spending	$7,265,509,960.00
Average household spends	61.91

	AVERAGE HOUSEHOLD SPENDING	BEST CUSTOMERS (index)	BIGGEST CUSTOMERS (market share)
AGE OF HOUSEHOLDER			
Average household	**$61.91**	**100**	**100.0%**
Under age 25	25.17	41	3.0
Aged 25 to 34	57.48	93	15.5
Aged 35 to 44	81.58	132	26.8
Aged 45 to 54	68.57	111	23.0
Aged 55 to 64	76.15	123	19.0
Aged 65 to 74	65.77	106	10.4
Aged 75 or older	14.92	24	2.3

	AVERAGE HOUSEHOLD SPENDING	BEST CUSTOMERS (index)	BIGGEST CUSTOMERS (market share)
HOUSEHOLD INCOME			
Average household	**$61.91**	**100**	**100.0%**
Under $20,000	16.79	27	6.2
$20,000 to $39,999	33.97	55	13.4
$40,000 to $49,999	36.43	59	5.7
$50,000 to $69,999	39.24	63	9.2
$70,000 to $79,999	64.65	104	6.0
$80,000 to $99,999	93.23	151	12.1
$100,000 or more	199.62	322	47.4
HOUSEHOLD TYPE			
Average household	**61.91**	**100**	**100.0**
Married couples	89.82	145	73.4
Married couples, no children	74.66	121	26.0
Married couples, with children	100.47	162	40.8
Oldest child under 6	86.46	140	6.7
Oldest child 6 to 17	119.22	193	25.4
Oldest child 18 or older	75.35	122	8.7
Single parent with child under 18	36.62	59	3.5
Single person	28.73	46	13.6
RACE AND HISPANIC ORIGIN			
Average household	**61.91**	**100**	**100.0**
Asian	33.08	53	2.0
Black	34.31	55	6.6
Hispanic	57.19	92	9.8
Non-Hispanic white and other	66.76	108	83.6
REGION			
Average household	**61.91**	**100**	**100.0**
Northeast	60.63	98	18.7
Midwest	50.92	82	18.9
South	57.73	93	33.5
West	81.28	131	28.9
EDUCATION			
Average household	**61.91**	**100**	**100.0**
Less than high school graduate	26.13	42	6.5
High school graduate	42.72	69	17.9
Some college	68.67	111	23.9
Associate's degree	53.23	86	8.5
College graduate	98.01	158	43.3
Bachelor's degree	83.59	135	23.3
Master's, professional, doctoral degree	122.68	198	20.0

Note: Market shares may not sum to 100.0 because of rounding and missing categories by household type. "Asian" and "black" include Hispanics and non-Hispanics who identify themselves as being of the respective race alone. "Hispanic" includes people of any race who identify themselves as Hispanic. "Other" includes people who identify themselves as non-Hispanic and as Alaska Native, American Indian, Asian (who are also included in the "Asian" row), Native Hawaiian or other Pacific Islander, as well as non-Hispanics reporting more than one race.
Source: Calculations by New Strategist based on the Bureau of Labor Statistics' 2005 Consumer Expenditure Survey

Appendix: Spending by Product and Service Ranked by Amount Spent, 2005

(average annual spending of consumer units on products and services, ranked by amount spent, 2005)

1.	Deductions for Social Security	$3,652.81
2.	Vehicle purchases (net outlay)	3,543.95
3.	Groceries (also shown by individual category)	3,296.88
4.	Mortgage interest (or rent, $2,270.86)	3,079.05
5.	Restaurants (also shown by meal category)	2,183.86
6.	Gasoline and motor oil	2,013.32
7.	Federal income taxes	1,696.16
8.	Property taxes	1,540.62
9.	Health insurance	1,360.74
10.	Electricity	1,154.97
11.	Dinner at restaurants	1,039.81
12.	Vehicle insurance	913.35
13.	Lunch at restaurants	760.84
14.	Cash contributions to church, religious organizations	706.81
15.	Vehicle maintenance and repairs	671.34
16.	Women's clothes	632.81
17.	Deductions for private pensions	612.16
18.	Maintenance and repair services, owned home	591.75
19.	Residential phone service	570.06
20.	College tuition	564.10
21.	State and local income taxes	534.32
22.	Cable TV and community antenna	518.94
23.	Natural gas	473.45
24.	Non-payroll deposit to retirement plans	468.50
25.	Cellular phone service	454.83
26.	Alcoholic beverages (beer and wine also shown separately)	426.32
27.	Drugs, prescription	405.19
28.	Life and other personal insurance	381.07
29.	Men's clothes	348.63
30.	Cash gifts to people in other households	331.93
31.	Homeowners insurance	329.05
32.	Vehicle finance charges	296.75
33.	Lodging on trips	293.77
34.	Cigarettes	292.16
35.	Airline fares	284.79
36.	Personal care services	267.57
37.	Water and sewerage maintenance	260.69
38.	Dental services	254.33
39.	Interest paid, home equity loan or line of credit	237.52
40.	Leased vehicles	237.03
41.	Restaurant meals on trips	236.49
42.	Beef	227.69
43.	Day care centers, nursery, and preschools	225.01
44.	Breakfast at restaurants	207.61
45.	Cash contributions to charities and other organizations	200.26
46.	Child support expenditures	195.84
47.	Decorative items for the home	189.76
48.	Finance charges other than mortgage and vehicle	188.95
49.	Fresh fruits	181.55
50.	Taxes except federal, state, local, personal property, and property	177.10
51.	Elementary and high school tuition	176.56
52.	Snacks at restaurants	175.59
53.	Fresh vegetables	174.70
54.	Expenses for other properties	161.65
55.	Movie, theater, opera, ballet tickets	155.94
56.	Computer information services	153.94

57.	Physician's services	$153.87
58.	Pork	153.31
59.	Motorized recreational vehicles	151.60
60.	Women's footwear	148.95
61.	Computers and computer hardware nonbusiness use	147.96
62.	Owned vacation homes	146.31
63.	Jewelry	140.70
64.	Prepared foods except frozen, salads, and desserts	135.10
65.	Poultry	134.36
66.	Laundry and cleaning supplies	134.13
67.	Carbonated drinks	132.74
68.	Cosmetics, perfume, bath preparations	132.31
69.	Pet food	132.24
70.	Fresh milk	130.74
71.	Social, recreation, civic club membership	124.79
72.	Legal fees	124.73
73.	Girls' (aged 2 to 15) clothes	120.82
74.	Beer and ale at home	119.50
75.	Cheese	114.27
76.	Fish and seafood	113.42
77.	Television sets	112.26
78.	Sofas	106.91
79.	Fees for participant sports	106.37
80.	Trash and garbage collection	100.84
81.	Men's footwear	99.34
82.	Gardening, lawn care service	95.73
83.	Cleansing and toilet tissue, paper towels and napkins	94.91
84.	Hospital room and services	94.44
85.	Lawn and garden supplies	94.26
86.	Bedroom furniture except mattress and springs	93.86
87.	Housekeeping services	92.14
88.	Potato chips and other snacks	91.84
89.	Support for college students	91.71
90.	Boys' (aged 2 to 15) clothes	91.11
91.	Veterinary services	89.43
92.	Vehicle registration state	89.14
93.	Fees for recreational lessons	88.77
94.	Ready-to-eat and cooked cereals	88.14
95.	Toys, games, arts and crafts, and tricycles	88.05
96.	Frozen prepared foods, except meals	86.92
97.	Athletic gear, game tables, and exercise equipment	86.88
98.	Deductions for government retirement	85.92
99.	Stationery, stationery supplies, giftwraps	85.27
100.	Maintenance and repair materials, owned home	82.96
101.	Children under age 2 clothes	82.31
102.	Fuel oil	80.82
103.	Nonalcoholic beverages (except carbonated, coffee, fruit-flavored drinks, and tea) and ice	80.59
104.	Beer and ale at bars, restaurants	79.06
105.	Wine at home	77.07
106.	Lotteries and gambling losses	76.70
107.	Catered affairs	76.67
108.	Candy and chewing gum	74.99
109.	Lunch meats (cold cuts)	73.99
110.	Drugs, nonprescription	72.04
111.	School lunches	71.60
112.	Babysitting and child care	70.25
113.	Pet purchase, supplies, medicine	70.05
114.	Unmotored recreational vehicles	68.55
115.	Postage	67.89
116.	Bedroom linens	65.03
117.	School books, supplies, equipment for college	63.90
118.	Funeral expenses	62.95
119.	Ice cream products	62.14
120.	Wall units, cabinets, and other occasional furniture	61.91

121.	Admission to sporting events	$61.91
122.	Housing while attending school	61.73
123.	Refrigerators, freezers	60.91
124.	Professional laundry and dry cleaning	60.68
125.	Mattress and springs	57.86
126.	Books	57.43
127.	Alimony expenditures	56.13
128.	Accounting fees	55.09
129.	Eyeglasses and contact lenses	54.10
130.	Power tools	53.67
131.	Canned and bottled fruit juice	53.55
132.	Bread, other than white	52.87
133.	Living room chairs	52.57
134.	Newspaper and magazine subscriptions	52.56
135.	Bottled gas	52.45
136.	Intracity mass transit fares	51.51
137.	Service by professionals other than physician	51.45
138.	Lawn and garden equipment	50.96
139.	Kitchen, dining room furniture	50.19
140.	Recreational expenses on trips	50.16
141.	Hair care products	49.65
142.	Cookies	48.80
143.	Coffee	48.52
144.	Sauces and gravies	46.53
145.	Indoor plants, fresh flowers	45.53
146.	Video cassettes, tapes, and discs	45.27
147.	Vitamins, nonprescription	43.96
148.	Ground rent	43.26
149.	Lab tests, x-rays	43.20
150.	Frozen meals	42.82
151.	Occupational expenses	42.40
152.	School expenses and supplies (except tuition, books)	42.22
153.	Ship fares	41.82
154.	Alcoholic beverages purchased on trips	41.80
155.	Cooking stoves, ovens	41.49
156.	Groceries on trips	41.34
157.	Biscuits and rolls	41.23
158.	Canned and packaged soups	40.80
159.	Rented vehicles	39.19
160.	Food or board at school	39.00
161.	Rent as pay	38.68
162.	Compact discs, records, and audio tapes	38.09
163.	Cash contribution to educational institutions	37.46
164.	Coin-operated apparel laundry and dry cleaning	37.33
165.	Photographic equipment and supplies (except film)	37.31
166.	Boys' footwear	37.29
167.	Canned vegetables	36.93
168.	Eyecare services	36.74
169.	Moving, storage, freight express	36.44
170.	Wine at bars, restaurants	36.42
171.	Girls' footwear	34.63
172.	Gift of stocks, bonds, and mutual funds to people in other households	34.18
173.	Cakes and cupcakes	33.29
174.	Window coverings	33.13
175.	School tuition (except college, elementary, high school)	33.10
176.	Rental of video cassettes, tapes, discs, films	32.64
177.	Eggs	32.61
178.	Property management, owner	32.58
179.	Prepared salads	32.39
180.	Washing machines	32.27
181.	White bread	32.04
182.	Parking fees, except at own home	31.81
183.	Musical instruments and accessories	31.72
184.	Crackers	31.50
185.	Telephones and accessories	31.18

186.	Pet services	$30.65
187.	Nuts	30.08
188.	Floor coverings, nonpermanent	29.87
189.	Baby food	29.80
190.	Video game hardware and software	29.78
191.	Deodorants, feminine hygiene, miscellaneous personal care	29.51
192.	Topicals and dressings	29.26
193.	Outdoor equipment	28.69
194.	Hunting and fishing equipment	28.27
195.	Oral hygiene products	28.24
196.	Frozen vegetables	28.02
197.	Fats and oils	27.77
198.	Care in convalescent or nursing home	27.38
199.	Meals as pay	26.78
200.	Salad dressings	26.58
201.	Wall-to-wall carpeting	26.34
202.	Sound equipment	25.56
203.	Care for elderly, invalids, handicapped, etc	24.79
204.	Electric floor cleaning equipment	24.70
205.	Frozen and refrigerated bakery products	24.42
206.	Taxi fares and limousine services	24.41
207.	Tobacco products except cigarettes	24.21
208.	Watches	23.63
209.	Tableware, nonelectric kitchenware	23.51
210.	Salt, spices, other seasonings	23.37
211.	Clothes dryers	22.94
212.	Jams, preserves, other sweets	22.91
213.	Baking needs	22.78
214.	Tea	22.78
215.	Pasta, cornmeal and other cereal products	21.93
216.	Bathroom linens	21.86
217.	Phone cards	21.08
218.	VCRs and video disc players	20.63
219.	Nonelectric cookware	20.50
220.	Sweetrolls, coffee cakes, doughnuts	20.47
221.	Frankfurters	20.27
222.	Photo processing	20.16
223.	Checking accounts, other bank service charges	20.08
224.	Photographer fees	19.86
225.	Computer software and accessories for nonbusiness use	19.70
226.	Lamps and lighting fixtures	19.67
227.	Butter	19.46
228.	Intercity train fares	19.41
229.	Tolls	18.92
230.	Small electric kitchen appliances	18.66
231.	Curtains and draperies	18.61
232.	Canned fruits	18.60
233.	Noncarbonated fruit-flavored drinks	18.12
234.	Outdoor furniture	18.02
235.	Automobile service clubs	17.87
236.	Living room tables	17.81
237.	Fresh fruit juice	16.79
238.	Dishwashers (built-in), garbage disposals, range hoods	16.49
239.	Home security system service fee	16.48
240.	Cemetery lots, vaults, maintenance fees	16.48
241.	Laundry and cleaning equipment	16.47
242.	Home maintenance and repair services, renter	16.35
243.	Rice	16.27
244.	Sugar	15.94
245.	Newspapers and magazines, nonsubscription	15.73
246.	Services for termite/pest control	15.55
247.	School books, supplies, equipment for elementary, high school	15.53
248.	Cream	15.20
249.	Shaving needs	14.84
250.	Appliance repair, including service center	14.47

251. Closet and storage items	$14.34
252. Bicycles	14.07
253. Infants' equipment	13.99
254. Security services, owned home	13.77
255. Personal digital audio players	13.39
256. Pies, tarts, turnovers	13.34
257. Prepared desserts	13.20
258. China and other dinnerware	13.06
259. Olives, pickles, relishes	12.96
260. Hearing aids	12.61
261. Intercity bus fares	12.10
262. Vegetable juice	11.93
263. Glassware	11.92
264. Dried vegetables	11.87
265. Prepared flour mixes	11.68
266. Peanut butter	11.43
267. Nondairy cream and imitation milk	11.32
268. Local transportation on out-of-town trips	11.27
269. Electric personal care appliances	11.12
270. Microwave ovens	10.77
271. Film	10.32
272. Maintenance and repair materials, renter	10.13
273. Sewing materials for slipcovers, curtains, other sewing materials for the home	10.09
274. Office furniture for home use	9.93
275. Vehicle inspection	9.76
276. Cash contribution to political organizations	8.97
277. Tenant's insurance	8.91
278. Lamb, organ and other meat	8.82
279. Camping equipment	8.77
280. Kitchen and dining room linens	8.63
281. Material for making clothes	8.62
282. Reupholstering, furniture repair	8.36
283. Coal, wood, and other fuels	8.31
284. Infants' furniture	8.30
285. Margarine	7.86
286. Shopping club membership fees	7.49
287. Drivers' license	7.43
288. Parking at owned home	7.38
289. Dried fruit	7.31
290. Slipcovers, decorative pillows	6.93
291. Luggage	6.88
292. Repairs/rentals of lawn and garden equipment, hand or power tools, other household equipment	6.50
293. Portable heating and cooling equipment	6.43
294. Stamp and coin collecting	6.36
295. Hand tools	6.22
296. Hair accessories	6.01
297. Docking and landing fees	5.73
298. Window air conditioners	5.66
299. Frozen fruit juice	5.64
300. Alteration, repair and tailoring of apparel and accessories	5.46
301. Sewing patterns and notions	5.28
302. Water sports equipment	5.03
303. Towing charges	5.01
304. Repair of computer systems for nonbusiness use	4.98
305. Clocks	4.95
306. Rental and repair of musical instruments	4.94
307. Artificial sweeteners	4.91
308. Flour	4.90
309. Silver serving pieces	4.84
310. Rental of recreational vehicles	4.54
311. Delivery services	4.27
312. Watch and jewelry repair	4.24
313. Septic tank cleaning	4.22
314. School books, supplies, equipment for day care, nursery, other	4.21

315.	Frozen fruits	$4.20
316.	Medical equipment for general use	4.19
317.	Bread and cracker products	4.15
318.	Water softening service	4.13
319.	Tape recorders and players	4.12
320.	Safe deposit box rental	4.09
321.	Internet services away from home	3.59
322.	Personal digital assistants	3.49
323.	Deductions for railroad retirement	3.44
324.	Supportive and convalescent medical equipment	3.43
325.	Fireworks	3.34
326.	Playground equipment	3.26
327.	Flatware	3.23
328.	Winter sports equipment	3.18
329.	Coin-operated laundry and dry cleaning (nonclothing)	3.12
330.	Sewing machines	3.10
331.	Radios	3.06
332.	Rental of furniture	3.01
333.	Repair of TV, radio, and sound equipment	2.98
334.	Business equipment for home use	2.85
335.	School bus	2.57
336.	Smoking accessories	2.41
337.	Streaming and downloading audio	2.34
338.	Termite/pest control products	2.25
339.	Rental and repair of miscellaneous sports equipment	2.22
340.	Clothing rental	2.17
341.	Credit card memberships	2.17
342.	Pinball, electronic video games	2.14
343.	Appliance rental	1.74
344.	Plastic dinnerware	1.72
345.	Wigs and hairpieces	1.72
346.	Pager service	1.66
347.	Global positioning services	1.46
348.	Shoe repair and other shoe service	1.33
349.	Telephone answering devices	1.20
350.	Smoke alarms	1.11
351.	Professional laundry and dry cleaning (nonclothing)	1.04
352.	Rental of medical equipment	0.84
353.	Rental of supportive, convalescent medical equipment	0.73
354.	Satellite dishes	0.72
355.	Clothing storage	0.59
356.	Portable dishwasher	0.57
357.	Streaming and downloading video	0.56
358.	Rental of television sets	0.54
359.	Repair and rental of photographic equipment	0.47
360.	Dating services	0.38
361.	Rental of VCR, radio, and sound equipment	0.28

Source: Calculations by New Strategist based on the 2005 Consumer Expenditure Survey

Glossary

alcoholic beverages Includes beer and ale, wine, whiskey, gin, vodka, rum, and other alcoholic beverages.

annual spending The annual amount spent per household. The Bureau of Labor Statistics calculates the annual average for all households in a segment, not just for those purchasing an item. The averages are calculated by integrating the results of the diary (weekly) and interview (quarterly) portions of the Consumer Expenditure Survey. For items purchased by most households—such as bread—average annual spending figures are a fairly accurate account of actual spending. For products and services purchased by few households during a year's time—such as cars—the average annual amount spent is much less than what purchasers spend. See the weekly and quarterly spending tables in each chapter for the percentage of consumer units reporting an expenditure during an average week or quarter and the amount spent by purchasers during the week or quarter. For more about the methodology of the Consumer Expenditure Survey, see Appendix A.

apparel, accessories, and related services Includes the following:

• *men's and boys' apparel* Includes coats, jackets, sweaters, vests, sport coats, tailored jackets, slacks, shorts and short sets, sportswear, shirts, underwear, nightwear, hosiery, uniforms, and other accessories.

• *women's and girls' apparel* Includes coats, jackets, furs, sport coats, tailored jackets, sweaters, vests, blouses, shirts, dresses, dungarees, culottes, slacks, shorts, sportswear, underwear, nightwear, uniforms, hosiery, and other accessories.

• *infants' apparel* Includes coats, jackets, snowsuits, underwear, diapers, dresses, crawlers, sleeping garments, hosiery, footwear, and other accessories for children.

• *footwear* Includes articles such as shoes, slippers, boots, and other similar items. It excludes footwear for babies and footwear used for sports such as bowling or golf shoes.

• *other apparel products and services* Includes material for making clothes, shoe repair, alterations and sewing patterns and notions, clothing rental, clothing storage, dry cleaning, sent-out laundry, watches, jewelry, and repairs to watches and jewelry.

cash contributions Includes cash contributed to persons or organizations outside the consumer unit including court-ordered alimony, child support payments, and support for college students, and contributions to religious, educational, charitable, or political organizations.

consumer unit Defined as follows:

• All members of a household who are related by blood, marriage, adoption, or other legal arrangements.

• A person living alone or sharing a household with others or living as a roomer in a private home or lodging house or in permanent living quarters in a hotel or motel, but who is financially independent.

• Two persons or more living together who pool their income to make joint expenditure decisions. Financial independence is determined by the three major expense categories: housing, food, and other living expenses. To be considered financially independent, at least two of the three major expense categories have to be provided by the respondent. For convenience, called households in the text of this report.

education Includes tuition, fees, books, supplies, and equipment for public and private nursery schools, elementary and high schools, colleges and universities, and other schools.

entertainment Includes the following:

• *fees and admissions* Includes fees for participant sports; admissions to sporting events, movies, concerts, plays; health, swimming, tennis, and country club memberships, and other social recreational and fraternal organizations; recreational lessons or instructions; and recreational expenses on trips.

• *audio and visual equipment and services* Includes televisions; radios; cable TV; tape recorders and players; video cassettes, tapes, and discs; VCRs and video disc players; video game hardware and software; personal digital audio players; streaming and downloading audio and video; sound components; CDs, records, and tapes; musical instruments; and rental and repair of TV and sound equipment.

• *pets, toys, hobbies, and playground equipment* Includes pet food, pet services, veterinary expenses, toys, games, hobbies, and playground equipment.

• *other entertainment equipment and services* Includes indoor exercise equipment, athletic shoes, bicycles, trailers, campers, camping equipment, rental of cameras and trailers, hunting and fishing equipment, sports equipment, winter sports equipment, water sports equipment, boats, boat motors and boat trailers, rental of boat, landing and docking fees, rental and repair of sports equipment, photographic equipment, film, photo processing, photographer fees, repair and rental of photo equipment, fireworks, pinball and electronic video games.

expenditure The transaction cost including excise and sales taxes of goods and services acquired during the survey period. The full cost of each purchase is recorded even though full payment may not have been made at the date of purchase. Expenditure estimates include gifts. Excluded from expenditures are purchases or portions of purchases directly assignable to business purposes and periodic credit or installment payments on goods and services already acquired.

federal income tax Includes federal income tax withheld in the survey year to pay for income earned in survey year plus additional tax paid in survey year to cover any underpayment or under withholding of tax in the year prior to the survey.

financial products and services Includes accounting fees, legal fees, union dues, professional dues and fees, other occupational expenses, funerals, cemetery lots, dating services, shopping club memberships, and unclassified fees and personal services.

food Includes the following:

• *food at home* Refers to the total expenditures for food at grocery stores or other food stores during the interview period. It is calculated by multiplying the number of visits to a grocery or other food store by the average amount spent per visit. It excludes the purchase of nonfood items.

• *food away from home* Includes all meals (breakfast, lunch, brunch, and dinner) at restaurants, carry-outs, and vending machines, including tips, plus meals as pay, special catered affairs such as weddings, bar mitzvahs, and confirmations, and meals away from home on trips.

gifts for people in other households Includes gift expenditures for people living in other consumer units. The amount spent on gifts is also included in individual product and service categories.

health care Includes the following:

• *health insurance* Includes health maintenance plans (HMOs), Blue Cross/Blue Shield, commercial health insurance, Medicare, Medicare supplemental insurance, long-term care insurance, and other health insurance.

• *medical services* Includes hospital room and services, physicians' services, services of a practitioner other than a physician, eye and dental care, lab tests, X-rays, nursing, therapy services, care in convalescent or nursing home, and other medical care.

• *drugs* Includes prescription and non-prescription drugs, internal and respiratory over-the-counter drugs.

• *medical supplies* Includes eyeglasses and contact lenses, topicals and dressings, antiseptics, bandages, cotton, first aid kits, contraceptives; medical equipment for general use such as syringes, ice bags, thermometers, vaporizers, heating pads; supportive or convalescent medical equipment such as hearing aids, braces, canes, crutches, and walkers.

household According to the Census Bureau, all the people who occupy a household. A group of unrelated people who share a housing unit as roommates or unmarried partners is also counted as a household. Households do not include group quarters such as college dormitories, prisons, or nursing homes. A household may contain more than one consumer unit. The terms "household" and "consumer unit" are used interchangeably in this report.

household furnishings and equipment Includes the following:

• *household textiles* Includes bathroom, kitchen, dining room, and other linens, curtains and drapes, slipcovers and decorative pillows, and sewing materials.

• *furniture* Includes living room, dining room, kitchen, bedroom, nursery, porch, lawn, and other outdoor furniture.

• *carpet, rugs, and other floor coverings* Includes installation and replacement of wall-to-wall carpets, room-size rugs, and other soft floor coverings.

• *major appliances* Includes refrigerators, freezers, dishwashers, stoves, ovens, garbage disposals, vacuum cleaners, microwaves, air-conditioners, sewing machines, washing machines and dryers, and floor cleaning equipment.

• *small appliances and miscellaneous housewares* Includes small electrical kitchen appliances, portable heating and cooling equipment, china and other dinnerware, flatware, glassware, silver and other serving pieces, nonelectric cookware, and plastic dinnerware. Excludes personal care appliances.

• *miscellaneous household equipment* Includes computer hardware and software, luggage, lamps and other lighting fixtures, window coverings, clocks, lawn mowers and gardening equipment, hand and power tools, telephone answering devices, personal digital assistants, Internet services away from home, office equipment for home use, fresh flowers and house plants, rental of furniture, closet and storage items, household decorative items, infants' equipment, outdoor equipment, smoke alarms, other household appliances and small miscellaneous furnishing.

household services Includes the following:

• *personal services* Includes baby sitting, day care, and care of elderly and handicapped persons.

• *other household services* Includes computer information services; housekeeping services; gardening and lawn care services; coin-operated laundry and dry-cleaning of household textiles; termite and pest control products; moving, storage, and freight expenses;

repair of household appliances and other household equipment; reupholstering and furniture repair; rental and repair of lawn and gardening tools; and rental of other household equipment.

housekeeping supplies Includes soaps, detergents, other laundry cleaning products, cleansing and toilet tissue, paper towels, napkins, and miscellaneous household products; lawn and garden supplies, postage, stationery, stationery supplies, and gift wrap.

income before taxes The total money earnings and selected money receipts accruing to a consumer unit during the 12 months prior to the interview date. Income includes the following components:

• *wages and salaries* Includes total money earnings for all members of the consumer unit aged 14 or older from all jobs, including civilian wages and salaries, Armed Forces pay and allowances, piece-rate payments, commissions, tips, National Guard or Reserve pay (received for training periods), and cash bonuses before deductions for taxes, pensions, union dues, etc.

• *self-employment income* Includes net business and farm income, which consists of net income (gross receipts minus operating expenses) from a profession or unincorporated business or from the operation of a farm by an owner, tenant, or sharecropper. If the business or farm is a partnership, only an appropriate share of net income is recorded. Losses are also recorded.

• *Social Security, private and government retirement* Includes the following: payments by the federal government made under retirement, survivor, and disability insurance programs to retired persons, dependents of deceased insured workers, or to disabled workers; and private pensions or retirement benefits received by retired persons or their survivors, either directly or through an insurance company.

• *interest, dividends, rental income, and other property income* Includes interest income on savings or bonds; payments made by a corporation to its stockholders, periodic receipts from estates or trust funds; net income or loss from the rental of property, real estate, or farms, and net income or loss from roomers or boarders.

• *unemployment and workers' compensation and veterans' benefits* Includes income from unemployment compensation and workers' compensation, and veterans' payments including educational benefits, but excluding military retirement.

• *public assistance, supplemental security income, and food stamps* Includes public assistance or welfare, including money received from job training grants; supplemental security income paid by federal, state, and local welfare agencies to low-income persons who are aged 65 or older, blind, or disabled; and the value of food stamps obtained.

• *regular contributions for support* Includes alimony and child support as well as any regular contributions from persons outside the consumer unit.

• *other income* Includes money income from care of foster children, cash scholarships, fellowships, or stipends not based on working; and meals and rent as pay.

indexed spending The indexed spending figures compare the spending of each demographic segment with that of the average household. To compute an index, the amount spent on an item by a demographic segment is divided by the amount spent on the item by the average household. That figure is then multiplied by 100. An index of 100 is the average for all households. An index of 132 means average spending by households in a segment is 32 percent above average (100 plus 32). An index of 75 means average spending by households in a segment is 25 percent below average (100 minus 25). Indexed spending figures identify the consumer units that spend the most on a product or service.

life and other personal insurance Includes premiums from whole life and term insurance; endowments; income and other life insurance; mortgage guarantee insurance; mortgage life insurance; premiums for personal life liability, accident and disability; and other non-health insurance other than homes and vehicles.

market share The market share is the percentage of total household spending on an item that is accounted for by a demographic segment. Market shares are calculated by dividing a demographic segment's total spending on an item by the total spending of all households on the item. Total spending on an item for all households is calculated by multiplying average spending by the total number of households. Total spending on an item for each demographic segment is calculated by multiplying the segment's average spending by the number of households in the segment. Market shares reveal the demographic segments that account for the largest share of spending on a product or service.

pensions and Social Security Includes all Social Security contributions paid by employees; employees' contributions to railroad retirement, government retirement and private pensions programs; retirement programs for self-employed.

personal care Includes products for the hair, oral hygiene products, shaving needs, cosmetics and bath products, suntan lotions and hand creams, electric personal care appliances, incontinence products, other personal care products, personal care services such as hair care services (haircuts, bleaching, tinting, coloring, conditioning treatments, permanents, press, and curls), styling and other services for wigs and hairpieces, body massages or slenderizing treatments, facials, manicures, pedicures, shaves, electrolysis.

quarterly spending Quarterly spending data are collected in the interview portion of the Consumer Expenditure Survey. The quarterly spending tables show the percentage of households purchasing an item during an average quarter, and the amount spent during the quarter on the item by purchasers. Not all items are included in the interview portion of the Consumer Expenditure Survey. For more about the methodology of the Consumer Expenditure Survey, see Appendix A.

reading Includes subscriptions for newspapers, magazines, and books through book clubs; purchase of single-copy newspapers and magazines, books, and encyclopedias and other reference books.

reference person The first member mentioned by the respondent when asked to "Start with the name of the person or one of the persons who owns or rents the home." It is with respect to this person that the relationship of other consumer unit members is determined. Also called the householder or head of household.

shelter Includes the following:

• *owned dwellings* Includes interest on mortgages, property taxes and insurance, refinancing and prepayment charges, ground rent, expenses for property management/security, homeowners' insurance, fire insurance and extended coverage, landscaping expenses for repairs and maintenance contracted out (including periodic maintenance and service contracts), and expenses of materials for owner-performed repairs and maintenance for dwellings used or maintained by the consumer unit, but not dwellings maintained for business or rent.

• *rented dwellings* Includes rent paid for dwellings, rent received as pay, parking fees, maintenance, and other expenses.

• *other lodging* Includes all expenses for vacation homes, school, college, hotels, motels, cottages, trailer camps, and other lodging while out of town.

• *utilities, fuels, and public services* Includes natural gas, electricity, fuel oil, coal, bottled gas, wood, and other fuels; residential telephone service; cell phone service; phone cards; water, garbage and trash collection; sewerage maintenance; septic tank cleaning; and other public services.

state and local income taxes Includes state and local income taxes withheld in the survey year to pay for income earned in survey year plus additional taxes paid in the survey year to cover any underpayment or under withholding of taxes in the year prior to the survey.

tobacco and smoking supplies Includes cigarettes, cigars, snuff, loose smoking tobacco, chewing tobacco, and smoking accessories such as cigarette or cigar holders, pipes, flints, lighters, pipe cleaners, and other smoking products and accessories.

transportation Includes the following:

• *vehicle purchases (net outlay)* Includes the net outlay (purchase price minus trade-in value) on new and used domestic and imported cars and trucks and other vehicles, including motorcycles and private planes.

• *gasoline and motor oil* Includes gasoline, diesel fuel, and motor oil.

• *other vehicle expenses* Includes vehicle finance charges, maintenance and repairs, vehicle insurance, and vehicle rental licenses and other charges.

• *vehicle finance charges* Includes the dollar amount of interest paid for a loan contracted for the purchase of vehicles described above.

• *maintenance and repairs* Includes tires, batteries, tubes, lubrication, filters, coolant, additives, brake and transmission fluids, oil change, brake adjustment and repair, front-end alignment, wheel balancing, steering repair, shock absorber replacement, clutch and transmission repair, electrical system repair, repair to cooling system, drive train repair, drive shaft and rear-end repair, tire repair, vehicle video equipment, other maintenance and services, and auto repair policies.

• *vehicle insurance* Includes the premium paid for insuring cars, trucks, and other vehicles.

• *vehicle rental, licenses, and other charges* Includes leased and rented cars, trucks, motorcycles, and aircraft, inspection fees, state and local registration, drivers' license fees, parking fees, towing charges, tolls on trips, and global positioning services.

• *public transportation* Includes fares for mass transit, buses, trains, airlines, taxis, private school buses, and fares paid on trips for trains, boats, taxis, buses, and trains.

weekly spending Weekly spending data are collected in the diary portion of the Consumer Expenditure Survey. The data show the percentage of households purchasing an item during an average week, and the amount spent per week on the item by purchasers. Not all items are included in the diary portion of the Consumer Expenditure Survey. For more about the methodology of the Consumer Expenditure Survey, see Appendix A.